BEHAVIOR A puffin uses twigs to build a nest in its burrow.

CHARACTERISTICS Puffins have been called "sea parrots" and "clowns of the sea" for their colorful bills and short, round bodies.

REPRODUCTION A female puffin lays a single egg each year. If the egg breaks, she may lay another.

YOUNG Puffin chicks are called pufflings. The chick hatches about 45 days after the egg is laid.

California
Science

Harcourt
SCHOOL PUBLISHERS

Visit *The Learning Site!*
www.harcourtschool.com

California Science

Tufted puffin

Series Consulting Authors

Michael J. Bell, Ph.D.
Assistant Professor of Early
    Childhood Education
College of Education
West Chester University of
    Pennsylvania
West Chester, Pennsylvania

Michael A. DiSpezio
Curriculum Architect
JASON Academy
Cape Cod, Massachusetts

Marjorie Frank
Former Adjunct, Science
    Education
Hunter College
New York, New York

Gerald H. Krockover, Ph.D.
Professor of Earth and
    Atmospheric Science
    Education
Purdue University
West Lafayette, Indiana

Joyce C. McLeod
Adjunct Professor
Rollins College
Winter Park, Florida

Barbara ten Brink, Ph.D.
Science Specialist
Austin Independent School
    District
Austin, Texas

Carol J. Valenta
Senior Vice President
St. Louis Science Center
St. Louis, Missouri
Former teacher, principal,
    and Coordinator
    of Science Center
    Instructional Programs
Los Angeles Unified School
    District
Los Angeles, California

Barry A. Van Deman
President and CEO
Museum of Life and Science
Durham, North Carolina

Series Consultants

Catherine Banker
Curriculum Consultant
Alta Loma, California

Robin C. Scarcella, Ph.D.
Professor and Director, Program
of Academic English and ESL
University of California, Irvine
Irvine, California

Series Content Reviewers

Paul Asimow, Ph.D.
Associate Professor, Geology
and Geochemistry
California Institute of
Technology
Pasadena, California

Larry Baresi, Ph.D.
Associate Professor
California State University,
Northridge
Northridge, California

John Brockhaus, Ph.D.
Department of Geography and
Environmental Engineering
United States Military Academy
West Point, New York

Mapi Cuevas, Ph.D.
Professor of Chemistry
Santa Fe Community College
Gainesville, Florida

William Guggino, Ph.D.
Professor of Physiology and
Pediatrics
Johns Hopkins University,
School of Medicine
Baltimore, Maryland

V. Arthur Hammon
Pre-College Education Specialist
Jet Propulsion Laboratory
Pasadena, California

Steven A. Jennings, Ph.D.
Associate Professor in
Geography
University of Colorado at
Colorado Springs
Colorado Springs, Colorado

James E. Marshall, Ph.D.
Professor and Chair,
Department of Curriculum
and Instruction
California State University,
Fresno
Fresno, California

Joseph McClure, Ph.D.
Associate Professor Emeritus
Department of Physics
Georgetown University
Washington, D.C.

Dork Sahagian, Ph.D.
Professor of Earth and
Environmental Science
Lehigh University
Bethlehem, Pennsylvania

Curriculum and Classroom Reviewers

Kelly Barrett
Curriculum Specialist
Anaheim City School District
Anaheim, California

Kenneth A. Collard
Associate Principal
Mueller Charter School
Chula Vista, California

Ruth M. Landmann
Teacher
Rio del Mar Elementary School
Aptos, California

Michael Lebda
Science Specialist
Fresno Unified School District
Fresno, California

Tonya C. Lee
Teacher
Meridian Elementary School
El Cajon, California

Ana G. Lopez
Science Specialist
Fresno Unified School District
Fresno, California

SCHOOL PUBLISHERS

Science and Technology features
provided by

*Science Content Standards for
California Public Schools* reproduced by
permission, California Department of
Education, CDE Press, 1430 N Street,
Suite 3207, Sacramento, CA 95814.

Printed in the United States of America

ISBN 13: 978-0-15-347119-3
ISBN 10: 0-15-347119-0

3 4 5 6 7 8 9 10 048 13 12 11 10 09 08 07

Big Idea Scientists learn about the world by asking questions and doing investigations.

Essential Questions

surfer in northern California

iv

PHYSICAL SCIENCE

UNIT 1 — Energy and Matter — 50

Big Idea Matter and energy have different forms. One form can change into another.

Essential Questions

UNIT 2 — Light — 144

Big Idea Light has a source and travels in straight lines.

Essential Questions

LIFE SCIENCE

caribou

EARTH SCIENCE

UNIT 4 — Patterns in the Sky 272

Big Idea We can predict where the sun, the moon, the stars, and the planets will be in the sky.

References

GETTING READY FOR SCIENCE

Getting Ready for Science

California Standards in This Unit

5 Scientific progress is made by asking meaningful questions and conducting careful investigations.

5.a Repeat observations to improve accuracy and know that the results of similar scientific investigations seldom turn out exactly the same because of differences in the things being investigated, methods being used, or uncertainty in the observation.

5.b Differentiate evidence from opinion and know that scientists do not rely on claims or conclusions unless they are backed by observations that can be confirmed.

5.c Use numerical data in describing and comparing objects, events, and measurements.

5.d Predict the outcome of a simple investigation and compare the result with the prediction.

5.e Collect data in an investigation and analyze those data to develop a logical conclusion.

What's the Big Idea?

Scientists learn about the world by asking questions and doing investigations.

Essential Questions

Science in California

Yosemite National Park

Dear Wen-Li,

Greetings from Yosemite National Park! Our field trip was a lot of fun. We went hiking and saw all kinds of plants and animals. A ranger answered a lot of my questions about the park. There are huge mountains and big waterfalls here. We're taking lots of pictures!

See you next week!
Jason

USA

How do you think scientists learn about the world around us? How do you think that relates to the

Big Idea?

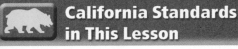
Investigation and Experimentation

5.a Repeat observations to improve accuracy and know that the results of similar scientific investigations seldom turn out exactly the same because of differences in the things being investigated, methods being used, or uncertainty in the observation.

5.d Predict the outcome of a simple investigation and compare the result with the prediction.

5.e Collect data in an investigation and analyze those data to develop a logical conclusion.

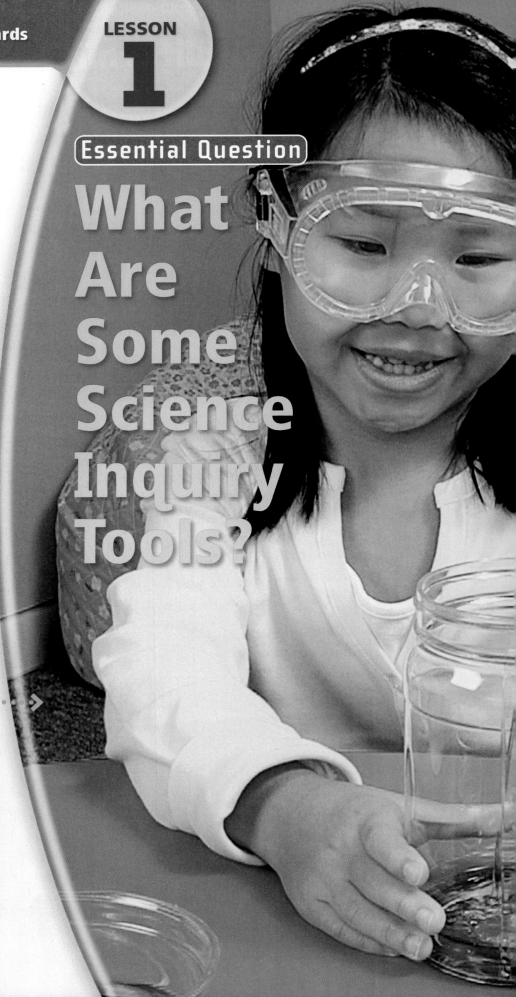

LESSON

1

Essential Question

What Are Some Science Inquiry Tools?

California Fast Fact

Measuring Up

The first humans probably used body parts for measuring tools! For example, the foot measurement was probably based on the length of a person's foot. In the Investigate, you will learn more about measurement.

2

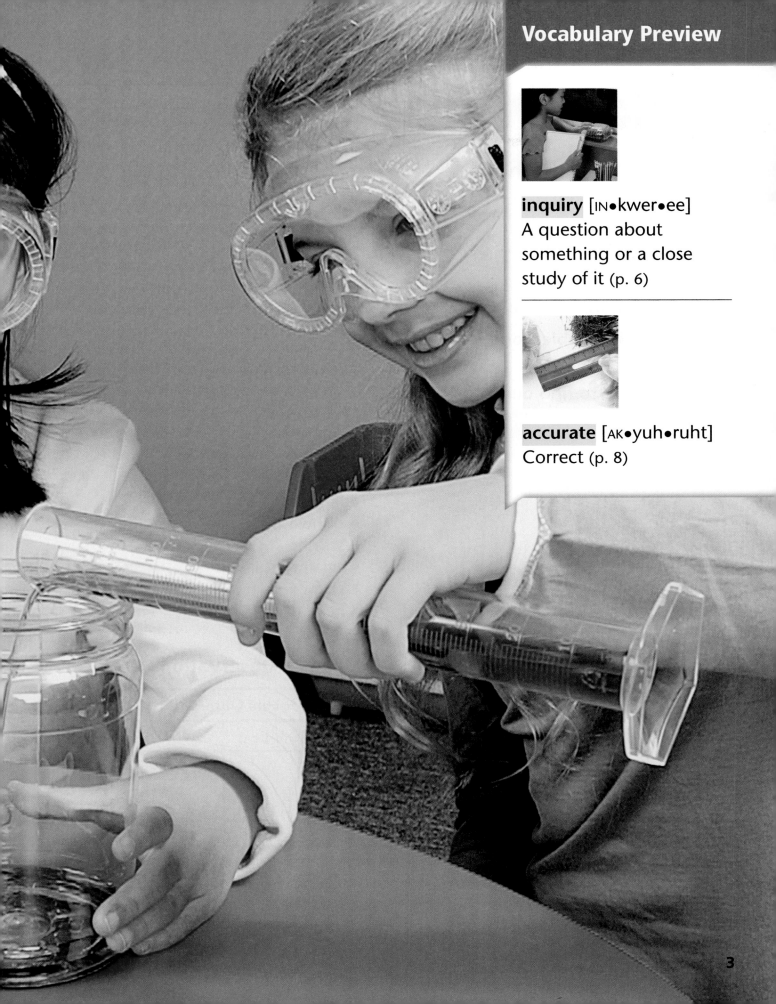

inquiry [IN•kwer•ee]
A question about
something or a close
study of it (p. 6)

accurate [AK•yuh•ruht]
Correct (p. 8)

3

Making Bubbles

Start with Questions

Do you like to blow bubbles? Blowing bubbles is fun!

- Are all bubbles alike?

- What do bubbles look like up close?

Investigate to find out. Then read to find out more.

Prepare to Investigate

Investigation Skill Tip

When you observe something, you study it closely. You can observe size, shape, color, smell, sound, and any other information that comes to your senses.

Materials
- safety goggles
- metric measuring cup
- water
- large container
- dishwashing soap
- stirring stick
- small container
- straw
- hand lens

Make an Observation Chart

Bubble Observations	
Without Hand Lens	With Hand Lens

Follow This Procedure

CAUTION: **Put on the safety goggles.**

1 Use the measuring cup to measure 1 L (1,000 mL) of water. Pour the water into a large container.

2 Measure 50 mL of dishwashing soap. Stir it into the water in the container. Pour some of the liquid into a small container.

3 Use the straw to blow air into the liquid in the small container. Observe the bubbles. Record your observations.

4 Observe the bubbles with a hand lens. Record those observations.

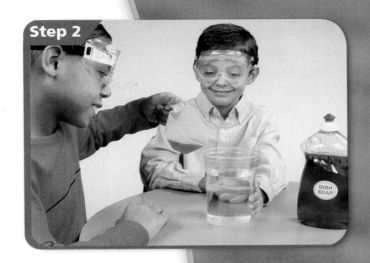

Step 2

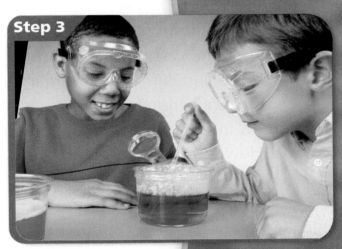

Step 3

Draw Conclusions

1. How did the hand lens help you observe the bubbles?

2. **Standards Link** From your data, can you conclude that all bubbles are alike? `5.e`

3. **Investigation Skill** We often use our eyes to observe. Describe a time when you used another body part to observe something. `5.a`

Independent Inquiry   **Make Predictions**

Add 60 mL of glycerine and 8 mL of sugar to the liquid in the small container. Predict what the bubbles you will blow with this mixture will be like. Then blow some bubbles. How do your results compare with your prediction? `5.d`

5.a, 5.d, 5.e

VOCABULARY
inquiry p. 6
accurate p. 8

SCIENCE CONCEPTS
▶ what some measurement tools are
▶ how these measurement tools are used

Focus Skill MAIN IDEA AND DETAILS
Look for details about tools used for measuring things.

Main Idea

detail | detail | detail

Tools Used for Inquiry

A scientist tries to answer questions about how things work. An **inquiry** is a question that is asked about something or an organized study of something. Investigations and experiments are inquiries.

In most science inquiries, you use tools to collect data. These tools help you observe, measure, and compare objects. However, you must use these tools properly.

Focus Skill MAIN IDEA AND DETAILS What is an inquiry?

Hand Lens

What It Is: A hand lens is a tool that makes an object look bigger.

How to Use It: Hold a hand lens near the object that you want to observe closely. Look at the object through the lens. You can move the lens closer to or farther from the object to see it more clearly.

Safety: Be careful not to drop or scratch a hand lens.

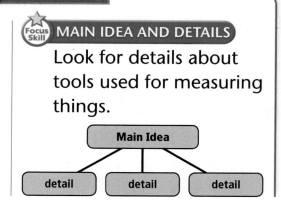

Forceps

What They Are: Forceps are a tool that is used to pick up and hold on to small objects or objects that break easily.

How to Use Them: Place the tips of the forceps around the object you want to pick up. Squeeze the forceps' handles gently, and lift the object.

Safety: The tips of the forceps may be sharp. Always clean the forceps after you use them.

Dropper

What It Is: A dropper is a tool that picks up and releases small amounts of liquid.

How to Use It: Squeeze the dropper's bulb to get the air out. Keep squeezing as you place the end of the dropper in a liquid. Then stop squeezing. Some of the liquid will move up into the dropper. To release the liquid, squeeze the bulb again.

Safety: Droppers should be cleaned after each use.

Magnifying Box

What It Is: Like a hand lens, a magnifying box can magnify an object, or make it look bigger.

How to Use It: Place the object you want to observe inside the magnifying box. Look through the clear part of the box.

Safety: Some magnifying boxes have a glass lens. Be careful not to drop the box.

Insta-Lab

Use a Magnifying Box
Place a magnifying box on this page. Use it to look at the text and some of the photographs. What do you observe? Then look at other objects, such as leaves or paper clips.

Measuring Tools

The tools on this page can be used to take measurements in an inquiry. If you do not use a tool properly, your measurements will be wrong. You want your measurements to be **accurate**, or correct.

Using the right tool will make your measurements more accurate. You should also check each measurement more than once. Taking measurements two or three times can help you make sure they are accurate.

 MAIN IDEA AND DETAILS Which tool would you use to measure how tall you are?

Measuring Cup

What It Is: A measuring cup measures volume, or the amount of space that something takes up. Measuring cups are usually used for liquids and for loose solids such as powders.

How to Use It: Pour the substance you want to measure into the measuring cup. Use the marks on the outside of the cup to see how much is in it. To be accurate, bend down so that your eyes are at the same level as the marks on the cup.

Safety: Do not drop the measuring cup. Ask your teacher for help with spills.

Spring Scale

What It Is: A spring scale is a tool that measures an object's weight.

How to Use It: Attach the object you want to weigh to the hook at the bottom of the spring scale. Allow the object to hang as you hold the spring scale up. The scale will show the weight of the object.

Safety: Weigh objects on a spring scale only when your teacher asks you to do so.

Thermometer

What It Is: A thermometer is a tool that measures temperature, or how hot or cold something is.

How to Use It: Put the thermometer in the place where you want to measure the temperature. Wait about five minutes. Then find the top of the liquid in the thermometer's tube. Use the markings along the side of the tube to read the temperature.

Safety: If a thermometer breaks, do not touch it. Ask your teacher for help.

Ruler

What It Is: A ruler is a tool used to measure length, width, height, or depth.

How to Use It: Place the ruler against the object you want to measure. Use the markings on the ruler to see how long, wide, high, or deep the object is. To take accurate measurements, make sure the end of the ruler or the 0 mark is exactly at one edge of the object.

Safety: Do not use rulers to measure hot objects. You could get hurt or damage the ruler.

Measuring Tape

What It Is: A measuring tape is like a ruler, but it can measure curved objects.

How to Use It: Place the measuring tape along the object that you would like to measure. Use the markings on the tape to see how long, wide, high, or deep the object is.

Safety: Do not use plastic measuring tapes to measure hot objects.

Some Other Tools Used in Science

Many science tools have similar uses. For example, measuring cups, measuring spoons, and graduates (GRA•joo•itz) all measure how much space something takes up. The tool that you use depends on how much you have to measure.

Your measurements will be more accurate if you use the proper tool. If you want to measure how much water is in a sink, for example, you would need a big enough tool. You would need a measuring cup, not a measuring spoon.

 **MAIN IDEA AND DETAILS** Why is it important to use the proper tool to measure something?

Measuring Spoon

What It Is: A measuring spoon can be used to measure ingredients before combining them. The spoons come in a set.

How It Is Used: A measuring spoon can be used to measure liquids or powders. Choose the spoon that will measure the amount you need. Then pour the liquid into the spoon or dip the spoon into the powder.

Safety: Measuring spoons should not be used to measure hot liquids.

Graduate

What It Is: Like a measuring cup, a graduate measures volume, or the amount of space that something takes up. A graduate is used to measure liquids. Note: A graduate is sometimes called a *graduated cylinder*.

How It Is Used: Pour the liquid into the graduate. To make an accurate measurement, bend down so that your eyes are even with the top of the liquid. Then read the measurement on the outside of the cylinder.

Safety: Handle glass graduates carefully so they do not break.

Pan Balance

What It Is: A pan balance is used to measure mass, or the amount of matter in an object.

How It Is Used: Make sure the pointer is in the middle. Place the object you want to measure in the left pan. Add standard masses to the right pan until the pointer comes back to the middle mark. Then add the numbers on the standard masses to find the mass of the object.

Safety: Use the pan balance only when your teacher asks you to do so.

Microscope

What It Is: A microscope is a tool that is used to make very small objects look larger. It helps you see details that are too small to see with just your eyes.

How It Is Used: Place the object on the platform under the lens. Look through the eyepiece. Turn the knob until you can see the object clearly.

Safety: Always use two hands when you carry a microscope. Do not touch the lenses with your fingers.

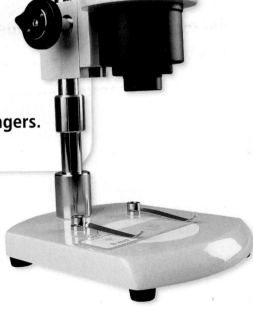

Standards Wrap-Up and Lesson Review

Essential Question

What are some science inquiry tools?

In this lesson, you learned about tools that can help you observe and measure things. Scientists use these tools in inquiries.

 Investigation and Experimentation Standards in This Lesson

5.a Repeat observations to improve accuracy and know that the results of similar scientific investigations seldom turn out exactly the same because of differences in the things being investigated, methods being used, or uncertainty in the observation.

5.d Predict the outcome of a simple investigation and compare the result with the prediction.

5.e Collect data in an investigation and analyze those data to develop a logical conclusion.

1. **(Focus Skill) MAIN IDEA AND DETAILS** Draw and complete a graphic organizer. Show the supporting details of the main idea *Many tools can be used in science inquiries.* **5.e**

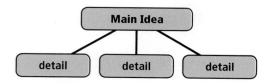

2. **SUMMARIZE** Make a table. List at least five of the tools in this lesson. Name a use for each tool. **5.e**

3. **DRAW CONCLUSIONS** You want to know whether a tiny animal that you found has six or eight legs. What tools could you use to help you find out? **5.e**

4. **VOCABULARY** Which of the following is **not** an inquiry?
   A asking a question
   B studying something closely
   C cleaning science tools
   D doing an investigation **5.d**

5. **Investigate and Experiment** What should you always do to make accurate measurements?
   A use two kinds of tools
   B take the measurement twice to make sure it's correct
   C use a tool made of plastic
   D make sure your measurement matches someone else's **5.a**

6. Explain how tools help scientists. **5.e**

 **The Big Idea**

 Writing ELA–W 1.1

Write a Paragraph

Choose a science tool that you have used. Write a paragraph about the tool you chose. Make sure your paragraph has a topic sentence and supporting details.

 Math MG 1.1

Select Unit of Measure

Look at the photograph on the left. Make a list of five things that you could measure, using science tools. For each thing on your list, tell what tool you would use to measure it. Also name the units for each measurement on your list.

 Health

How Many Are Enough?

We should eat five servings of fruit and vegetables each day. One serving of dried fruit is $\frac{1}{4}$ cup. Ask a classmate to predict how many raisins are in $\frac{1}{4}$ cup. Then measure $\frac{1}{4}$ cup, and count to check the prediction.

 For more links and activities, go to **www.hspscience.com**

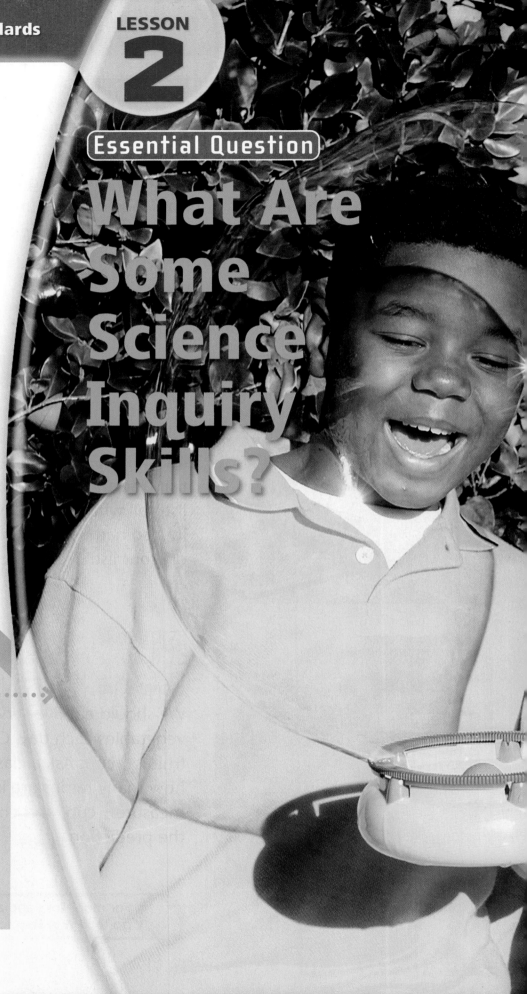

Investigation and Experimentation

5.b Differentiate evidence from opinion and know that scientists do not rely on claims or conclusions unless they are backed by observations that can be confirmed.

5.d Predict the outcome of a simple investigation and compare the result with the prediction.

5.e Collect data in an investigation and analyze those data to develop a logical conclusion.

LESSON

2

Essential Question

What Are Some Science Inquiry Skills?

California Fast Fact

Blowing Bubbles

The longest bubble ever blown and measured was about 32 meters (105 ft) long! What shape do you think this huge bubble was? In the Investigate, you will learn about bubble shapes.

Wow! How can a bubble get so big?

predict [pree•DIKT] To tell what you think will happen in the future (p. 20)

evidence [EV•uh•duhns] Information collected in a scientific inquiry (p. 23)

Cats are the best pets.

opinion [uh•PIN•yuhn] A personal belief that is not based on evidence (p. 23)

15

Shapes of Bubbles

Start with Questions

Have you ever seen fancy-shaped wands for blowing bubbles? They look very interesting.

- Can you blow bubbles that have different shapes?

- Do bubble wands that have different shapes make bubbles that have different shapes?

Investigate to find out. Then read to find out more.

Prepare to Investigate

Investigation Skill Tip

When you predict, you tell what you think will happen in an investigation. A prediction is not just a guess. Predictions should be based on what you know and have observed. You should always be able to tell why you made your prediction.

Materials
- safety goggles
- wire hangers
- plastic flying disk
- bubble solution

Make an Observation Chart

Bubble Shapes		
Shape of Wand	Predicted Bubble Shape	Actual Bubble Shape

Follow This Procedure

CAUTION: **Put on safety goggles.**

① Use the hangers to make bubble wands of different shapes.

② Predict the shape of the bubbles that each wand will make. Record your prediction.

③ Turn the flying disk upside down. Pour some bubble solution into it. Dip a wand into the solution, and make bubbles. Observe and record their shapes. Repeat with all the wands. Try each wand at least twice.

Step 1

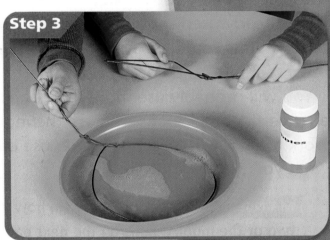

Step 3

Draw Conclusions

1. What information did you use to make your predictions?

2. **Standards Link** How did you know if your predictions were correct? `5.d`

3. **Investigation Skill** Use your observations to predict the shape of a bubble blown with a heart-shaped wand. `5.d`

Independent Inquiry → **Tell Evidence from Opinion**

Your friend says that a bubble will be the same color as the wand. This is her opinion. Plan an investigation to test her opinion. Try it. Did you gather evidence that supported her opinion? `5.b`

VOCABULARY
predict p. 20
evidence p. 23
opinion p. 23

SCIENCE CONCEPTS
▶ what some inquiry skills are
▶ how inquiry skills are used

MAIN IDEA AND DETAILS
Look for details about skills for science inquiry.

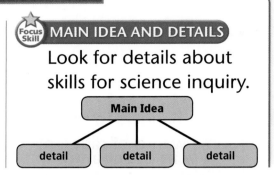

Skills Used for Inquiry

When scientists try to answer a question, they use thinking tools called inquiry skills. You have already used some of these skills. In the Investigates, you have observed, measured, recorded data, and compared.

You will probably use more than one skill in an investigation. That's because the inquiry skills work together. The skills that you use depend on what you are trying to find out.

MAIN IDEA AND DETAILS Explain how you used two of the inquiry skills on the next page during the Investigate.

These students are setting up an investigation. They will need to use inquiry skills to complete the investigation. ▼

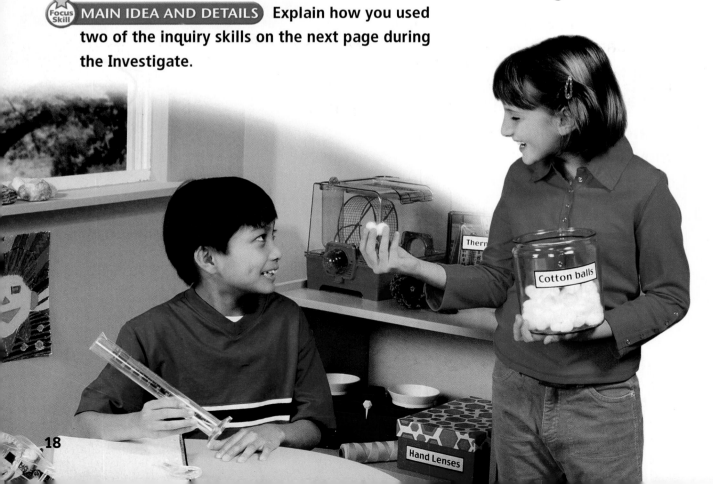

Observe

When you observe, you study something closely. You might observe the way something looks, smells, tastes, feels, or sounds. It is important to repeat your observations to make sure they are correct.

Infer

When you infer, you assume something that you did not actually observe. You might observe people wearing coats outside. You could infer that it is cold, but you could not be sure unless you went outside.

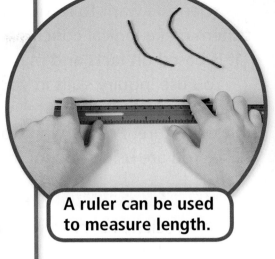

A ruler can be used to measure length.

Use Numbers

Scientists use numbers when they collect and display data. Understanding numbers and using them to show the results of investigations are important skills.

Measure

You use numbers when you measure something. To take measurements, you use tools such as thermometers, spring scales, measuring tapes, and measuring cups.

Collect, Record, Analyze, and Display Data

When you measure or observe something, you are collecting data. Data is information. When you record data, you write it down. Recording data can help you *analyze*, or figure out, what the data is telling you. Data can be displayed in charts, tables, and graphs.

This student has collected data. He is making a bar graph to display it.

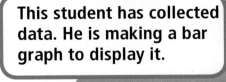

More Skills Used for Inquiry

Scientists want to learn new things. Inquiry skills help them make logical conclusions. A conclusion is logical if it is based on facts and makes sense.

You use inquiry skills in your life, too. For example, when you **predict**, you tell what you think will happen in the future. Predict what tomorrow's weather will be like. You are using an inquiry skill!

 **MAIN IDEA AND DETAILS** Explain how two of the inquiry skills on these two pages are connected.

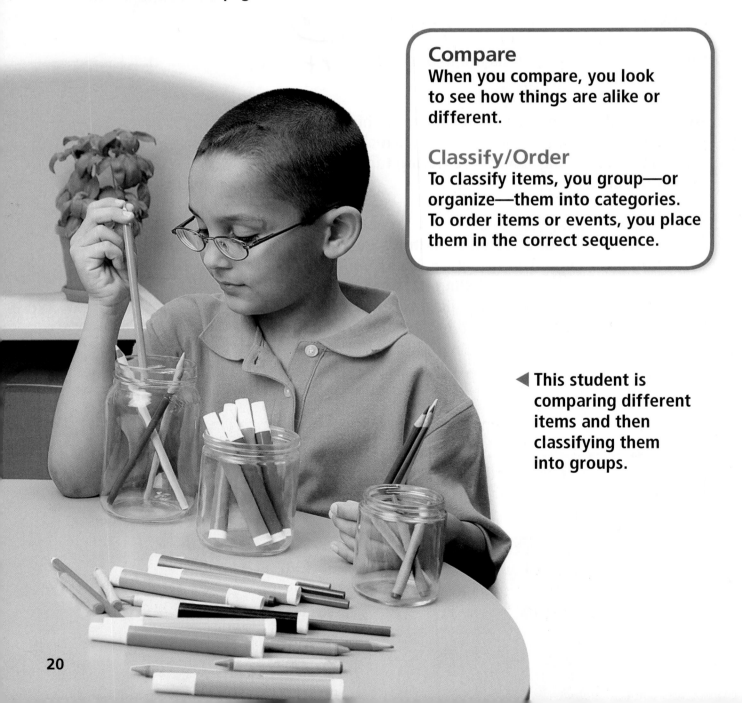

Compare
When you compare, you look to see how things are alike or different.

Classify/Order
To classify items, you group—or organize—them into categories. To order items or events, you place them in the correct sequence.

◀ This student is comparing different items and then classifying them into groups.

20

This student is using a stopwatch to time her classmate. She will use numbers—minutes and seconds—to tell how long something takes. Timing something involves using a time/space relationship. ▼

Use Time/Space Relationships
Where were you at noon yesterday? By answering this question, you are using a time/space relationship. In fact, every time that you identify where something is at a certain time, you classify that object according to the time and space that it is in.

Predict
When you predict something, you use what you observe and what you know to tell what might happen in the future. Then you see what happens and compare your prediction with the actual result. What do you predict will happen to the water in the photograph?

Using Models

You might want to study something that is very big or very small, such as the solar system or an ant. Perhaps you want to learn about something that is dangerous, such as an earthquake.

You can use a model of what you want to study. A model can help you learn how something works. A good model works the same way as the thing that the model represents.

MAIN IDEA AND DETAILS Name two things that scientists might use models to study.

Insta-Lab

Make a Model
Use modeling clay to make a model of a plant or an animal that interests you. How does your model compare to the real plant or animal?

Use Models
Models are often used in science to study things that are too big or too small to see easily in real life. Some models are made by computers. For example, computer models help people predict the weather.

These students are learning more about volcanoes by building a model of one. ▼

22

Ashley records that the bug is pretty. Erin records that the bug has six legs. Which student is recording her opinion? Which student is recording evidence?

Evidence and Opinion

Evidence is information collected in a scientific inquiry. You know that evidence is true if the inquiry always has the same results. An **opinion** is a personal belief that is not based on evidence.

Scientists do not draw conclusions based on opinions. They use facts and evidence to understand the world.

Focus Skill MAIN IDEA AND DETAILS Give an example of an opinion and an example of evidence about an apple.

Draw Conclusions

To draw conclusions, you think about everything you learned in an inquiry. Then you make a statement about it. Your conclusion should be based on data you gathered and information you already know. In an inquiry, a conclusion must be supported by the data.

23

Essential Question

What are some science inquiry skills?

In this lesson, you learned why inquiry skills, or thinking skills, are important. They include making observations, using numbers, measuring, collecting and analyzing data, inferring, comparing, predicting, and drawing conclusions. They also include using models and telling the difference between evidence and opinion. Scientists use these skills to help answer their questions.

Investigation and Experimentation Standards in This Lesson

5.b Differentiate evidence from opinion and know that scientists do not rely on claims or conclusions unless they are backed by observations that can be confirmed.

5.d Predict the outcome of a simple investigation and compare the result with the prediction.

5.e Collect data in an investigation and analyze those data to develop a logical conclusion.

1. **MAIN IDEA AND DETAILS** Draw and complete a graphic organizer. Show the details that support the main idea *Many skills can be used in science inquiries.* **5.d**

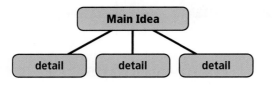

2. **SUMMARIZE** List five inquiry skills. Explain how each one might be used. **5.d**

3. **DRAW CONCLUSIONS** Two scientists conduct the same investigation. They use different inquiry skills. What might be true of their results? **5.a**

4. **VOCABULARY** Describe how someone *predicts*, and give an example. **5.d**

5. **Critical Thinking** You want to find out how the heights of third graders differ from the heights of second graders. Which inquiry skills will you use? **5.e**

6. Which of these is an opinion?
   A The weather is nice today.
   B It rained 6 cm today.
   C It was 2 degrees colder yesterday.
   D Clouds are covering the sun. **5.b**

The **Big** Idea

 Writing ELA–W1.1

Write a Paragraph

Which do you think are the three most useful inquiry skills? Write a paragraph explaining how these skills can help scientists get accurate results in an investigation.

 Math MR 2.3

Compare Data

Read question 5 in the Lesson Review again. Make a chart or table that would help you collect and record the heights of students in the second and third grades. Allow space for recording at least 10 observations for each of the grades. Compare your observations of each grade.

 Social Studies HSS 3.5.2

Evidence or Opinion?

Someone says that oranges grown in Orange County have more juice than other oranges. Tell how you would find out whether this statement is a fact or an opinion. Which inquiry skills would you use?

 For more links and activities, go to **www.hspscience.com**

Investigation and Experimentation

5.c Use numerical data in describing and comparing objects, events, and measurements.

5.d Predict the outcome of a simple investigation and compare the result with the prediction.

LESSON **3**

Essential Question

How Do We Use Numbers in Science?

California Fast Fact

Number What?

Ancient Greeks used the first letter of words as numbers. *Pente* means "five" in Greek, so *P* stood for 5. *Deka* means "ten," so D stood for 10. DP stood for 15. What did DDDP stand for?

What makes some bubbles so large and others so small?

data table [DAY•tuh TAY•buhl] A display that organizes data into rows and columns (p. 32)

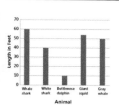

bar graph [BAR GRAF] A graph that uses bars to display data (p. 32)

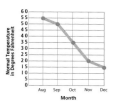

line graph [LYN GRAF] A graph that uses a line to display data (p. 33)

Numbers of Bubbles

Directed Inquiry

Start with Questions

A bubble bath is made when liquid soap is mixed with water in a bathtub.

- What happens if you add too much soap?

- What happens if you don't add enough soap?

- Does the amount of soap in the water make a difference?

Investigate to find out. Then read to find out more.

Prepare to Investigate

Investigation Skill Tip

When you analyze your data, you look for a pattern. It might help to make a graph. A graph organizes your data and can help you see patterns.

Materials
- 3 plastic jars with lids
- marker
- water
- graduate
- dropper
- dishwashing soap
- ruler

Make a Data Table

Heights of Bubbles		
Jar	Height, Trial 1	Height, Trial 2
A		
B		
C		

Follow This Procedure

Step 2

1. Mark the jars A, B, and C. Using the graduate, measure and pour 50 mL of water into each jar.

2. Use the dropper to put 5 drops of soap in Jar A, 10 drops in Jar B, and 15 drops in Jar C. Put the lids on the jars.

3. Shake Jar A five times. Use the ruler to measure the height of the bubbles. Record the number. Repeat with the other two jars.

Step 3

4. Rinse the jars, and repeat Steps 1–3. Record your results.

Draw Conclusions

1. Which container had the most bubbles? The least?

2. **Standards Link** Use the data you collected to make a bar graph. `5.c`

3. **Investigation Skill** Analyze the data you collected. Use the graph to write a summary of your data. `5.c`

Independent Inquiry > **Make Predictions**

What do you think would happen if you shook the containers more than five times? Predict how the outcome of the investigation would change. Try it, and compare the results with the results of the original investigation. Was your prediction correct? `5.d`

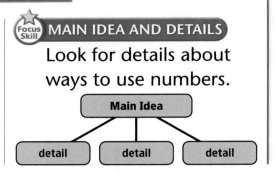
VOCABULARY
data table p. 32
bar graph p. 32
line graph p. 33

SCIENCE CONCEPTS
▶ how to use numbers to collect data
▶ ways to display data

Focus Skill **MAIN IDEA AND DETAILS**
Look for details about ways to use numbers.

Main Idea
detail   detail   detail

Using Numbers to Collect Data

How old are you? How tall are you? You can use numbers to measure yourself. You also use numbers to measure objects, count time, and compare things.

Without numbers, for example, we could not measure the distance to the moon. We would just have to say it is a long, long way from Earth.

This student is using a ruler to measure how long these roots are.

We can use minutes and seconds to measure how much time has gone by.

We also couldn't compare distances. We wouldn't know how much farther away the sun is than the moon. We couldn't measure temperatures, either. We would just say that the moon is cold and the sun is hot. We couldn't learn much without numbers!

Focus Skill MAIN IDEA AND DETAILS **Explain three ways in which we use numbers.**

We can use degrees to measure temperature.

We can use centimeters to compare two diameters.

Displaying Data

There are many ways to display the data you collect. A **data table** is a display that organizes data into rows and columns. A data table should have a title, and each column needs a heading.

You can also display data in graphs. Graphs also need titles and labels. A **bar graph** is a graph that uses bars to display data. A bar graph works for data that is in categories.

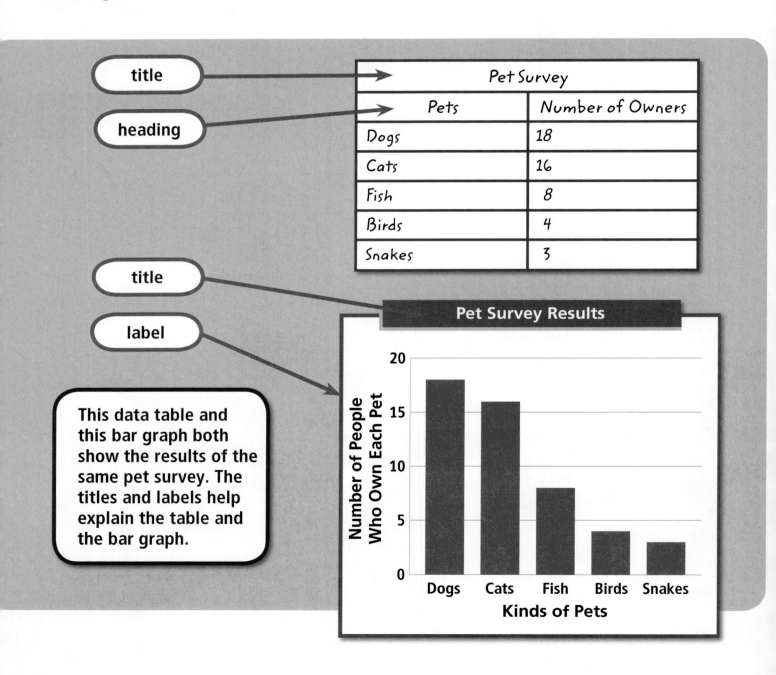

title

heading

Pet Survey	
Pets	Number of Owners
Dogs	18
Cats	16
Fish	8
Birds	4
Snakes	3

title

label

This data table and this bar graph both show the results of the same pet survey. The titles and labels help explain the table and the bar graph.

Pet Survey Results

Number of People Who Own Each Pet

Kinds of Pets

Dogs   Cats   Fish   Birds   Snakes

Average High Temperatures in Sacramento	
Month	Temperature (°C)
January	11
February	16
March	18
April	22
May	27
June	31
July	34
August	33
September	30
October	25
November	18
December	11

This data table and line graph display the same data.

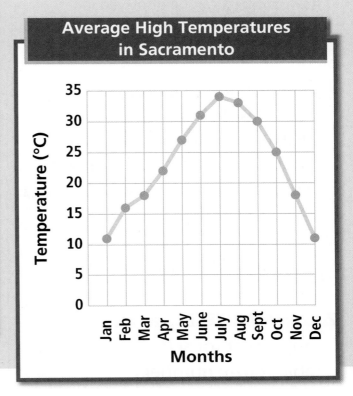

Average High Temperatures in Sacramento

A **line graph** is a graph that uses a line to display data. The line graph above shows the average temperature in each month. Using the graph, it is easy to see how temperature and the month are related.

 **MAIN IDEA AND DETAILS** What parts should all data tables and graphs have?

Make a Bar Graph
Go through this lesson, and count the number of times the words *measure* and *numbers* appear. Make a bar graph to show your data.

Standards Wrap-Up and Lesson Review

Investigation and Experimentation Standards in This Lesson

5.c Use numerical data in describing and comparing objects, events, and measurements.

5.d Predict the outcome of a simple investigation and compare the result with the prediction.

1. (Focus Skill) **MAIN IDEA AND DETAILS** Draw and complete a graphic organizer. Show details that support the main idea *We use numbers in many ways.* 5.c

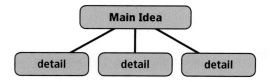

2. **SUMMARIZE** Explain why it's important for scientists to be able to use numbers. 5.c

3. **DRAW CONCLUSIONS** Describe two ways in which your life would change if no one used numbers. 5.c

4. **VOCABULARY** How is a line graph similar to a bar graph? How are they different? 5.c

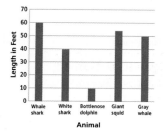

5. **Investigate and Experiment** Predict what the temperature will be in your town tomorrow morning. Explain how you will know if your prediction was correct. 5.d

6. Which is **not** a use for numbers in science?

   A to measure width

   B to find out how long a change takes

   C to describe a smell

   D to determine which rock is heavier 5.c

The Big Idea

Writing   ELA–W 2.1

Write a Narrative

Write a short story about a detective who measures the sizes of animal tracks to solve a mystery. Give details about where the mystery takes place and why solving it is important.

9÷3 Math   MR 2.3

Make a Graph

Make a list of measuring tools that you often use. Include *ruler, measuring cup, thermometer, measuring tape,* and *clock or watch.* Next, ask 10 people which of the tools they have used this week. Then make a bar graph to display the data you have collected.

Art   VPA–VA 2.2

Paint by Numbers

Use a few colors of tempera paints to make many other colors. For example, mix 1 teaspoon of blue with 2 teaspoons of yellow. Make a key that shows how you used numbers to make each color. Then make a painting with the colors you made.

For more links and activities, go to **www.hspscience.com**

Investigation and Experimentation

5.a Repeat observations to improve accuracy and know that the results of similar scientific investigations seldom turn out exactly the same because of differences in the things being investigated, methods being used, or uncertainty in the observation.

5.d Predict the outcome of a simple investigation and compare the result with the prediction.

5.e Collect data in an investigation and analyze those data to develop a logical conclusion.

Essential Question

What Is the Scientific Method?

California Fast Fact

Bubble Art

These students added tempera paint to bubble solution to make art. Bubbles don't need paint added to be colorful, however. In the Investigate, you will observe bubble colors.

You can make a piece of art by adding paint to bubbles.

scientific method

[sy•uhn•TIF•ik METH•uhd]
An organized plan that scientists use to conduct an investigation (p. 40)

investigation

[in•ves•tuh•GAY•shuhn]
A scientific study (p. 40)

experiment

[ek•SPEHR•uh•muhnt]
A test done to find out if a hypothesis is correct (p. 41)

Bubble Colors

Directed Inquiry

Start with Questions

You probably have never seen bubbles that are different colors.

- Can you blow bubbles in different colors?

- Can you make bubbles change colors?

Investigate to find out. Then read to find out more.

Prepare to Investigate

Investigation Skill Tip

To compare things, you name ways the things are the same and ways the things are different. In this investigation, you will do the same thing three times. Compare the results you get each time.

Materials
- safety goggles
- clear tape
- clear plastic lid
- flashlight
- cotton ball
- bubble solution
- spoon
- straw

Make an Observation Chart

Bubble Color Observations		
	Large Bubble	After Blowing
Observation 1		
Observation 2		
Observation 3		

Follow This Procedure

CAUTION: Put on safety goggles.

1. Tape the lid over the lit end of the flashlight.

2. Dip a cotton ball in bubble solution. Wipe it on the lid. Put a spoonful of solution on the lid.

3. Use a straw to blow a bubble. Turn off the lights. Record your observations of the bubble.

4. Dip the straw in solution. Then dip it in the bubble. Blow gently. Record your observations.

5. Break the bubble. Repeat Steps 3 and 4.

Step 1

Step 4

Draw Conclusions

1. Why was it important to wear safety goggles?

2. **Standards Link** What kinds of things might make each of your three observations turn out differently? 5.a

3. **Investigation Skill** Compare the colors in the bubble when you first watched it to the color you saw right before the bubble popped.

Independent Inquiry | **Make a Prediction**

Predict how adding some tempera paint to the bubble solution would change your results. Plan and conduct a simple investigation to find out. How did your results compare with your prediction? 5.d

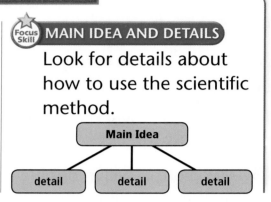
VOCABULARY
scientific method p. 40
investigation p. 40
experiment p. 41

SCIENCE CONCEPTS
▶ what the scientific method is
▶ how to use the scientific method

(Focus Skill) MAIN IDEA AND DETAILS
Look for details about how to use the scientific method.

Main Idea

detail · detail · detail

Planning an Investigation

How do scientists answer a question or solve a problem? They use an organized plan called the **scientific method** to conduct a study. A scientific study is called an **investigation**. In this lesson, you will learn how the scientific method can be used to plan an investigation to study bubbles.

(Focus Skill) MAIN IDEA AND DETAILS What plan do scientists use to help them answer questions?

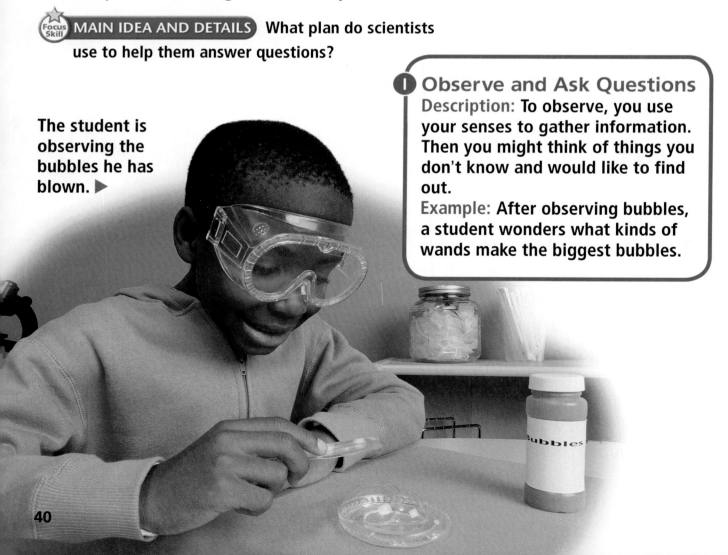

The student is observing the bubbles he has blown. ▶

① Observe and Ask Questions
Description: **To observe, you use your senses to gather information. Then you might think of things you don't know and would like to find out.**
Example: **After observing bubbles, a student wonders what kinds of wands make the biggest bubbles.**

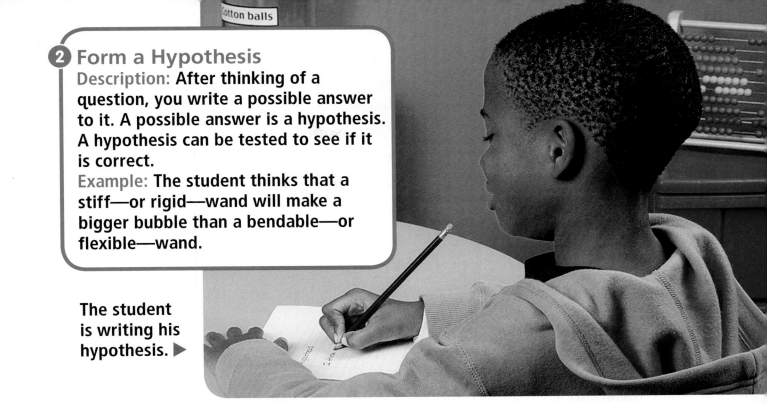

❷ Form a Hypothesis

Description: **After thinking of a question, you write a possible answer to it. A possible answer is a hypothesis. A hypothesis can be tested to see if it is correct.**

Example: **The student thinks that a stiff—or rigid—wand will make a bigger bubble than a bendable—or flexible—wand.**

The student is writing his hypothesis. ▶

❸ Plan an Experiment

Description: **An experiment is a test done to find out if a hypothesis is correct. When you plan an experiment, you describe the steps and list the equipment you need. Decide how to gather and record your data.**

Example: **The student will test his hypothesis by making a stiff wand and a bendable wand.**

Safety: **Include any safety equipment you need, such as goggles.**

Now the student is planning an experiment to study bubble size. ▼

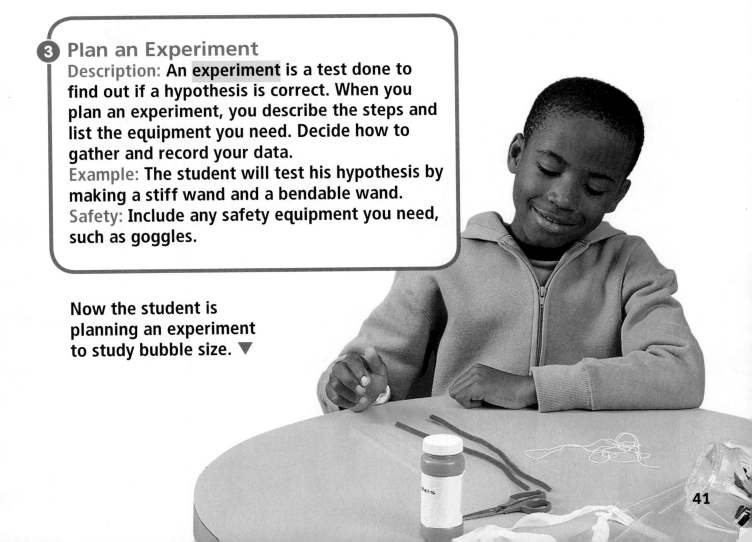

41

Conducting an Investigation

To conduct an investigation, follow the steps in your plan. Your results may not be exactly the same as a classmate's results. Using different tools and recording different observations can lead to different results. The more times you perform an experiment, the more accurate your observations will be.

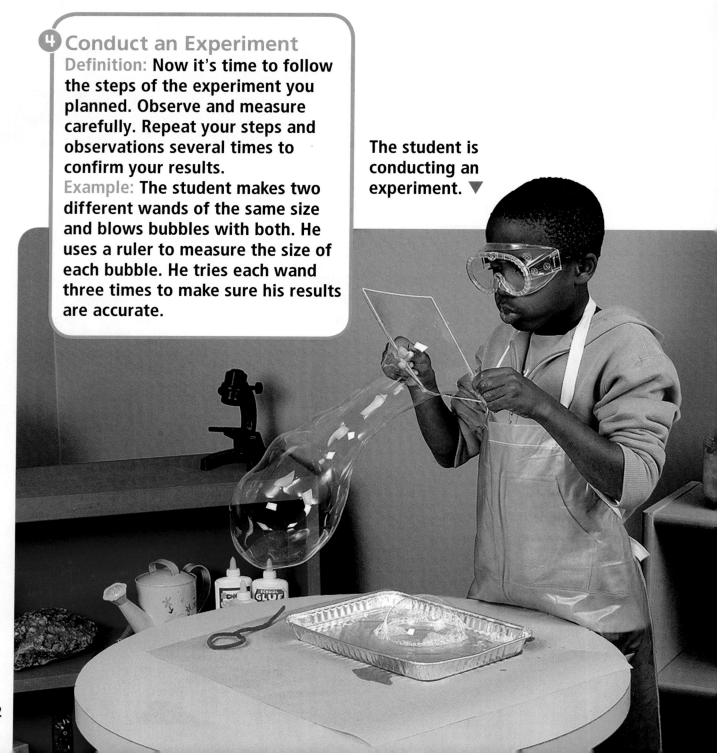

4 Conduct an Experiment

Definition: Now it's time to follow the steps of the experiment you planned. Observe and measure carefully. Repeat your steps and observations several times to confirm your results.

Example: The student makes two different wands of the same size and blows bubbles with both. He uses a ruler to measure the size of each bubble. He tries each wand three times to make sure his results are accurate.

The student is conducting an experiment. ▼

5 **Draw Conclusions and Communicate Results**
Definition: Analyze the data you gathered and write a conclusion. Make charts, tables, or graphs to show your data.
Example: The student studies the data he collected. He realizes that he blew bigger bubbles with the flexible wand. His results do not support his hypothesis. Many times the first hypothesis may be wrong. When it is wrong, a scientist will make a new hypothesis and test it.

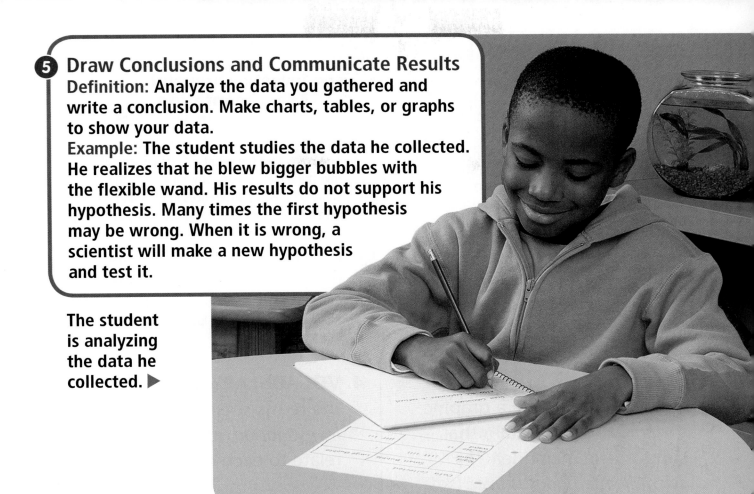

The student is analyzing the data he collected. ▶

Next, you use your results to draw a conclusion. A conclusion is a decision based on what you know and on your results. Your results might show that your hypothesis was correct.

What if your results show that your hypothesis is wrong? You still learned something. Now you can write a new hypothesis. You can plan a new experiment to test it.

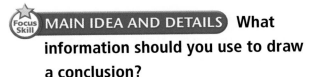 **MAIN IDEA AND DETAILS** What information should you use to draw a conclusion?

Insta-Lab

Blow a Super Bubble!
Thread a 90-cm string through two straws. Tie the ends of the string together to make a wand. Hold the straws so that the string is tight. Dip the wand in bubble solution, and blow bubbles. What do your bubbles look like?

Essential Question

What is the scientific method?

In this lesson, you learned the steps in planning and conducting an investigation. These steps, called the scientific method, make up an organized plan that you can follow to conduct a study or answer a question.

Investigation and Experimentation Standards in This Lesson

5.a Repeat observations to improve accuracy and know that the results of similar scientific investigations seldom turn out exactly the same because of differences in the things being investigated, methods being used, or uncertainty in the observation.

5.d Predict the outcome of a simple investigation and compare the result with the prediction.

5.e Collect data in an investigation and analyze those data to develop a logical conclusion.

---

1. **(Focus Skill) MAIN IDEA AND DETAILS**
   Draw and complete a graphic organizer. Show details that support the main idea *The scientific method has five main parts.* **5.a**

   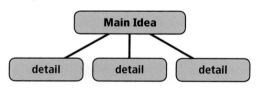

2. **SUMMARIZE** Explain in your own words each step in the scientific method. **5.e**

3. **DRAW CONCLUSIONS** Is it possible to complete the steps in the scientific method in a different order? Why or why not? **5.e**

4. **VOCABULARY** Explain how the terms *scientific method, investigation,* and *experiment* relate to each other. **5.d**

5. **Critical Thinking** A scientist hypothesizes that cats prefer fish to chicken. She experiments with one cat. The results do not support her hypothesis. What are some possible reasons? **5.a**

6. **Investigate and Experiment** In which steps of the scientific method do you predict an outcome and then compare the results with your prediction? **5.d**

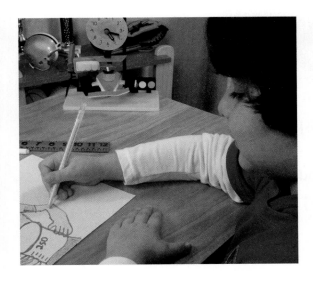

 Writing ELA–W 2.2

Write a Description

Write a how-to booklet about the scientific method. Include illustrations and examples. Also, explain why scientists use the scientific method.

Wand Size	Bubble Size
1 cm	2 cm
2 cm	4 cm
3 cm	6 cm
4 cm	8 cm
5 cm	

 Math AF 2.2

Analyze Patterns

The table at the left shows the sizes of bubbles made by bubble wands of different sizes. What size bubble will the 5-cm bubble wand make?

 Health

Getting Fit

Which exercise makes the heart beat faster, jumping jacks or sit-ups? Make a prediction. Then write a hypothesis to answer this question. Conduct an experiment to test your hypothesis. Compare your results to your prediction.

 For more links and activities, go to **www.hspscience.com**

Wrap-Up

▶ Visual Summary

Tell how each picture helps explain the **Big Idea**.

The Big Idea Scientists learn about the world by asking questions and doing investigations.

5.a, 5.b

Aiming for Accuracy
To be accurate, scientists measure carefully and repeat their observations.

5.c

Using Numbers
Scientists use numbers when they measure, describe, and order things.

5.d

Predicting and Comparing
Scientists compare the results of an investigation with their prediction.

5.e

Drawing Conclusions
Scientists analyze data from investigations to draw conclusions.

Show What You Know

Write a Report

Choose a scientist, and learn more about him or her. For example, when and where did this person live? What was he or she interested in? How did this scientist work to solve problems? What tools did he or she use? How did others treat this scientist? Write a report to share what you learned. Include a picture of the scientist.

Unit Project

Plan and Conduct an Investigation

Use the steps of the scientific method to plan and conduct an investigation. First, think of a question that interests you that you could test. For example, you might ask "What kinds of flowers do butterflies like?" or "What kind of soap works best?" Then follow the rest of the steps of the scientific method to answer your question.

Review

California Science Standards ■

Vocabulary Review

Use the terms below to complete the sentences. The page numbers tell you where to look in the unit if you need help.

accurate p. 8   data table p. 32

predict p. 20   bar graph p. 32

evidence p. 23   scientific method p. 40

opinion p. 23   experiment p. 41

1. A tool that organizes data into rows and columns is a _____. 5.e

2. A personal belief that is not based on evidence is an _____. 5.b

3. Scientists use an organized plan called the _____. 5.e

4. Measuring more than once helps make sure the measurement is correct, or _____. 5.a

5. A graph that uses bars to display data is a _____. 5.c

6. Information collected in a scientific inquiry is _____. 5.a

7. To _____, you tell what you think will happen in the future. 5.d

8. To answer a question, you can conduct an _____. 5.e

Check Understanding

Choose the best answer.

9. **MAIN IDEA AND DETAILS** Which tool would you use to measure the length of a pencil? 5.c
   A forceps   C measuring cup
   B ruler   D balance

10. What is the purpose of the tool in the picture? 5.e
    A magnifying
    B measuring
    C predicting
    D weighing

11. Which of these is an opinion? 5.b
    A The dog is brown and white.
    B The dog's name is Cody.
    C The dog is 45 centimeters tall.
    D The dog's color is beautiful.

12. **MAIN IDEA AND DETAILS** Which statement is a prediction? 5.d
    A The ice melted in 4 minutes.
    B Only the temperature changed in the experiment.
    C The ice in the sunlight will melt faster than the ice in the shade.
    D Each chunk of ice has the same shape.

13. Which inquiry skill would **most likely** be used with the tool below? `5.c`

A classify
B infer
C predict
D use numbers

14. After you have the results of your investigation, what should you do first? `5.d`

A Think of a new question.
B Compare them to your prediction.
C Communicate them to others.
D Conduct another experiment.

15. Which of these should you **not** use to draw a conclusion? `5.e`

A evidence   C observations
B facts   D opinion

16. Which of the following is **true** about a logical conclusion? `5.e`

A It should be based on data from an investigation.
B It should match the prediction.
C It should be an opinion.
D It should tell what you expected in an investigation.

Investigation Skills

17. Use the numbers in the table below to make a bar graph that displays the data. `5.e`

Eye Colors of Students in My Class	
Color	Number of Students
Brown	12
Green	4
Blue	6

18. Analyze the data in the graph below. Predict how the temperature will change from December to August. `5.c`

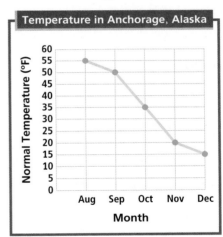

Critical Thinking

19. What tools could you use to measure the size of this book? Explain your answer. `5.c`

20. Why do scientists follow the scientific method to answer their questions?

The Big Idea

Energy and Matter

What's the Big Idea?

Matter and energy have different forms. One form can change into another.

California Standards in This Unit

1 Energy and matter have multiple forms and can be changed from one form to another.

1.a *Students know* energy comes from the Sun to Earth in the form of light.

1.b *Students know* sources of stored energy take many forms, such as food, fuel, and batteries.

1.c *Students know* machines and living things convert stored energy to motion and heat.

1.d *Students know* energy can be carried from one place to another by waves, such as water waves and sound waves, by electric current, and by moving objects.

1.e *Students know* matter has three forms: solid, liquid, and gas.

1.f *Students know* evaporation and melting are changes that occur when the objects are heated.

1.g *Students know* that when two or more substances are combined, a new substance may be formed with properties that are different from those of the original materials.

1.h *Students know* all matter is made of small particles called atoms, too small to see with the naked eye.

1.i *Students know* people once thought that earth, wind, fire, and water were the basic elements that made up all matter. Science experiments show that there are more than 100 different types of atoms, which are presented on the periodic table of the elements.

This unit also includes these Investigation and Experimentation Standards:
5.b **5.c** **5.d** **5.e**

Essential Questions

Science in California

San Diego

Dear Jose,

I went to the beach today with my family. Dad said that water, people, and sand are all made of tiny pieces that are too small to see? Did you know that?

When I finished, I had to run back to the car because the sand was so hot! If you had been here, you would have run too!

Your friend,
Franny

What "tiny pieces" is Franny talking about? How does the sun affect Earth? How do these things relate to the **Big Idea?**

Unit Inquiry

Battery Test

You use batteries in many things you own. You may know that batteries store energy. How long do batteries last? Plan and conduct an experiment to find out.

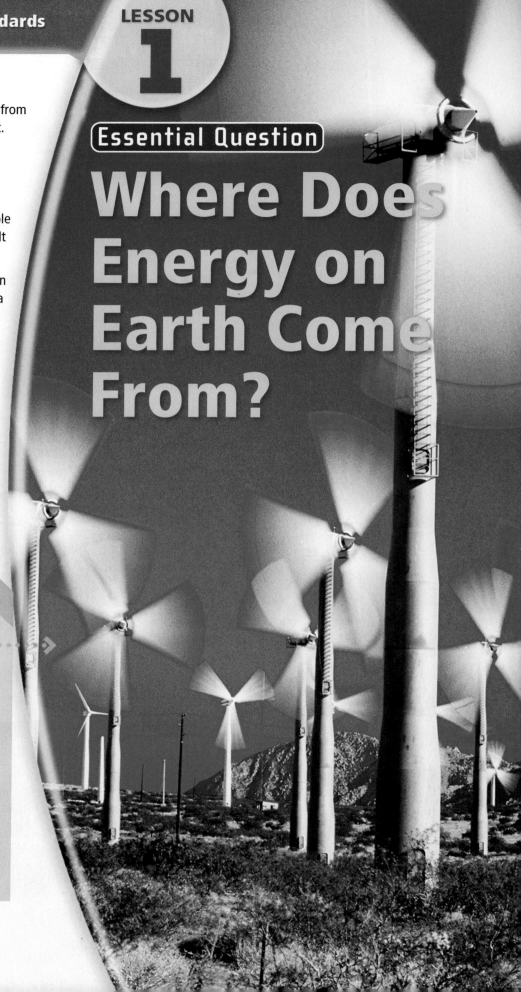

Science Content

1.a *Students know* energy comes from the Sun to Earth in the form of light.

Investigation and Experimentation

5.d Predict the outcome of a simple investigation and compare the result with the prediction.

5.e Collect data in an investigation and analyze those data to develop a logical conclusion.

LESSON 1

Essential Question

Where Does Energy on Earth Come From?

California Fast Fact

Using the Wind's Energy

These space-age windmills, called turbines, stand near Palm Springs. They use the energy of wind to produce electricity. This wind farm can produce enough electricity for an entire city.

energy [EN•er•jee] The ability to cause change (p. 56)

light [LYT] A form of energy you can see (p. 57)

heat [HEET] Energy that warms objects (p. 60)

53

What Solar Energy Does

Start with Questions

You may have seen panels such as this on the roof of a house or business.

- What are they for?

- Why do they face the sun?

Investigate to find out. Then read to find out more.

Prepare to Investigate

Investigation Skill Tip

Before you carry out an investigation, you predict what you think will happen. To make a prediction, you combine what you already know with things you have observed.

Materials
- thermometer
- clock

Make a Data Table

Temperatures in a Sunny Place	
Time	Temperature (in °C)

Follow This Procedure

1 In the morning, place the thermometer where it will be in the sun all day. Place the thermometer on the ground, face up.

2 Wait five minutes. Then record the temperature.

3 Predict what will happen to the temperature through the day.

4 Observe the thermometer each hour. Record the temperature.

5 Communicate your observations in a line graph.

Draw Conclusions

1. What did you observe? Was your prediction correct?

2. **Standards Link** What caused the change in temperature? `1.a`

3. **Investigation Skill** Scientists use their observations to predict what will happen. What do you predict will happen to the temperature after the sun sets? Why? `5.d`

Step 1

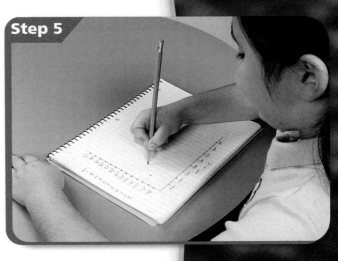

Step 5

Independent Inquiry

Predict the Outcome of an Investigation

Think about the outcome of this investigation. Next, predict what would happen if you put the thermometer in a shady place.

Try it! Collect and analyze the data. Then come up with a conclusion based on the data. `5.d, 5.e`

VOCABULARY
energy p. 56
light p. 57
heat p. 60

SCIENCE CONCEPTS
▸ what energy is
▸ what some forms of energy are

MAIN IDEA AND DETAILS

Look for information about where energy comes from.

Main Idea

detail | detail | detail

What Energy Does

Think about this morning. You got dressed and ate breakfast. You walked from the bus into your school. Each action needed energy.

Energy is the ability to cause change. Energy makes things move, stretch, and grow. You use energy to run, play ball, or cook food.

MAIN IDEA AND DETAILS What are some things you do that need energy?

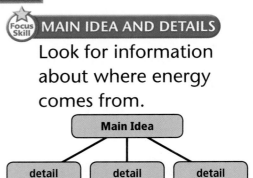

Moving water supplies the energy to turn the water wheel.

Lightning is a kind of electrical energy.

Some Sources of Energy

Wind blows, making sailboats move and flags wave. When gasoline is burned, it provides energy to move cars. Waves carry energy that can change the shape of a beach. The food you eat supplies your body with the energy it needs to grow and change.

Most of Earth's energy comes from millions of miles away! It comes from the sun. **Light** is a form of the sun's energy that you can see. You feel another form of the sun's energy as heat. Energy from the sun lights and warms everything on Earth.

Focus Skill **MAIN IDEA AND DETAILS** What are some sources of energy?

You know that the clock produces sound energy because you hear its bell ring.

Waves and wind carry energy that makes the windsurfer move.

Electrical energy makes this sign light up.

Light from the Sun

Living things depend on the sun's energy. What would happen if the sun stopped shining? There would be no light to provide energy for plants, animals, and people.

Plants need light to grow. If there were no light, all of Earth's plants would soon die. If there were no plants, what would mice, rabbits, and cows eat? Animals such as these get their energy by eating plants. Without plants, there would be no animals.

In a forest, young plants must grow quickly to get the sunlight they need.

Light from the sun allows the girl to see the pages of the book.

People get energy from the things they eat and drink. Milk comes from cows, and cheese is made from milk. Bread is made from wheat. Fruits grow on trees. Everything you eat comes from a plant or an animal. Without plants and animals, there would be no food for people.

You may say that people could use lamps to see and to grow plants for food. However, where would the energy to light those lamps come from? To answer this question, remember where most of Earth's energy comes from—the sun!

 **MAIN IDEA AND DETAILS** What would happen to plants without light from the sun?

Heat from the Sun

You know that when sunlight touches your skin, you feel warm. The sun's energy warms everything on Earth. Millions of living things can live on Earth because of the sun's energy. The form of energy that warms objects is called **heat**.

Earth would be a very different place without the sun's heat. The rivers and oceans would turn to ice. Earth would be too cold for any life.

Heat changes snow to water. What will happen to the snow figure if the sun keeps shining on it?

What kinds of energy are shown in this picture? ▶

Energy from the sun changes Earth. The sun's energy makes the wind blow. It also causes water to move into the air. This water returns to Earth as rain. Millions of years ago, living things took in the sun's energy. After a long time, their bodies became coal and oil under the ground.

Today, people use many sources of energy. They use wind energy to produce electricity. They burn fuels made from oil to get light and heat. All of these started with the sun.

MAIN IDEA AND DETAILS How can the sun's energy become other kinds of energy?

Insta-Lab

Color Matters

Place equal-size pieces of red, black, and white paper on a cookie sheet. Put an ice cube on each piece of paper. Place the cookie sheet in a sunny area. Observe the ice cubes every three minutes. Record your observations. How does color affect how fast the ice cubes melt?

61

Essential Question

Where does energy on Earth come from?

In this lesson, you learned that energy is the ability to cause change. Most of Earth's energy comes from the sun as light and heat.

 Science Content Standards in this Lesson

1.a *Students know* energy comes from the Sun to Earth in the form of light.

1. **Focus Skill** MAIN IDEA AND DETAILS

   Draw and complete a graphic organizer. Give details that support this main idea: Most of Earth's energy comes from the sun. **1.a**

   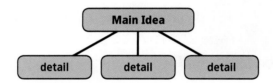

2. **SUMMARIZE** Use the details in the organizer to write three sentences about the main idea in this lesson. **1.a**

3. **DRAW CONCLUSIONS** Describe two ways that you use energy from the sun each day. **1.a**

4. **VOCABULARY** Write three sentences using the word *energy*. **1.a**

5. **Investigate and Experiment** Predict how the results of the Investigate might change if you put a sheet of black paper under the thermometer. **5.d**

6. Describe several ways energy from the sun can change into other forms of energy. **1.a**

   The Big Idea

  Writing ELA–W 2.3

Write a Letter

Write a friendly letter to a friend or relative. Tell what you learned about different forms of energy.

 Math NS 2.1

Solve Problems

In order for a wind turbine to produce electricity, wind speeds must be at least 12 miles per hour. If the speed of the wind is 5 miles per hour, how much faster does the wind need to be?

 Social Studies HSS 3.1.2

Using Energy

Make a chart that lists ways people in your community use energy from the sun. Begin by reviewing the ideas presented in the lesson. Then do research to learn more about specific uses, such as raising crops and producing electricity.

 For more links and activities, go to **www.hspscience.com**

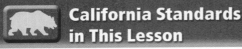

Science Content

1.b *Students know* sources of stored energy take many forms, such as food, fuel, and batteries.

1.c *Students know* machines and living things convert stored energy to motion and heat.

Investigation and Experimentation

5.c Use numerical data in describing and comparing objects, events, and measurements.

5.e Collect data in an investigation and analyze those data to develop a logical conclusion.

California Fast Fact

Something's Cooking!

When people first learned to use fire, they did much of their cooking outdoors. In California today, people still sometimes cook outdoors for fun.

LESSON **2**

Essential Question

How Is Energy Stored and Used?

fuel [FYOOL] A substance that is burned to produce energy (p. 68)

battery [BAT•er•ee] An object that changes stored chemical energy into electrical energy (p. 73)

electricity [ee•lek•TRIS•uh•tee] A kind of energy that moves through a wire (p. 73)

Stored and Moving Energy

Directed Inquiry ## Start with Questions

When the player bats the ball, she transfers, or moves, some of her energy to the ball. The ball changes direction and moves away from her.

- How far will it travel?

- How can she make it travel even farther?

Investigate to find out. Then read to find out more.

Prepare to Investigate

Investigation Skill Tip

To draw a conclusion, use the data you have collected and what you already know. Then decide what seems to be logical.

Materials
- rubber ball or tennis ball
- meterstick

Make a Data Table

Bouncing Ball Investigation			
	Height of Drop (in centimeters)		
	30 cm	60 cm	90 cm
First measurement			
Second measurement			
Third measurement			

Follow This Procedure

1 One team member should hold the meterstick with the 0-cm end on the floor.

2 A second member should hold the ball at the 30-cm mark. When this member drops the ball, a third member should observe how high it bounces. Record the measurement. Repeat two more times.

3 Repeat Step 2 from 60 cm and 90 cm. Observe. Record the measurements.

Draw Conclusions

1. How did the height from which the ball was dropped affect how high it bounced?

2. Standards Link Where did the ball get the energy to move? How did the amount of energy it had affect how high it bounced? **1.b**

3. Investigation Skill Scientists combine their observations with what they already know to draw conclusions. What can you conclude about the ball's energy just before it was dropped? **5.e**

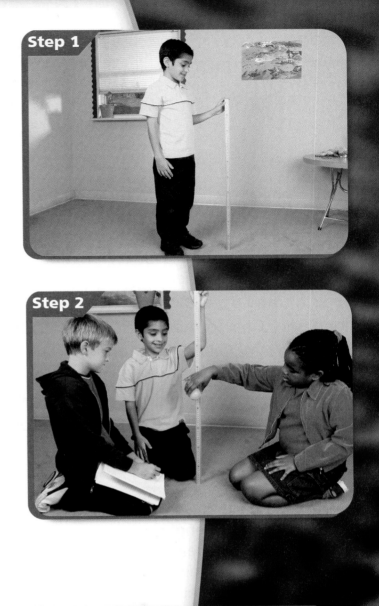

Step 1

Step 2

Independent Inquiry **Use Numerical Data**

What would happen if you dropped the ball from heights of 120 cm and 150 cm?

Figure out a way to measure these heights. Then drop the ball. Compare the measurements you make with your data from the Investigate. **5.c**

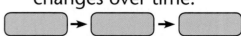
VOCABULARY
fuel p. 68
battery p. 73
electricity p. 73

SCIENCE CONCEPTS
▶ where energy is stored
▶ how energy is used

Focus Skill **SEQUENCE**
Look for information about how energy changes over time.

☐ → ☐ → ☐

Energy from Fuels

Coal, oil, and natural gas are fuels. A **fuel** is a substance that is burned to release the energy stored in it. These fuels formed from the remains of living things that died long ago. Coal formed from plants that stored energy from the sun. Oil and gas formed from tiny living things in ancient oceans.

Gasoline is a fuel made from oil. A car's engine releases the energy stored in the gasoline. This energy can cause the car to move.

The gasoline in the tank is fuel. The car's engine burns the fuel, releasing its stored energy. The energy then turns the wheels to move the car.

Natural gas is another fuel. Gas stoves and furnaces change the energy stored in the fuel to heat. The heat can then be used to cook your food and warm your home.

Not all fuels are old. Trees store energy from the sun as they grow. People cut down the trees and then burn the wood. The energy that is released by burning wood can be used for light, warmth, or cooking food.

Focus Skill SEQUENCE How did energy from the sun change to the energy that moves a car?

When natural gas is burned, its stored energy is released.

Energy is stored in chemical fuels such as wax. Burning a wax candle releases the energy as heat and light.

What sources of energy can you find in this picture?

Energy from Food

How do you get the energy you need to move and grow? Animals and people get energy from food. First, plants store the sun's energy in their leaves, stems, seeds, roots, and fruits. Then, people eat these plant parts.

Oak trees store the sun's energy in their acorns. Squirrels that eat the acorns store this energy in their bodies. When a fox eats a squirrel, the fox gets the energy that is stored in the squirrel's body.

Suppose you eat an apple. When your body digests the apple, it breaks it down into tiny particles. Then, the particles travel to different parts of your body, such as your muscles. Next, the energy that was stored in the apple is released. Your muscles use some of this energy to move your body.

Your body also uses some of the energy to keep you warm. Energy you don't need right away is stored as fat.

Focus Skill **SEQUENCE** **Tell how the energy stored in food becomes available to your muscles.**

The bear gets its energy from eating berries, insects, and fish. ▼

This girl and her father get the energy to play from the foods they eat.

The girl pushes the cat into the box and turns the crank.

Energy from Machines and Batteries

In nature, the sun's energy is stored in fuel and food. People have learned ways to use energy to make machines do work. You can use energy to move the pedals of a bike. The bike uses the energy to cause a larger movement in the wheels. The bike moves forward.

People have also learned how to store energy in different ways. When you close the lid and push the spring down, you store energy in the spring. When you turn the crank, it releases the lid. This causes the spring to unwind, and the toy moves. It stops when the spring has no more energy.

The energy from the girl's muscles is stored in the spring.

When the lid is released, the spring pushes the cat out of the box.

How a Battery Works

Chemicals in the battery contain stored energy. One end of the battery touches the powder inside the battery. The other end touches the brass tube that runs through the battery.

To use the energy, you put the battery in a *circuit* (SER•kit). The stored chemical energy changes to electricity that can light a flashlight or make a toy move.

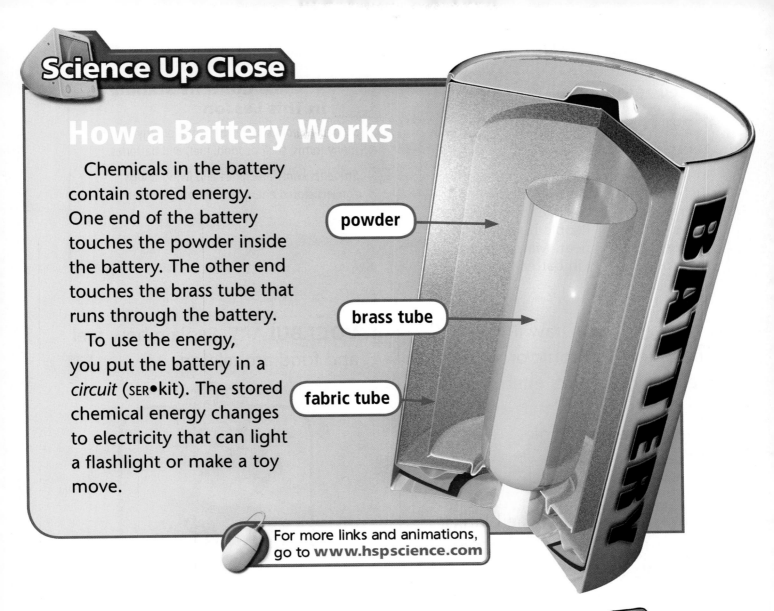

powder

brass tube

fabric tube

For more links and animations, go to **www.hspscience.com**

A **battery** is an object that stores energy in chemicals. When the battery is used, its chemical energy changes to electricity. **Electricity** is a kind of energy that moves through a wire. In a flashlight bulb, electricity changes to light and heat. After a while, the light goes out because the battery has no more stored energy. Time to buy a new battery!

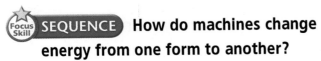 **SEQUENCE** How do machines change energy from one form to another?

Insta-Lab

Make It Go

Place on the floor a toy that uses batteries. Turn it on and let it go. Record your observations. Then take the battery out of the toy. How can you make the toy move now? What kinds of energy can move the toy?

Essential Question

How is energy stored and used?

In this lesson, you learned that food, fuel, and batteries store energy. Food energy makes it possible for people to move and grow. People burn fuel to release light and heat. Machines use the stored energy in batteries and in fuel.

Science Content Standards in This Lesson

1.b *Students know* sources of stored energy take many forms, such as food, fuel, and batteries.

1.c *Students know* machines and living things convert stored energy to motion and heat.

1. **Focus Skill** **SEQUENCE** Draw and complete a graphic organizer to tell how the sun's energy moves to plants and animals and is then used by people. **1.b**

2. SUMMARIZE Fill in the blanks. Energy from the _____ is stored in plants as food or _____. When the stored energy is _____, it changes form. The _____ energy stored in batteries changes to electricity. **1.b, 1.c**

3. DRAW CONCLUSIONS What kinds of energy can be used to make a lawn mower work? **1.c**

4. VOCABULARY Explain how fuel and food are related. **1.b**

5. Critical Thinking What kind of energy change takes place when you put batteries in a CD player and turn it on?

A electrical changes to chemical

B chemical changes to electrical

C electrical changes to heat

D heat changes to electrical **1.b**

6. Describe three ways people change energy from one form to another.

The **Big Idea** **1.b, 1.c**

 Writing ELA–W 1.1

Write a Paragraph

Use ideas from this lesson to write a paragraph that describes three ways you and your family use sources of stored energy.

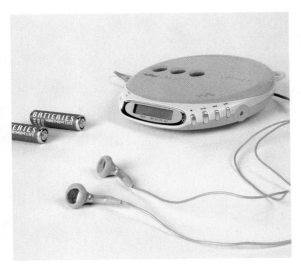

 Math NS 3.3

Solve Problems

A CD player needs three batteries. Each battery costs $0.75. How much will the three batteries cost altogether?

 Drama VPA–T 2.2

Write a Script

Write a short script for a skit that shows how energy moves from the sun to plants and animals and then to people.

 For more links and activities, go to **www.hspscience.com**

A New Source of Energy?

People in the United States use a lot of electricity. Televisions, computers, toasters, and lights all use electricity. Energy companies have to produce all that electricity. Unfortunately, making electricity can cause the air to become polluted. An energy company in Georgia is testing a way to make electricity that doesn't give off much pollution.

Most energy stations burn coal or oil. Burning these fuels gives off gases that pollute the air.

Generating Energy

Electricity is produced at energy stations, which are sometimes called power plants. Energy stations have huge machines called generators. These machines generate electricity and send it across wires to your home and school.

Mixing Fuel

A company in Georgia is testing a fuel that is a mixture of grass and coal. The grass, called switchgrass, is a kind of prairie grass that grows in the South.

To make the fuel, the company mixes switchgrass and coal. The mixture is then formed into cubes. As the cubes burn, they release almost as much energy as the same amount of coal would produce. However, the cubes give off less pollution than other fuels.

Think and Write

1. What are the sources of the electricity that you use at school and at home?

   1.d

2. How could you use less electricity?

Find out more. Log on to
www.hspscience.com

LESSON 3

Essential Question

How Does Energy Move?

Science Content

1.d *Students know* energy can be carried from one place to another by waves, such as water waves and sound waves, by electric current, and by moving objects.

Investigation and Experimentation

5.d Predict the outcome of a simple investigation and compare the result with the prediction.

5.e Collect data in an investigation and analyze those data to develop a logical conclusion.

California Fast Fact

Surf's Up!

Surfers at Half Moon Bay use the energy carried by ocean waves to move across the water. The speed of a wave depends on water depth and wind speed.

Half Moon Bay, California

wave [WAYV] A disturbance that moves energy to other places (p. 82)

vibrations [vy•BRAY•shuhnz] A series of quick back-and-forth movements (p. 84)

friction [FRIK•shuhn] A force that slows the motion of objects that are touching (p. 87)

Investigate

Making Waves

Directed Inquiry

Start with Questions

The bobber on a fishing line floats on the water.

- What happens to it when a passing boat makes waves?
- How do waves carry energy?

Investigate to find out. Then read to find out more.

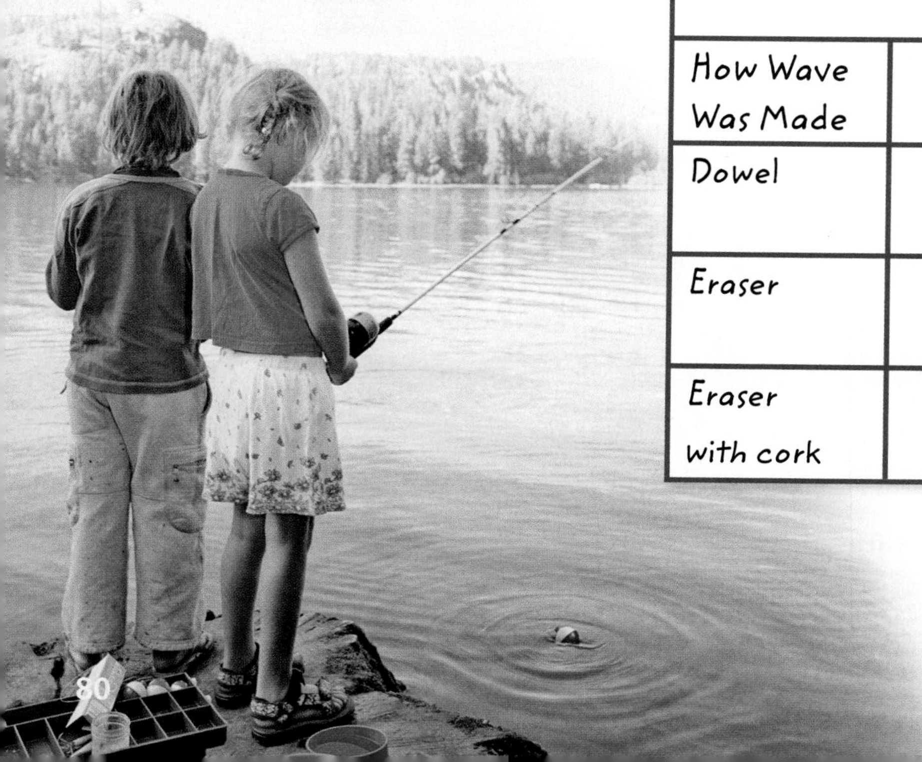

Prepare to Investigate

Investigation Skill Tip

Using models is a good way to learn about things that would be hard to study directly. When you make a model, it should be as much like the real thing as possible.

Materials

- water
- clear rectangular glass pan
- dowel
- pencil with eraser
- small cork

Make an Observation Chart

Making Waves	
How Wave Was Made	Drawing of Observation
Dowel	
Eraser	
Eraser with cork	

Follow This Procedure

1. Put 1 cm of water in the pan.

2. Set the dowel in the pan near one of the short sides.

3. Slowly roll the dowel back and forth about a half turn. Observe and draw the waves you see. Remove the dowel.

4. After the water stops moving, dip the eraser end of the pencil up and down near the middle of the pan. Observe and draw the waves.

5. Place the cork halfway between the middle and an end of the pan. Repeat Step 4. Record how the cork moves.

Step 3

Step 5

Draw Conclusions

1. What caused the waves to form?

2. **Standards Link** How did the movement of the waves compare with the movement of the cork?   1.d

3. **Investigation Skill** Scientists use models to understand how larger objects behave. What does this model of waves tell you about how a boat on the ocean might be affected by the waves?

Independent Inquiry   **Collect Data in an Investigation**

Think about the waves you observed when you moved the dowel.

Predict what would happen if you used a larger dowel. Then try it. Use the data you collect to reach a conclusion about how the waves made by the two dowels are different.   5.d, 5.e

VOCABULARY
wave p. 82
vibrations p. 84
friction p. 87

SCIENCE CONCEPTS
► how waves carry energy
► how energy moves in other ways

(Focus Skill) COMPARE AND CONTRAST
Compare the ways sound and light waves travel.

| alike | different |

Waves Carry Energy

Wind blowing across the surface of water makes waves. A **wave** is a disturbance that moves energy. Waves in water are up-and-down motions. A drawing of a water wave might look like the rope in the picture. The waves transfer, or carry, the wind's energy. Which way does the energy move?

In the Investigate, you made waves by adding energy to water. The waves caused energy to move across the pan, but the water moved only up and down, not across. The waves, not the water, carried energy.

As energy moves from one end of the rope to the other, a point on the rope moves up and down. ►

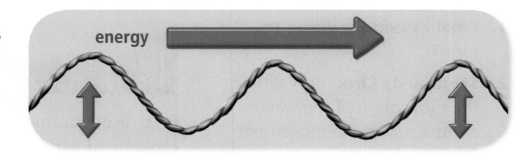

energy

◄ As a wave carries energy past these penguin toys, they bob up and down.

82

The sun's light and heat travel to Earth in waves. Like water waves, these are up-and-down waves. Unlike water waves, you can't see them.

During an earthquake, part of Earth's surface moves. This releases energy. The energy travels through the ground in waves. The ground and the buildings on it can't move and bend. As the energy waves pass, the ground may crack and the buildings may break.

Focus Skill **COMPARE AND CONTRAST** **How are the effects of water waves different from those of earthquake waves?**

This tool is called a *seismograph* (SYZ•muh•graf). It records the strength of the energy waves in an earthquake. ▼

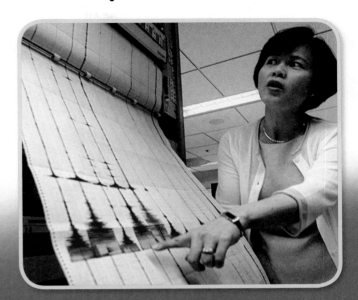

Building walls break and fall down because they can't move freely as the wave passes.

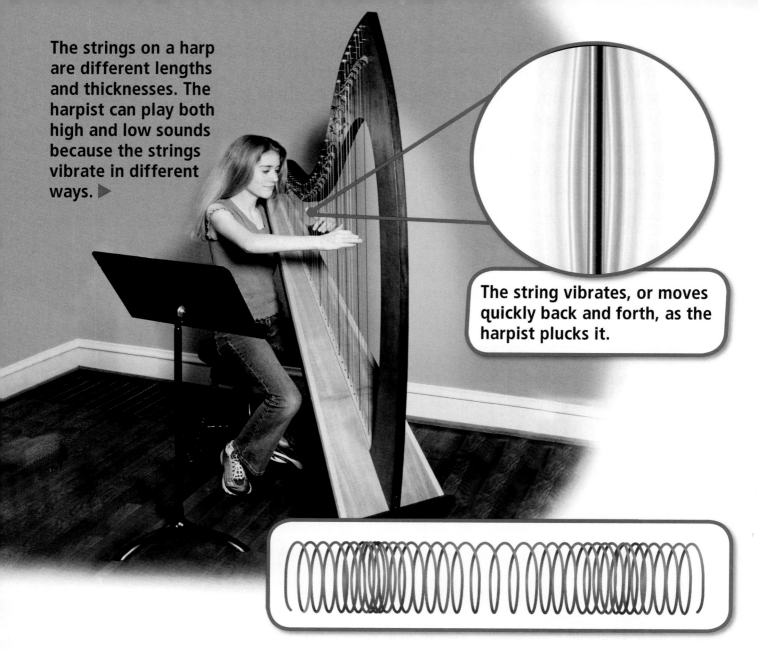

The strings on a harp are different lengths and thicknesses. The harpist can play both high and low sounds because the strings vibrate in different ways. ▶

The string vibrates, or moves quickly back and forth, as the harpist plucks it.

▲ In a back-and-forth wave, the energy moves in a straight line away from the source. The spring vibrates.

Sound Waves

Sound is energy you can hear. Like light and heat, sound travels in waves. However, sound does not travel in up-and-down waves.

What happens when you tap the end of a spring toy? As you see in the picture, the energy moves along the spring. This is similar to the way energy moves across water. However, the coils of the spring don't move up and down the way water does. Instead, they move back and forth. The back-and-forth motions are **vibrations**.

Touch your throat as you talk. Do you feel the vibration? When objects vibrate, they make sound waves. The air vibrates back and forth as energy moves away from the source, or the place where it came from. A human voice, a trumpet, and a singing bird all make vibrations.

Your *eardrum* is a thin, skin-like sheet inside your ear. It is like the flat part of a drum. When sound energy strikes the eardrum, it vibrates. Your brain recognizes the vibrations as sounds.

COMPARE AND CONTRAST

How are sound waves different from waves that carry light from the sun?

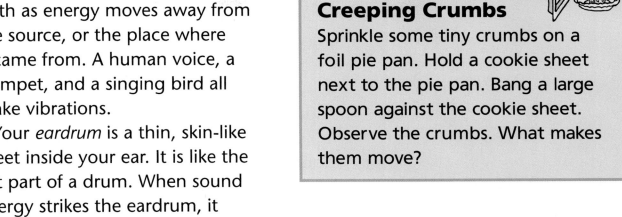

Insta-Lab

Creeping Crumbs

Sprinkle some tiny crumbs on a foil pie pan. Hold a cookie sheet next to the pie pan. Bang a large spoon against the cookie sheet. Observe the crumbs. What makes them move?

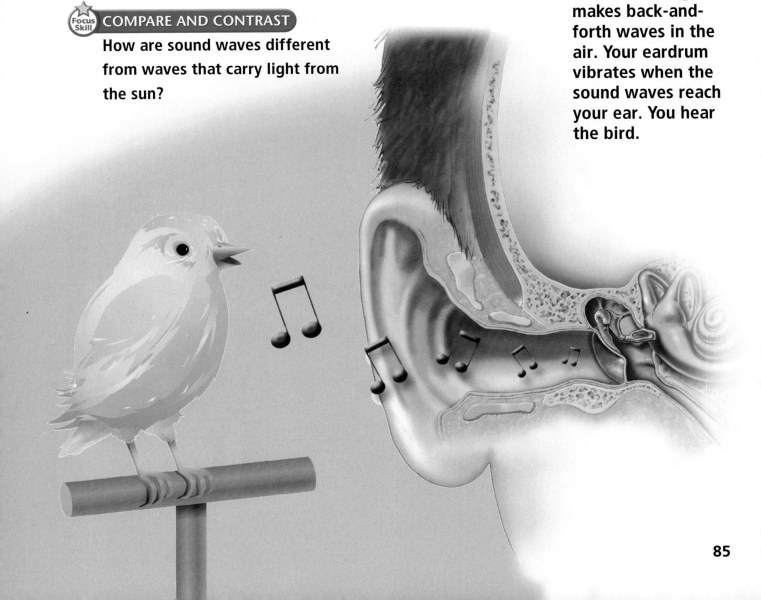

◄ The bird's song makes back-and-forth waves in the air. Your eardrum vibrates when the sound waves reach your ear. You hear the bird.

Other Ways Energy Moves

Electricity is a form of energy that does not travel in waves. How does it move from place to place?

Energy stations change the energy of wind, falling water, or burning fuel to electricity. The electricity travels through wires to your home. When you turn on a radio, electricity changes to sound energy. In a toaster, it changes to heat energy and light energy. In a fan, it changes to the motion of the fan's blades.

Electricity travels through wires from the energy station to your home. ▼

Heat energy under the ground is transferred to water, which then shoots up into the air.

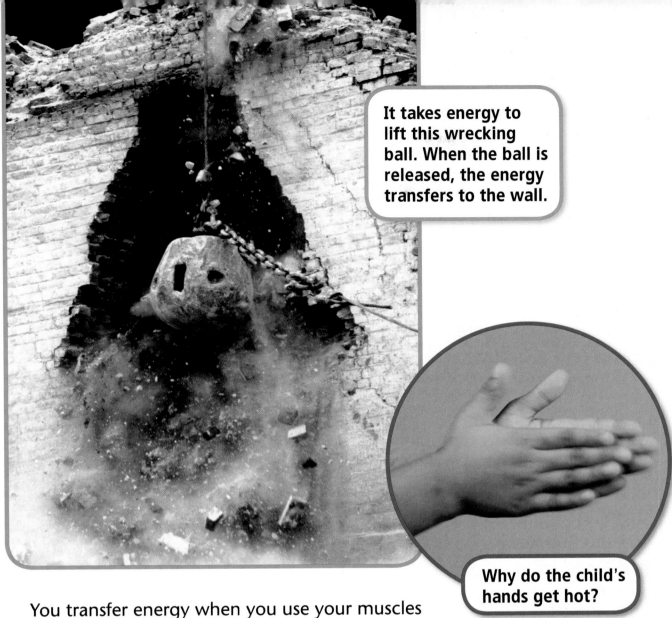

It takes energy to lift this wrecking ball. When the ball is released, the energy transfers to the wall.

Why do the child's hands get hot?

You transfer energy when you use your muscles to move objects. If you lift a ball and then drop it, it bounces. If you lift it higher, you give it more energy. It bounces higher.

Suppose you throw a ball at a bottle. Energy is transferred to the ball. When the ball hits the bottle, its energy knocks the bottle over.

Friction is a force that slows the motion of objects that are touching. Rub your hands together. What do you feel? Friction changes the energy of motion to heat energy.

 **COMPARE AND CONTRAST** How is electricity like light? How is it different?

Standards Wrap-Up and Lesson Review

How does energy move?

In this lesson, you learned that there are different kinds of waves that all carry energy from place to place. Energy is also carried by electricity and by moving objects.

 Science Content Standards in This Lesson

1.d *Students know* energy can be carried from one place to another by waves, such as water waves and sound waves, by electric current, and by moving objects.

1. (Focus Skill) **COMPARE AND CONTRAST** Draw and complete a graphic organizer to compare light waves and sound waves. **1.d**

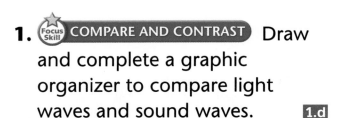

2. **SUMMARIZE** Fill in the blanks. Energy _____ in several different ways. Light, heat, and sound travel in _____. Electricity travels through _____. Energy produced by your _____ transfers to things you push or pull. Friction changes motion to _____. **1.d**

3. **DRAW CONCLUSIONS** Which has more stored energy, a book on a high shelf or one on a low shelf? Why? **1.d**

4. **VOCABULARY** How do *vibrations* produce sound? **1.d**

5. **Critical Thinking** Why do you think some sounds are louder than others? **1.d**

6. Explain how energy changes its form as it transfers from the sun to your muscles to a ball that you throw. **1.d**

The **Big Idea**

 Writing ELA–W 1.1

Write a Paragraph

Write a paragraph that uses at least three of these words: *energy, waves, light, sound,* and *motion.* Be sure you use each word in the same way that it is used in the lesson.

 Math NS 2.8

Solve Problems

A student counts the waves as they wash past an old post. In 10 seconds, 2 waves pass. How many waves will pass in 30 seconds?

 Art VPA–VA 2.4

Create a Work of Art

Create a work of art that shows one kind of energy that is carried by waves. Label your art to show how the waves move and to show the direction in which energy travels.

 For more links and activities, go to **www.hspscience.com**

Science Content

1.e *Students know* matter has three forms: solid, liquid, and gas.

Investigation and Experimentation

5.b Differentiate evidence from opinion and know that scientists do not rely on claims or conclusions unless they are backed by observations that can be confirmed.

5.d Predict the outcome of a simple investigation and compare the result with the prediction.

California Fast Fact

Sandy City

It seems there's no limit to the things clever people can build from sand! At Ocean Beach, everyone who saw this "city" of sand was amazed by its size and beauty.

LESSON 4

Essential Question

What Is Matter?

Ocean Beach,
California

matter [MAT•er] Anything that takes up space (p. 95)

solid [SAHL•id] A kind of matter that has a definite shape and a definite volume (p. 96)

liquid [LIK•wid] A kind of matter that has a definite volume but no definite shape (p. 96)

gas [GAS] A kind of matter that has no definite shape or volume (p. 97)

Measuring Volume

Start with Questions

Compare the glasses.

- Will the father and daughter get the same amount of milk?

- If not, who will get the most?

- How could they both get the same amount?

Investigate to find out. Then read to find out more.

Prepare to Investigate

Investigation Skill Tip

Before you carry out an investigation, you predict what you think will happen. To make a prediction, you combine what you already know with things you have observed.

Materials
- metric measuring cup
- water
- masking tape
- 3 clear containers of different shapes

Make an Observation Chart

	Measuring Volume		
	Container Number		
	1	2	3
Drawing of Container with 100 mL of Water			

Follow This Procedure

❶ Use the measuring cup to measure 100 mL of water. Pour the water into one of the containers.

❷ Use masking tape to mark the water level. Place the bottom edge of the tape at the water line.

❸ Repeat Steps 1 and 2 with the other two containers.

❹ Compare the water levels in the three containers. Record what you observe.

Draw Conclusions

1. How much water is in each container?

2. **Standards Link** Explain why the water levels are different in the three containers. 1.e

3. **Investigation Skill** Scientists use the data they collect and the observations they make to predict what will happen. What do you predict will happen if you pour the water from each container back into the measuring cup? 5.d

Step 1

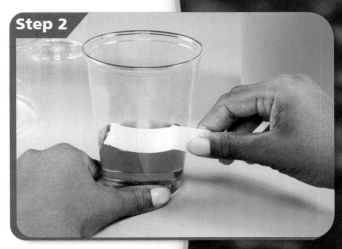

Step 2

Independent Inquiry

Separate Opinion from Evidence

A person might say that containers with different shapes hold different amounts of water. How might you get evidence to support this opinion?

Use two containers. Predict which one will hold more water. Then carry out your investigation and collect your data. Tell whether your prediction was correct. 5.b, 5.d

VOCABULARY

matter p. 95
solid p. 96
liquid p. 96
gas p. 97

SCIENCE CONCEPTS

▶ what matter is
▶ what forms matter has

Focus Skill **MAIN IDEA AND DETAILS**

Look for details about states of matter and properties.

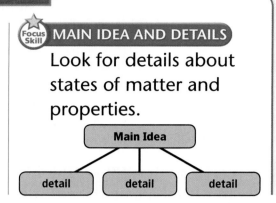

Matter

What do a book, the water in a cooking pot, and the air in a balloon have in common? Not much, you may say! They certainly are different, but they do have one thing in common. They all take up space.

Volume is the amount of space something takes up. You can figure out the volume of a book by using a ruler. In the Investigate, you used a measuring cup to measure the volume of water.

Everything you see in this picture is matter. How many different kinds of matter can you find?

▲ If you let the air out of these balloons, their volumes would decrease. The balloons would take up much less space.

You might not believe that air takes up space. After all, you can walk through the air in a room. If air doesn't take up space, though, why does a balloon get bigger when you blow into it? The only thing inside it is the air you put there. From this, you can tell that air does take up space.

Matter is anything that takes up space. The book, the water, and the air are all forms of matter. Look around you. What other forms of matter do you see?

 **MAIN IDEA AND DETAILS** What is matter?

These two horses have a lot in common, but one has a much larger volume.

Forms of Matter

Matter has different forms, or *states*. A **solid** is matter with a definite volume and a definite shape. Something that is definite does not change. A book is a solid. If you move it, it still has the shape of a book. It still takes up the same amount of space.

In the Investigate, you put the same volume of water into containers of different shapes. The water took a different shape in each container, but the volume of the water did not change. Water is a liquid. A **liquid** is matter that has a definite volume, but no definite shape. What are some other kinds of liquids?

The oil and the vinegar are both liquids. The salad pieces, the bowl, the bottles, and the table are solids. ▼

Water changes shape as it falls.

◄ The airplane and the mountains in this picture are solids. The water is a liquid. You can't see the air, which is a mixture of gases. Without it, however, the plane would not fly!

▲ If you popped the balloon, what would happen to the volume and shape of the air inside?

Air has no definite shape or volume. If you put it in a balloon, it spreads out to fill all the space inside. What happens if you open the balloon? The air spreads out all around you. It takes up more space than it did when it was inside the balloon.

Matter that has no definite shape or volume is a **gas**. As you know, some stoves cook with natural gas. You can't see the natural gas, but you can see a blue flame when it burns.

Focus Skill MAIN IDEA AND DETAILS What are three states of matter?

Properties of Matter

Matter can be a solid, a liquid, or a gas. How else can you describe matter? You might say that a cat's fur is soft. You could describe the color, taste, or smell of a lemon. Milk is a white liquid. A sheet of paper is thin and bends easily. A metal pan doesn't bend. The pan clangs when you hit it with a spoon.

The features described above are all properties of matter. You use one or more of your senses to observe these properties.

You need tools to observe some properties of matter. You can use a measuring cup to measure the volume of a liquid. You can use a ruler to measure an object's length or width.

A balance is used to measure a property called mass. *Mass* is the amount of matter in an object. To use a balance, you set a solid on one pan and add masses to the other until the pans balance. You can also use a balance to measure the mass of a certain volume of a liquid or gas.

 **MAIN IDEA AND DETAILS**

What are five properties of matter?

Science Up Close

Measuring Mass

The mass of the truck is 50 grams.

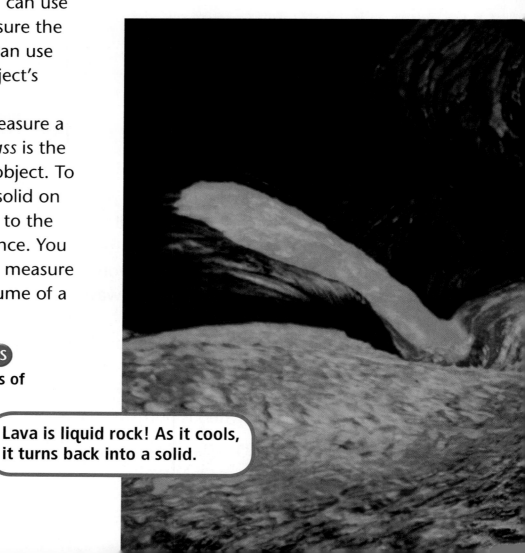

Lava is liquid rock! As it cools, it turns back into a solid.

The mass of the pebbles is 14 grams.

What is the mass of the truck and pebbles together?

For more links and animations, go to www.hspscience.com

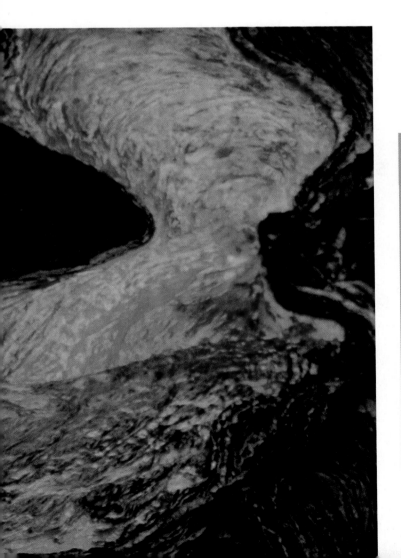

Insta-Lab

Comparing Mass and Volume

Fill one sandwich bag with marbles. Fill another with cotton balls. Seal the bags. Measure the mass of each bag. How do their volumes compare? Which matter has more mass in the same volume—marbles or cotton balls?

Standards Wrap-Up and Lesson Review

What is matter?

In this lesson, you learned that matter has different forms, or states. Properties of matter such as color, odor, and taste can be observed by using your senses. You need tools to measure other properties, such as mass and volume.

Science Content Standards in This Lesson

1.e *Students know* matter has three forms: solid, liquid, and gas.

1. (Focus Skill) **MAIN IDEA AND DETAILS** Draw and complete a graphic organizer to give details that support this main idea: Matter has properties you can observe. **1.e**

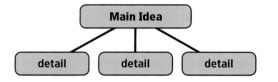

2. SUMMARIZE Fill in the blanks. Matter is anything that takes up _____. It has three forms, or _____. You use your _____ to observe properties such as color, odor, and taste. You use tools to measure _____ and _____. **1.e**

3. DRAW CONCLUSIONS Suppose you pour water from a cup into a glass. Name a property of the water that will change and one that will not change. **1.e**

4. VOCABULARY Describe the properties of the following forms of matter: *solid*, *liquid*, *gas*. **1.e**

5. Critical Thinking Think of your favorite food. What properties could you use to describe it? **1.e**

6. Which tool is used to measure the mass of an object?
A ruler   **C** measuring cup
B balance   **D** beaker   **1.e**

Make Connections

 Writing ELA–W 2.2

Write a Description

Write a description of a scene that contains solids, liquids, and gases. Be sure to include details that tell how things look, smell, sound, and feel.

 Math NS 2.2

Solve Problems

Each of 6 bottles holds 9 mL of water. When the water from all the bottles is poured into one container, what is the total volume?

 Health

Identify Properties

What properties should a helmet have to protect you from injury when you ride a bike? Identify these properties, and show them on a poster that you can share with your class.

 For more links and activities, go to **www.hspscience.com**

Science Content

1.e *Students know* matter has three forms: solid, liquid, and gas.

1.f *Students know* evaporation and melting are changes that occur when the objects are heated.

Investigation and Experimentation

5.c Use numerical data in describing and comparing objects, events, and measurements.

5.e Collect data in an investigation and analyze those data to develop a logical conclusion.

California Fast Fact

Wonderful Water

Icicles hanging from a lodge roof in the Sierra Nevada melt in the sun. Water is unusual. It can be a solid, a liquid, or a gas at temperatures found in nature.

LESSON 5

Essential Question

What Causes Matter to Change State?

melting [MELT•ing] The change of state from a solid to a liquid (p. 106)

evaporation [ee•vap•uh•RAY•shuhn] The change of state from a liquid to a gas (p. 107)

Mammoth Lakes, California

Temperature and Matter

Start with Questions

Liquid nitrogen boils at a temperature that's still cold enough to freeze water.

- How can matter boil at such a low temperature?

- What effect does cooling have on matter?

Investigate to find out. Then read to find out more.

Prepare to Investigate

Investigation Skill Tip

There are many ways to record data. You might use a data table or an observation chart. You communicate data by sharing it with others.

Materials
- safety goggles
- metric measuring cup
- hot water
- plastic jar or beaker
- thermometer
- 3 ice cubes of the same size
- plastic spoon

Make a Data Table

Water Temperatures		
	Temperature (°C)	Other Observations
Hot tap water		
After first ice cube		
After second ice cube		
After third ice cube		

Follow This Procedure

CAUTION: **Wear safety goggles when you pour hot water.**

1 Measure 200 mL of hot tap water. Pour it into the jar or beaker.

2 Measure the temperature of the water with the thermometer. Record the data.

3 Add an ice cube to the water. Stir. Record what you observe.

4 Measure the temperature of the water again. Record the data.

5 Repeat Steps 3 and 4 twice.

Draw Conclusions

1. What happened to the ice cubes in the water?

2. **Standards Link** What happened to the temperature of the water each time you added an ice cube? Why do you think this happened? **1.f**

3. **Investigation Skill** One way scientists communicate data is in a bar graph. Make a bar graph to communicate what happened to the temperature in this activity.

Step 2

Step 3

Independent Inquiry | **Collect Data in an Investigation**

Think about the data you collected during this investigation. How might the data be different if you put 100 mL of water in a pan in a freezer?

Measure the temperature of the water every 10 minutes. Interpret the data, and draw a conclusion that explains why the water changed. **5.c, 5.e**

1.e, 1.f

VOCABULARY
melting p. 106
evaporation p. 107

SCIENCE CONCEPTS
▶ how matter changes state
▶ what evaporation is

CAUSE AND EFFECT
Look for things that cause a change of state.

cause ⟶ effect

Melting and Evaporation

Matter can change when it is heated or cooled. Why? Matter is made up of small particles. In ice, the particles are close together. They vibrate, but they cannot move around. In the Investigate, you put ice cubes in hot water. Heat energy from the water moved to the ice. The energy caused the particles in the ice to move around freely.

The ice cubes melted. **Melting** is the change of a solid to a liquid. Any solid can melt. Even the pans you cook in can melt if they get hot enough!

Math in Science
Interpret Data

°C
100

50

0

At what temperature does ice melt? Between what temperatures is water a liquid?

Iron melts at 1,535°C (2,795°F). Liquid iron can be poured into molds to make different shapes.

Evaporation

The child's clothing and skin are wet. Heat from the sun speeds up the motion of the water particles.

Most of the water has evaporated.

Melting is not the only way matter can change when it is heated. Suppose that you hang wet clothes outside on a sunny day. The next time you check, they are dry! Energy from the sun caused the particles of water to move faster and faster. When the particles gained enough energy, they broke away from the water and entered the air. The water evaporated. **Evaporation** is the change of a liquid to a gas.

(Focus Skill) **CAUSE AND EFFECT** What causes a liquid to evaporate?

Insta-Lab

Disappearing Liquid

With a dropper, place one drop of water on a piece of plastic. Use a second dropper to place one drop of rubbing alcohol several centimeters away from the water. Observe the liquids for five minutes. What did you observe? How can you explain what happened?

Other Changes of State

Suppose a pan of water is heated on the stove. What happens? After a while, the water begins to bubble. A mist forms above it. The water boils. *Boiling* is a change from a liquid to a gas. Boiling changes a liquid to a gas faster than evaporation does.

What happens if you put water in the freezer? The air in the freezer is cold. This causes the water particles to lose energy. When the particles move slowly enough, the water freezes. *Freezing* is the change from a liquid to a solid. Freezing is the opposite of melting.

▲ Carbon dioxide is a gas. At very low temperatures, the gas changes directly into a solid called dry ice. It does not become a liquid first!

Freezing liquid juice makes a tasty treat. ▼

What happens when the frozen juice pop touches the girl's warm tongue?

Now, suppose you are drinking a glass of ice water on a hot day. Water appears on the outside of the glass. Why? Is it leaking through the glass? No! The air around the glass contains water vapor, which is the gas form of water. The particles of water vapor next to the cold glass lose energy. This causes the particles to slow down. When they slow down enough, the gas *condenses,* or turns back into a liquid. Condensation is the opposite of evaporation.

Focus Skill **CAUSE AND EFFECT** **What causes droplets of water to form on the outside of a cold soda can?**

The glass is colder than the air around it. This causes water vapor to condense on the outside of the glass.

◄ Water vapor in the boy's breath loses energy as it hits the cold window. The gas condenses, forming tiny drops of water.

Standards Wrap-Up and Lesson Review

What causes matter to change state?

In this lesson, you learned that adding or taking away heat energy can cause matter to change state.

Science Content Standards in This Lesson

1.e *Students know* matter has three forms: solid, liquid, and gas.

1.f *Students know* evaporation and melting are changes that occur when the objects are heated.

---

1. **Focus Skill** **CAUSE AND EFFECT** Draw and complete a graphic organizer to tell the effects of adding heat to a solid and to a liquid. **1.e, 1.f**

cause	→	effect

2. SUMMARIZE Fill in the blanks. Matter can change _____ when its particles gain or lose energy. When a solid is heated, it can _____. When a liquid is heated, it can _____ or _____. Melting is the opposite of _____. The opposite of evaporation is _____. **1.e, 1.f**

3. DRAW CONCLUSIONS Why doesn't water vapor condense on the outside of a cup of hot chocolate? **1.f**

4. VOCABULARY Draw pictures to show what happens during *evaporation* and *melting*. **1.f**

5. Critical Thinking Which change of state describes what happens when water vapor forms clouds?

A melting

B freezing

C condensation

D evaporation **1.f**

6. Investigate and Experiment In the Investigate, you made a bar graph to display your data. How else could you display this numerical data? **5.c**

 Writing ELA–W 1.1

Write a Paragraph

Write a paragraph in which you explain how the words *melt* and *freeze* and the words *evaporate* and *condense* are related.

 Math MG 1.4

Solve Problems

Maria bought a frozen treat to eat on a hot day. She forgot about the treat as she played with her friends. It melted in $\frac{3}{4}$ of an hour. How many minutes did it take to melt?

 Social Studies HSS 3.5.1

Think About Geography

Look in your social studies textbook to identify crops that are grown in different parts of California. Then pick one crop, and find out about the climate in the area where it grows. Write a short report to share with your class.

 For more links and activities, go to **www.hspscience.com**

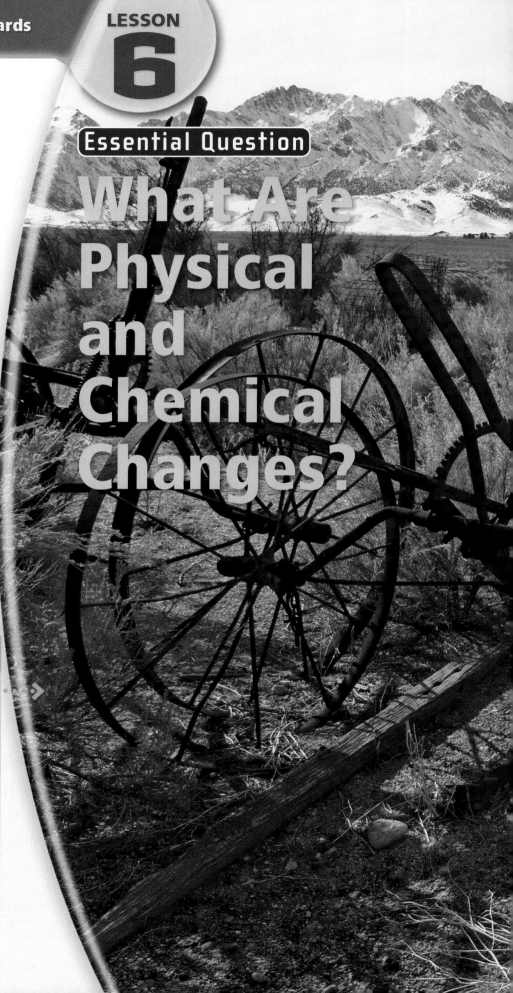

California Standards in This Lesson

Science Content

1.g *Students know* that when two or more substances are combined, a new substance may be formed with properties that are different from those of the original materials.

Investigation and Experimentation

5.e Collect data in an investigation and analyze those data to develop a logical conclusion.

Essential Question

What Are Physical and Chemical Changes?

California Fast Fact

A Change over Time

When the California gold rush began, in 1848, this equipment was made of smooth, shiny metal. Today, some of the metal has changed to a rough orange coating called rust.

mixture [MIKS•cher] A substance that contains different kinds of matter (p. 116)

Independence, California

Physical and Chemical Changes

Start with Questions

You have probably seen fireworks during Fourth of July celebrations.

- As the fireworks explode, how does the matter in them change?

- What signs show that matter is changing?

Investigate to find out. Then read to find out more.

Prepare to Investigate

Investigation Skill Tip

When you compare things, you tell how they are alike and how they are different. To compare two things, observe them carefully and make a short list that describes each one.

Materials

- safety goggles
- 2 plastic cups or beakers
- hot water
- 2 plastic spoons
- baking soda
- vinegar

Make an Observation Chart

My Observations	
Substances	Observations
Baking soda and water	
Baking soda and vinegar	

Follow This Procedure

Caution: **Put on safety goggles.**

1. Half-fill one cup or beaker with hot water.

2. Use one spoon to add a half-spoonful of baking soda to the water. Stir. Observe and record what happens.

3. Half-fill the other cup or beaker with vinegar.

4. Use the other spoon to add a half-spoonful of baking soda to the vinegar. Stir. Observe and record what happens.

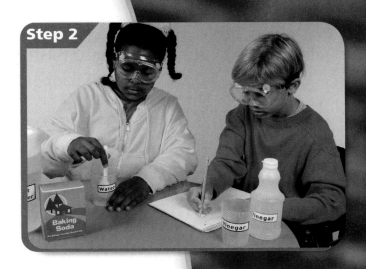
Step 2

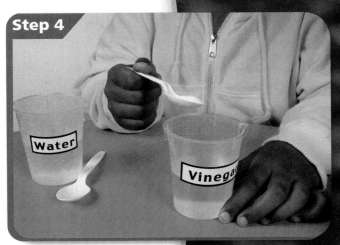
Step 4

Draw Conclusions

1. What was different about what happened to the baking soda in water and in vinegar?

2. **Standards Link** In which step did you see a new kind of matter form? How did you know it was new? **1.g**

3. **Investigation Skill** Scientists sometimes compare their observations during an experiment with something that they already know or understand. Compare other things you've seen with what happened to the baking soda in water and in vinegar.

Independent Inquiry

Collect Data in an Investigation

Think about your observations during this investigation. What other questions can you ask about the baking soda, water, and vinegar?

Write a plan to find the answer to one of your questions. What procedure will you follow? What data will you need to collect to draw a logical conclusion? **5.e**

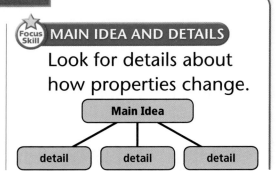
VOCABULARY
mixture p. 116

SCIENCE CONCEPTS
▶ what a mixture is
▶ what happens during a chemical change

Focus Skill MAIN IDEA AND DETAILS
Look for details about how properties change.

Main Idea

detail   detail   detail

Physical Changes

A glass breaks. You tear a strip of paper into pieces. An ice cube melts in your hand. These are all physical changes. A physical change happens when no new substance, or kind of matter, is formed. The glass and paper are in smaller pieces, but they are still glass and paper. The solid water in ice simply changed form to liquid water.

When you combine, or mix, salt and sand, you make a mixture. A **mixture** is a combination of two or more kinds of matter.

In a pure substance—such as water, salt, or sand—every particle is like every other particle. If you mix these substances together, their particles do not change into new matter.

salt crystals

sand

This bowl holds a mixture of cereal, strawberries, and bananas. How could you separate the mixture?

The salt and sand haven't changed. You can still separate them. Becoming part of a mixture is a physical change.

What happens when you stir sugar into water until it disappears? We say that the sugar *dissolves.* Is this a physical change?

The sugar water tastes sweet—like sugar. If you let the sugar water evaporate, the sugar is left in the glass. When the sugar dissolved, it broke up into pieces that were too small to see. It did not change into a new substance. This means that dissolving is also a physical change.

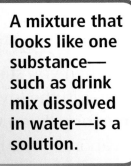

A mixture that looks like one substance—such as drink mix dissolved in water—is a solution.

Focus Skill MAIN IDEA AND DETAILS

What is a mixture?

117

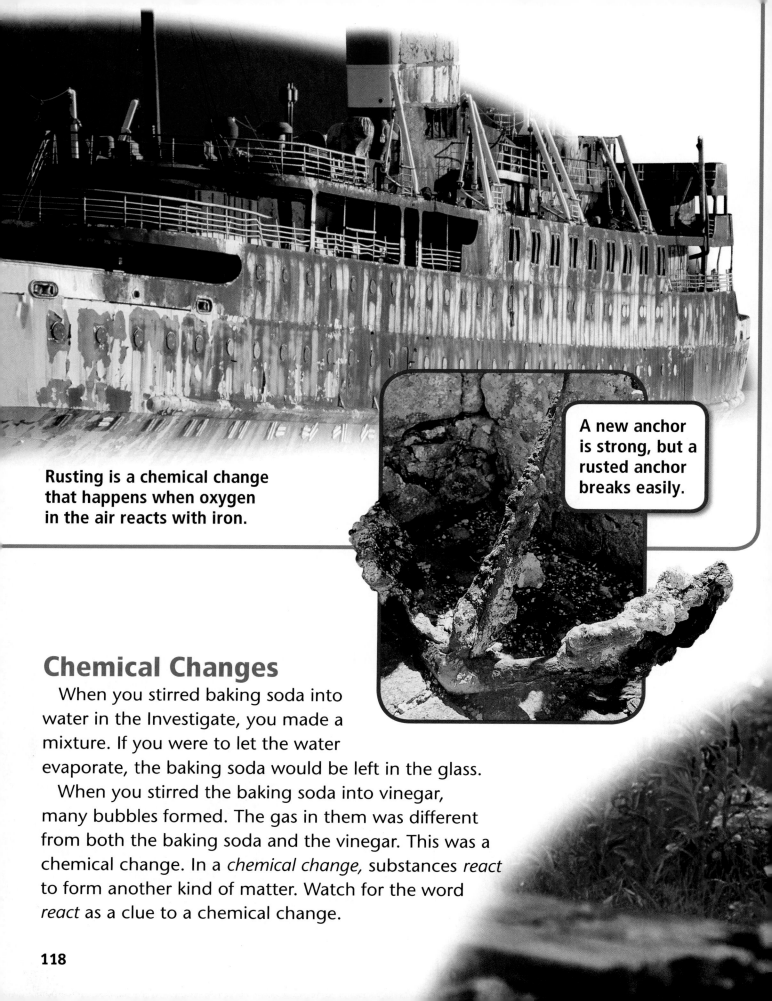

Rusting is a chemical change that happens when oxygen in the air reacts with iron.

A new anchor is strong, but a rusted anchor breaks easily.

Chemical Changes

When you stirred baking soda into water in the Investigate, you made a mixture. If you were to let the water evaporate, the baking soda would be left in the glass.

When you stirred the baking soda into vinegar, many bubbles formed. The gas in them was different from both the baking soda and the vinegar. This was a chemical change. In a *chemical change,* substances *react* to form another kind of matter. Watch for the word *react* as a clue to a chemical change.

You can see many chemical changes. Iron reacts with oxygen in the air. It forms the orange substance called rust. The rust can't be changed back into iron.

Slices of apple react with oxygen in the air and turn brown. This is another chemical change.

Burning is also a chemical change. When wood burns, it reacts with oxygen in the air. Ashes, smoke, and hot gases form. These kinds of matter are different from wood. You can't get the wood back.

 **MAIN IDEA AND DETAILS** Describe some chemical changes.

A chemical reaction causes the apple to turn brown.

Burning is a chemical change. Light and heat are released. Smoke, ash, and hot gases are produced.

Changes in Properties

To solve a mystery, you look for clues. What clues tell you that a chemical change has taken place?

Remember that you can use your senses to observe properties of matter. When iron rusts, it changes color. You also see a color change when apple slices are left out in the air.

When wood burns, there are many clues that a chemical change is taking place. The wood turns black. Smoke appears. Heat and light energy are released.

Candle wax melts when it is heated. This is a physical change. When the liquid wax burns, it forms water vapor, other gases, and carbon. ▼

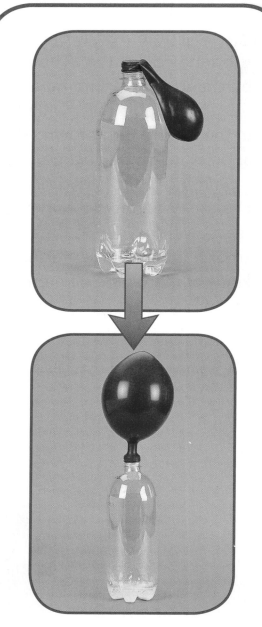

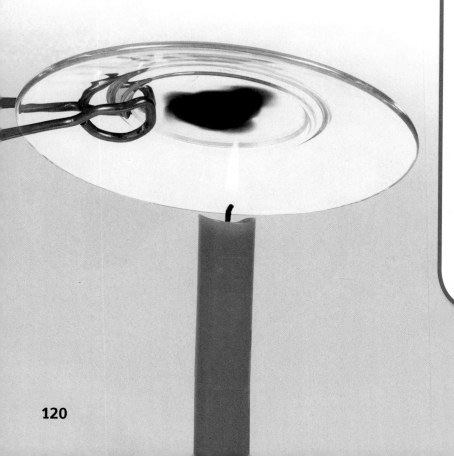

The bottle contains vinegar. The balloon contains some baking soda. When the balloon is lifted so that the baking soda mixes with the vinegar, the balloon begins to expand. Why does this happen?

This liquid has lead in it. It looks like water.

This liquid has iodine in it. It also looks like water.

When the two liquids are mixed, a yellow solid forms. This is an example of a chemical change.

In some chemical changes, bubbles of gas form. If the substances you mixed didn't include a gas, that's a clue. The gas shows that a new substance has formed. What if you mix two liquids, and a solid forms? What if the color changes? These are all clues that a chemical change has taken place.

Do the substances you started with still exist? Can you get them back? If the answer is no, you've probably observed a chemical change.

Focus Skill MAIN IDEA AND DETAILS **What kinds of properties can change during a chemical change?**

Insta-Lab

Make It Fizz

Place a piece of plastic wrap on a table. Put an antacid tablet in the center of the plastic. With a dropper, place one drop of water on the tablet. Observe, and record your observations. Did you observe a physical or a chemical change? How do you know?

Standards Wrap-Up and Lesson Review

What are physical and chemical changes?

In this lesson, you learned that in physical changes, substances keep their properties. When substances react in a chemical change, they form new matter with different properties. These new properties are clues that a chemical change has taken place.

 Science Content Standards in This Lesson

1.g *Students know* that when two or more substances are combined, a new substance may be formed with properties that are different from those of the original materials.

1. **MAIN IDEA AND DETAILS** Draw and complete a graphic organizer to give details that support this main idea: Physical changes are different from chemical changes. **1.g**

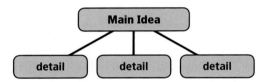

Main Idea

detail   detail   detail

2. **SUMMARIZE** Name and describe one physical change and one chemical change. **1.g**

3. **DRAW CONCLUSIONS** What are two clues that a chemical change has taken place? **1.g**

4. **VOCABULARY** Tell why sugar water is a *mixture*. **1.g**

5. **Critical Thinking** Suppose you mix two clear liquids, and a red solid forms. What type of change has taken place? Tell how you know. **1.g**

6. Which of the following is a chemical change?

The Big Idea

   A drying your hair in the sun
   B grinding wheat to make flour
   C burning gasoline in a car
   D making a paper airplane **1.g**

  Writing ELA–W 2.2

Write a Description

Tell what happens during two chemical changes. Be sure to describe the properties of the new substances.

 Math AF 2.2

Analyze Patterns

A mixture contains two times as many red beads as white beads. There are six white beads. How many red beads are in the mixture?

 Health

Keeping Food Safe

Food spoils because of chemical changes. Refrigerators keep food from spoiling quickly. Do research to find out how people kept food from spoiling before refrigerators were invented. Write a report to share with the class.

 For more links and activities, go to **www.hspscience.com**

Science Content

1.h *Students know* all matter is made of small particles called atoms, too small to see with the naked eye.

1.i *Students know* people once thought that earth, wind, fire, and water were the basic elements that made up all matter. Science experiments show that there are more than 100 different types of atoms, which are presented on the periodic table of the elements.

Investigation and Experimentation

5.e Collect data in an investigation and analyze those data to develop a logical conclusion.

Essential Question

What Are Atoms and Elements?

California Fast Fact

Bricks or Blocks?

From a distance, these buildings look like the ones along a busy San Francisco street. But everything in this scene, including the cable cars, is actually made from hundreds of small plastic blocks.

atom [AT•uhm] The smallest particle of matter that still has the properties of that matter (p. 128)

element [EL•uh•muhnt] A pure substance that is made of only one kind of atom (p. 130)

model of San Francisco, California

125

Combinations of Matter

Start with Questions

Everything in this picture is made of just a few substances.

- What are those substances?

- How can they combine into so many different things?

Investigate to find out. Then read to find out more.

Prepare to Investigate

Investigation Skill Tip

Using models is a good way to learn about things that would be hard to study directly. When you make a model, it should be as much like the real thing as possible.

Materials
- 3 dishes, labeled *water, salt,* and *salt water*
- masking tape
- 12 equal-sized pieces of white paper, labeled *H*
- scissors
- 3 index card halves of different colors
- transparent tape

Make an Observation Chart

Particles of Matter	
	Observations
Water	
Salt	
Salt water	

Follow This Procedure

1. Cut each half index card into six equal pieces. Label one color O, the second color Na, and the third color Cl.

2. Make "water" (H_2O) by taping two H pieces to one O piece. Repeat six times. Put the particles in the water dish.

3. Make "salt" (NaCl) by taping one Na piece to one Cl piece. Repeat six times. Put the particles in the salt dish.

4. Make "salt water" by mixing three particles each of water and salt in the dish labeled salt water.

5. Observe and record the differences between the water, the salt, and the salt water.

Step 2

Step 4

Draw Conclusions

1. What did you observe about all the water particles and all the salt particles? **5.e**

2. **Standards Link** How does the salt water differ from the water and the salt? **1.h**

3. **Investigation Skill** Use your models to separate the salt water into its original particles. Then tell how you did it.

Independent Inquiry **Collect and Analyze Data**

What other questions can you ask about the substances that make up salt water? Pick one question to investigate.

Build models, and carry out your investigation. Analyze the data you collect to draw a logical conclusion that answers your question. **5.e**

VOCABULARY
atom p. 128
element p. 130

SCIENCE CONCEPTS
▶ what atoms and elements are
▶ how elements are organized

MAIN IDEA AND DETAILS
Look for details about how atoms make up matter.

```
              Main Idea
           /     |      \
      detail   detail   detail
```

Atoms

Suppose you are on a hill above a beach. From there, the beach looks like a solid surface. Up close, you can see that it is made up of millions of tiny grains of sand.

Early Greek thinkers wondered if matter might also be made of smaller bits. A piece of iron looks solid. How many times could you cut it in half? Would you finally get a piece that couldn't be cut and still have the properties of iron?

The Greeks decided that there must be such a particle. They called the particle an *atom*. An **atom** is the smallest particle of matter that has the properties of that matter. An atom of gold is still gold. If you could split a gold atom in half, it would no longer be gold.

The grains of sand on a beach are very tiny, but you can still see them. The atoms in matter are millions of times smaller! Even with the strongest microscopes, scientists can barely see them.

MAIN IDEA AND DETAILS What is an atom?

The aluminum this foil is made of is a pure substance.

STOP AT THE SHOP-SMART

Insta-Lab

What Color Is It?

Observe a color cartoon from the newspaper. What colors do you see in the cartoon? Use a hand lens to look at the colors more closely. What do you see now? How is this like the atoms in matter?

The smallest piece of aluminum you can have is an aluminum atom.

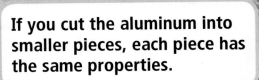

If you cut the aluminum into smaller pieces, each piece has the same properties.

129

Elements

All the atoms in a piece of gold are alike. All the atoms in oxygen gas are alike. Gold and oxygen are elements. An **element** is a pure substance that has only one kind of atom.

When early Greeks watched wood burn, they saw fire and ash. Hot gases were also released. Some of the gas condensed to form water. This made the Greeks think that matter must be made up of four elements—earth, air, fire, and water. This is not true, but elements are the building blocks of matter. Today, we know that there are more than 100 elements.

mercury (Hg)

gold (Au)

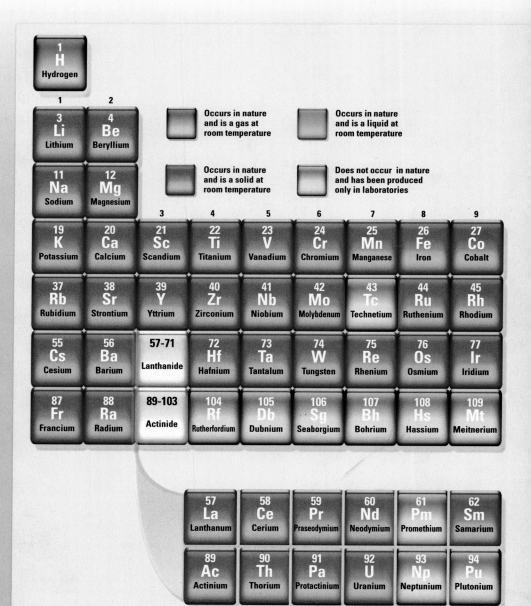

Occurs in nature and is a gas at room temperature		Occurs in nature and is a liquid at room temperature
Occurs in nature and is a solid at room temperature		Does not occur in nature and has been produced only in laboratories

1 H Hydrogen									
1	**2**								
3 Li Lithium	4 Be Beryllium								
11 Na Sodium	12 Mg Magnesium	**3**	**4**	**5**	**6**	**7**	**8**	**9**	
19 K Potassium	20 Ca Calcium	21 Sc Scandium	22 Ti Titanium	23 V Vanadium	24 Cr Chromium	25 Mn Manganese	26 Fe Iron	27 Co Cobalt
37 Rb Rubidium	38 Sr Strontium	39 Y Yttrium	40 Zr Zirconium	41 Nb Niobium	42 Mo Molybdenum	43 Tc Technetium	44 Ru Ruthenium	45 Rh Rhodium
55 Cs Cesium	56 Ba Barium	57-71 Lanthanide	72 Hf Hafnium	73 Ta Tantalum	74 W Tungsten	75 Re Rhenium	76 Os Osmium	77 Ir Iridium
87 Fr Francium	88 Ra Radium	89-103 Actinide	104 Rf Rutherfordium	105 Db Dubnium	106 Sg Seaborgium	107 Bh Bohrium	108 Hs Hassium	109 Mt Meitnerium

57 La Lanthanum	58 Ce Cerium	59 Pr Praseodymium	60 Nd Neodymium	61 Pm Promethium	62 Sm Samarium
89 Ac Actinium	90 Th Thorium	91 Pa Protactinium	92 U Uranium	93 Np Neptunium	94 Pu Plutonium

The elements are shown in a chart called the *periodic table.* Each one has a name and a *symbol*—one, two, or three letters that stand for the element. *H* is the symbol for hydrogen, and *Al* stands for aluminum.

Scientists who discover elements are allowed to name them. One group of scientists named their element after Albert Einstein, a famous scientist who studied matter and energy. Find this element, called einsteinium (Es), in the periodic table.

Focus Skill **MAIN IDEA AND DETAILS** What is an element?

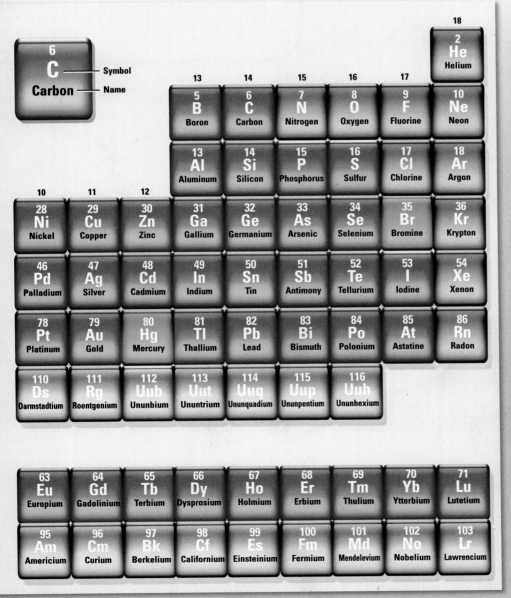

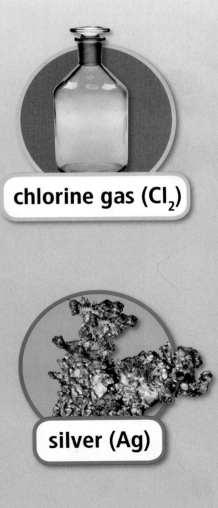

chlorine gas (Cl_2)

silver (Ag)

Combining Elements

Why aren't water and salt found on the periodic table? Think about how you made "water" in the Investigate. You joined two atoms of hydrogen and one atom of oxygen. Hydrogen and oxygen are elements. Water (H_2O) is made of two kinds of atoms, so it's not an element. Salt (NaCl) also contains two elements—sodium (Na) and chlorine (Cl).

Elements can combine in different ways to make thousands of substances. All living things are mostly combinations of carbon (C), oxygen (O), nitrogen (N), and hydrogen (H) atoms.

 MAIN IDEA AND DETAILS Why isn't water an element?

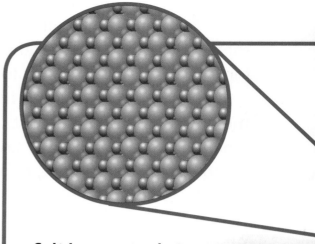

Salt is a pure substance made of the elements sodium and chlorine.

Each grain of sand is made of billions of tiny particles of SiO_2. What two elements are in sand? How many atoms does a sand particle contain?

132

Water is a pure substance. Every particle of water contains the same two elements.

Standards Wrap-Up and Lesson Review

Essential Question

What are atoms and elements?

In this lesson, you learned that all matter is made of tiny particles called atoms. Elements are substances that have only one kind of atom. The names and symbols of all the elements are shown in the periodic table.

Science Content Standards in This Lesson

1.h *Students know* all matter is made of small particles called atoms, too small to see with the naked eye.

1.i *Students know* people once thought that earth, wind, fire, and water were the basic elements that made up all matter. Science experiments show that there are more than 100 different types of atoms, which are presented on the periodic table of the elements.

1. (Focus Skill) **MAIN IDEA AND DETAILS** Draw and complete a graphic organizer to show details that support this main idea: Matter can be elements or combinations of elements. **1.i**

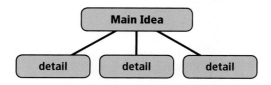

2. **SUMMARIZE** Fill in the blanks. Matter is made of tiny particles called _____. Each _____ in the periodic table has only one kind of atom. Elements can _____ in different ways to form many other kinds of matter. **1.h, 1.i**

3. **DRAW CONCLUSIONS** Why did the early Greeks think there were only four elements? **1.i**

4. **VOCABULARY** Explain how *atoms* and *elements* are related. **1.h, 1.i**

5. **Critical Thinking** Air is not on the periodic table. What does that tell you about air?
   A Air is an element.
   B Air is a particle.
   C Air is an atom.
   D Air is a mixture. **1.i**

6. Which of the following is **not** an element?
   A oxygen (O_2)
   B methane (CH_4)
   C neon (Ne)
   D iron (Fe) **1.i**

The **Big** Idea

  Writing ELA–W 1.1, 1.3

Write a Paragraph

Choose one of the following elements: copper, gold, mercury, or helium. Do research, and then write a paragraph to tell how this element got its name.

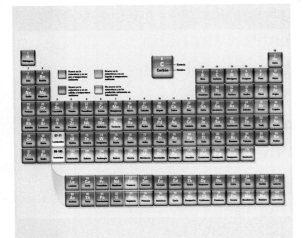

 Math AF 2.2

Solve Problems

Carbon dioxide (CO_2) is a gas that is given off when things burn. Each particle of carbon dioxide has 1 carbon (C) atom and 2 oxygen (O) atoms. How many carbon atoms are in 10 particles of carbon dioxide? How many oxygen atoms?

 Health

Stay Healthy

Look in your health textbook or other sources to identify the most common elements in your body. Find out which kinds of food contain these elements. Write a short report or make a poster to show what you have learned.

 For more links and activities, go to **www.hspscience.com**

Lise Meitner

▶ **DR. LISE MEITNER**

▶ **Physicist**

▶ Discovered that splitting an atom produces energy

Lise Meitner was a shy, quiet woman. In the late 1800s, most women didn't even go to high school, but Meitner insisted on going to college. There, she studied physics, or how matter and energy work. She was one of the first women to study that subject in college.

Together with scientist Otto Hahn, Meitner discovered the element that has atomic number 91. She also discovered that splitting uranium produces energy. However, she refused to take part in the development of the atomic bomb, which was partly based on her discovery. The element with atomic number 109—Meitnerium—was named in her honor.

 Think and Write

❶ Where on the periodic table is element 91 located?

1.i

❷ Do you think a scientist can control the way his or her discoveries are used? Explain.

A nuclear energy plant uses energy from splitting uranium to produce electricity.

Glenn Seaborg

▶ **DR. GLENN T. SEABORG**

▶ **University of California, Berkeley**

▶ Shared in the discovery of ten elements

Most scientists would be happy if they discovered just one element. Dr. Glenn Seaborg shared in the discovery of ten elements— atomic numbers 94 through 102 and atomic number 106. In 1997, element 106 was named in honor of Seaborg. It was the first element to be named after a living person. Seaborg said it was a greater honor than winning the Nobel Prize!

Seaborg also worked on the Manhattan Project, which developed the atomic bomb. He later led the Atomic Energy Commission (AEC). The AEC tried to control the use of atomic power for peaceful purposes.

✎ Think and Write

1. How did Seaborg change the periodic table? **1.i**

2. Why is it important to control the uses of atomic energy?

Seaborg and other scientists actually made the new elements in their lab. The elements don't exist in nature.

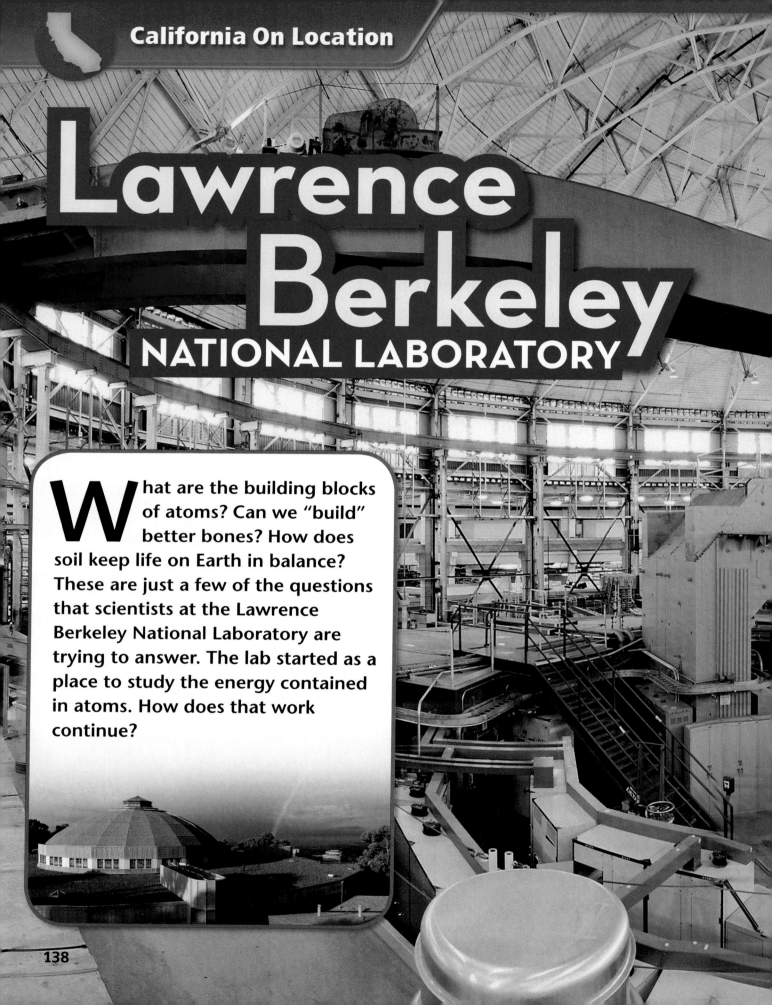

Lawrence Berkeley
NATIONAL LABORATORY

What are the building blocks of atoms? Can we "build" better bones? How does soil keep life on Earth in balance? These are just a few of the questions that scientists at the Lawrence Berkeley National Laboratory are trying to answer. The lab started as a place to study the energy contained in atoms. How does that work continue?

It's About Teamwork

In 1931, Ernest Lawrence built the lab. It held a machine that studied the particles that make up atoms. Lawrence hired teams of scientists to do research in different fields, such as physical science and life science. These teams worked together well. Lawrence and nine other scientists at the lab have won Nobel Prizes for their discoveries.

Science for the Future

Today, scientists at Berkeley Lab work with machines that make tiny gears less than one centimeter wide. Other scientists study tiny living things that eat harmful wastes. Other groups work to find ways to use new sources of energy, such as making cars that don't burn gasoline. The scientists at Lawrence Berkeley National Laboratory continue to make discoveries that will help everyone in the future.

 Think and Write

❶ How might a team of scientists do better research than one person working alone?

❷ Recall what you learned about atoms. What new information about atoms does this article present?

The Lawrence Berkeley National Laboratory has 17 divisions. Scientists study many things, including the tiniest parts of atoms and new ways to use energy.

139

Wrap-Up

▶ Visual Summary

Tell how each picture helps explain the **Big Idea**.

The Big Idea Matter and energy have different forms. One form can change into another.

1.a–1.d

Energy
The sun's light and heat travel to Earth as waves of energy. Machines and living things change stored energy into motion and heat.

1.e, 1.h, 1.i

Matter
Matter has three forms—solid, liquid, and gas. About 100 elements make up all matter. All matter is made of atoms.

1.f, 1.g

Changes in Matter
Matter changes forms when it melts or evaporates. When different kinds of matter combine, new kinds can form.

Show What You Know

 Unit Writing Activity

Write a Description

Think about a time when you saw energy from the sun change matter from one form to another. Maybe you saw crayons melt, a puddle evaporate, or the colors of a picture fade over time. Describe what happened, and tell how the sun's energy made the change happen.

Unit Project

Mixtures and Solutions

Work with three or four other students. Use water, two cups, sugar, rice, paper clips, dried beans, and a spoon. Make a mixture in one cup and a solution in the other. Explain how the mixture and the solution are different. Suggest a way to separate the mixture. Can you separate the solution? If so, tell how.

Vocabulary Review

Use the terms below to complete the sentences. The page numbers tell you where to look in the unit.

atom p. 128   evaporation p. 107

electricity p. 73   fuel p. 68

element p. 130   gas p. 97

energy p. 56   heat p. 60

1. The form of energy that warms objects is _____.   `1.a`

2. A pure substance that has only one kind of atom is an _____.   `1.i`

3. A form of matter with no fixed volume or shape is a _____.   `1.e`

4. The ability to cause change is known as _____.   `1.c`

5. A change from a liquid to a gas is _____.   `1.f`

6. Energy that moves through a wire is _____.   `1.d`

7. The smallest particle of matter is an _____.   `1.h`

8. A material that is burned to produce energy is a _____.   `1.b`

Check Understanding

Choose the best answer.

9. **MAIN IDEA AND DETAILS** Where does the energy stored in food come from?   `1.b`
   A soil   C the sun
   B water   D fertilizer

10. **CAUSE AND EFFECT** What causes clothes to dry when they are hung outside?   `1.a`
    A heat from a fire
    B energy from the sun
    C heat from the ground
    D energy from electricity

11. Which process occurs when iron changes from a solid to a liquid?   `1.f`
    A melting   C freezing
    B boiling   D evaporation

12. Look at the liquid below. What property is being measured?   `1.e`

    A color   C shape
    B mass   D volume

13. Which of the following is a chemical change? `1.g`
- **A** glass breaking
- **B** metal rusting
- **C** water freezing
- **D** paper being torn

14. How does the sound of a drum reach your ear? `1.d`
- **A** through the drumhead
- **B** through circular waves
- **C** in up-and-down waves
- **D** in back-and-forth waves

15. Which of the following is **not** an element? `1.i`
- **A** water (H_2O)
- **B** hydrogen (H_2)
- **C** silver (Ag)
- **D** copper (Cu)

16. Which kind of energy do plants need to grow? `1.a`
- **A** sound energy
- **B** light energy
- **C** wind energy
- **D** electrical energy

Investigation Skills

Use the picture below to answer questions 17 and 18.

17. How would you use the items in the picture to gather data about physical changes? `5.e`

18. Predict what will happen if you mix all four substances together. `5.d`

Critical Thinking

19. How is the food you eat like a battery? `1.b`

20. Explain how all the different kinds of matter in the world can be made up of just a few elements.

The **Big** Idea

Light

California Standards in This Unit

2 **Light has a source and travels in a direction. As a basis for understanding this concept:**

2.a *Students know* sunlight can be blocked to create shadows.

2.b *Students know* light is reflected from mirrors and other surfaces.

2.c *Students know* the color of light striking an object affects the way the object is seen.

2.d *Students know* an object is seen when light traveling from the object enters the eye.

This unit also includes these Investigation and Experimentation Standards: **5.d** **5.e**

What's the Big Idea?

Light has a source and travels in straight lines.

Essential Questions

Science in California

Hollywood

Dear Steven,

Last night a new movie opened at the theater near my house. There were big spotlights shining into the air. It was neat to see the big beams of light shining straight up into the night sky.

Your friend,
Kyle

USA

What is light? What does it do? How is what Kyle saw related to the **Big Idea?**

Unit Inquiry

At a Distance

You have probably used a flashlight in the dark to see things. How does the beam of light look if you shine it on objects that are close to you? How does it look if the objects are far away? Plan and conduct an investigation to discover how the light beam changes.

Science Content

2.a *Students know* sunlight can be blocked to create shadows.

2.b *Students know* light is reflected from mirrors and other surfaces.

Investigation and Experimentation

5.d Predict the outcome of a simple investigation and compare the result with the prediction.

Essential Question

How Does Light Travel?

California Fast Fact

Look to the Lighthouse

This lighthouse is 35 meters (115 ft) high. It is the second-tallest lighthouse on the Pacific coast. The light from its 1,000-watt bulb is very bright. It warns passing ships not to come too close to shore.

Pigeon Point lighthouse, on California Highway 1

shadow [SHAD•oh] A dark area that forms where an object blocks the path of light (p. 152)

reflect [rih•FLEKT] To bounce off a surface (p. 154)

147

Shadow Boxing

Start with Questions

On a sunny day, you can see your shadow.

- What makes your shadow?

- How does it change?

- What do you think causes your shadow to change?

Investigate to find out. Then read to find out more.

Prepare to Investigate

Investigation Skill Tip

To compare things, observe them carefully. Then make a short list or draw pictures to record your observations.

Materials
- large sheet of paper
- masking tape
- clay
- index card
- flashlight
- crayon
- scissors

Make an Observation Chart

Shadow Observations		
Flashlight Position	Whole Card	Cut-out Card
1		
2		

Follow This Procedure

1 Tape a large sheet of paper to a desk or table. Put a small ball of clay in the middle of the paper.

2 Set an index card in the clay so that the card stands up straight.

3 Hold the flashlight to one side of the card and a little above it. Shine the light on the card.

4 Record what you observe. Write whether the shadow is sharp or fuzzy. Use the crayon to trace the card's shadow on the paper.

5 Hold the flashlight in a different place. Repeat Step 4.

6 Cut a circle from your card. Repeat all the steps.

Step 2

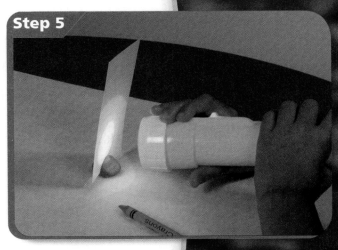
Step 5

Draw Conclusions

1. Compare the two tracings of the shadows of the whole card.

2. **Standards Link** What happened to the shadow when you moved the flashlight? **2.a**

3. **Investigation Skill** Compare the shadows of the whole card with the shadows of the cut-out card. Tell how they are alike and different.

Independent Inquiry

Predict the Outcome of an Investigation

Find out how the shadows of other shapes change.

Cut any shape you like from an index card. Predict the size and shape of its shadow before you turn on the flashlight. Was your prediction correct? Repeat with other shapes. Do your predictions improve? **5.d**

VOCABULARY
shadow p. 152
reflect p. 154

SCIENCE CONCEPTS
▶ what light is
▶ what light does

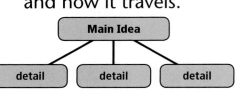 **MAIN IDEA AND DETAILS**
Look for details about where light comes from and how it travels.

Light Energy

Think about the last time your mom or dad cooked your favorite foods on an outdoor grill. Heat energy from the fire changed the food. The fire also changed the wood or coals to ashes. The food gave you energy to run and play. The fire also gave off light.

Light is a form of energy that you can see. Light comes from different things. Fire, light bulbs, and the sun all produce light.

The colors in this light tell drivers when to stop and go.

What are the sources of light in these pictures?

Like all energy, light can cause changes. Plants use sunlight to make food. The plants use the food to grow bigger. Doctors use laser light to do some operations. Light can even make some kinds of cars move. In space, satellites and the space station use light to produce electricity.

Without light, we couldn't see the things around us. We see colors because of differences in light energy. Because light is a kind of energy, it can make all these things happen.

Focus Skill **MAIN IDEA AND DETAILS** **How do you know that light is energy?**

The sun shines on the waves as they wash ashore.

The lights on these dune buggies allow the drivers to see at night.

Shadows

You are outside on a sunny day. You jump, and a dark spot on the sidewalk jumps with you. That spot is your shadow.

Light travels in straight lines. If something stops it, a shadow forms. A **shadow** is a dark area that is formed where something blocks the path of light.

Shadows can move and change. When you put your hand in front of a lamp, some of the light is stopped by your hand. Your hand forms a shadow. When you move your hand, the shadow moves because your hand blocks different lines of light.

Notice the shadow in this picture. What has caused it to form? ▶

▲ What causes the turtle's shadow to form?

In the Investigate, you saw that the size and shape of a shadow changed when you moved the light. You also saw that the shadows were sharper when the light was closer to the card.

When you are in the sun, your body blocks some of the sunlight. As the sun's position in the sky changes through the day, the size of your shadow changes. In early morning and late afternoon, the sun is low in the sky. Your shadow is long. At noon, the sun is high overhead, so your shadow is small and close to your feet.

 MAIN IDEA AND DETAILS What is a shadow? What makes a shadow change?

Bouncing Light

Look in a mirror. What do you see? Light bounces off your body and travels to the mirror. Then it bounces off the mirror and travels back to your eyes. We use the word **reflect** to describe the bouncing of light off a surface. Light reflects off your face and body. That's why you can see yourself in a mirror. It is why other people can see you, too.

The reflection in a mirror is opposite from left to right. Everything looks backward.

You can see the trees and the mountain reflected in the lake.

◀ **The boy sees himself and the reflections of the things that are around him.**

Light bounces off a mirror in straight lines. ▼

Light always moves in straight lines. When it hits a mirror, it bounces off. It travels away from the mirror in straight lines. Because a mirror is smooth and shiny, it reflects light in a way that lets you see your reflection.

Light reflects off the surfaces of objects it hits. The reflected light travels in straight lines to our eyes. It lets us see all the things around us.

 **MAIN IDEA AND DETAILS** Why can other people see you?

Insta-Lab

What Do You See?

Write the capital letters ABCD on a card. Hold the card in front of a mirror. Draw what you see in the mirror. Repeat, using BIRD and MOTH. Why do the words look different in the mirror?

How does light travel?

In this lesson, you learned that light travels in straight lines. When an object blocks light, it makes a shadow. Light reflects, or bounces off, mirrors and other surfaces.

 Science Content Standards in This Lesson

2.a *Students know* sunlight can be blocked to create shadows.

2.b *Students know* light is reflected from mirrors and other surfaces.

1. 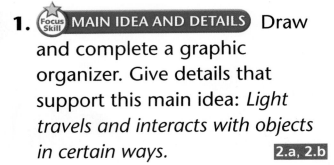 **MAIN IDEA AND DETAILS** Draw and complete a graphic organizer. Give details that support this main idea: *Light travels and interacts with objects in certain ways.* **2.a, 2.b**

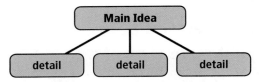

2. **SUMMARIZE** Fill in the blanks. Light travels in _____ lines. Light bounces, or _____, off mirrors and other smooth surfaces. We can see objects because light bounces off them and travels to our _____. **2.a, 2.b**

3. **DRAW CONCLUSIONS** Why can you see your reflection in a mirror but not in a brick wall? **2.b**

4. **VOCABULARY** Draw a picture that illustrates the vocabulary word *reflect*. **2.b**

5. **Critical Thinking** Can light travel around corners? Explain. **2.b**

6. Which is a true statement about light?

 The Big Idea

   A It makes you feel cold.
   B Its only source is the sun.
   C It travels in straight lines.
   D It can shine through any object. **2.b**

 Writing ELA–W 2.2

Write a Description

Think of a building. Write a description of what it would look like reflected in a pool.

 Math NS 2.1

How Many Watts?

The amount of electrical power used each second by light bulbs is measured in units called *watts*. How much more power would a 300-watt bulb use each second than a 50-watt bulb?

 Drama VPA–T 2.1

Shadow Puppets

Make a screen, using a white sheet. Shine a light behind it. Make shadow animals on the sheet. Use them to tell a story to the class. Then tell how you made the sizes and shapes of the shadows change.

 For more links and activities, go to **www.hspscience.com**

The Discovery Science Center

The Discovery Science Center in Santa Ana is a wonderful place! One part of the center, Techno Arts, has an exhibit called Shadow Garden: Sand. In this exhibit, computers use math to move shadows. Visitors can make their shadows dance along with the shadows of falling sand. They can use shadows to pass sand to one another. No, shadows can't really do those things, but at the center, they seem to!

A visitor to the Discovery Science Center makes shadows in the "Shadow Garden: Sand" exhibit.

Shadows Make Music

Lasers make a special kind of colored light. The center has a laser harp that visitors can play. The harp doesn't have strings. Instead, it has beams of laser light.

Here's how the harp works. A visitor puts a finger or a hand through a beam of laser light. A computer senses that the light is blocked and sends an electrical signal. The signal makes a musical note. That's using shadows to make music!

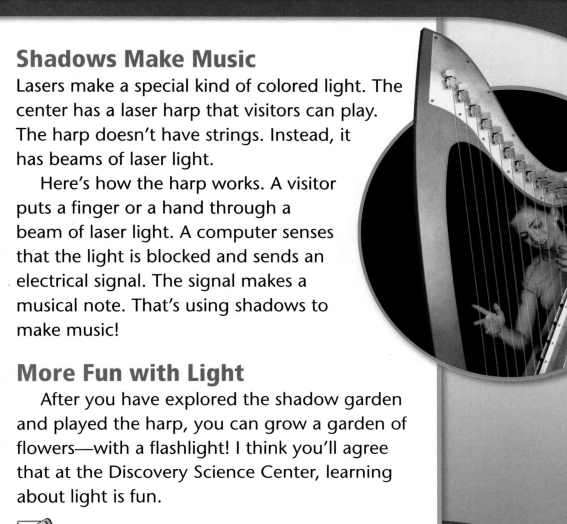

More Fun with Light

After you have explored the shadow garden and played the harp, you can grow a garden of flowers—with a flashlight! I think you'll agree that at the Discovery Science Center, learning about light is fun.

✎ Think and Write

❶ Why are shadows dark?   2.a

❷ *Techno* is short for *technology*. Why do you think the center's light exhibit is called Techno Arts?

This girl is using light to grow "flowers."

Essential Question

What Causes Color?

California Fast Fact

Over the Rainbow

This California rainbow is like rainbows in other places. The colors are always in the same order. They start with red at the top and end with violet at the bottom.

absorb [ab•SAWRB] To take in (p. 166)

Olmsted Point, in
Yosemite National Park

Making Rainbows

Start with Questions

The rainbow that appears after a shower or storm is beautiful. You have probably seen many rainbows.

- What do you think causes a rainbow?

- Why do you see different colors?

- Can you make your own rainbows?

Investigate to find out. Then read to find out more.

Prepare to Investigate

Investigation Skill Tip

Before you carry out an investigation, you predict what you think will happen. To make a prediction, use what you already know and things you have observed.

Materials
- scissors
- 3 sheets of paper—black, white, and red
- masking tape
- prism
- crayons

Make an Observation Chart

Prism Observations	
Paper Color	Colors Observed
White	
Red	

Follow This Procedure

1 Cut a narrow slit in the black sheet of paper.

2 Tape the paper at the bottom of a window. Pull down the blinds to let a narrow beam of sunlight shine through the slit.

3 Place the prism in the beam of light. Slowly turn the prism until you see colors.

4 Place a sheet of white paper under the prism. Use the crayons to record what you observe.

5 Predict what you will see on the red paper. Then repeat Steps 3 and 4 with the red paper.

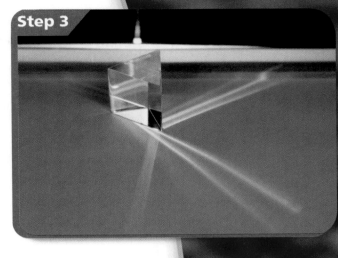
Step 3

Step 4

Draw Conclusions

1. How does a prism change sunlight?

2. Standards Link Compare the light you saw on the white paper with the light you saw on the red paper. **2.c**

3. Investigation Skill Scientists compare the results of an investigation with their prediction. Was your prediction correct for the red paper? If not, how was the result different from your prediction? **5.d**

Independent Inquiry

Predict the Outcome of an Investigation

Think about how the light looked on the red paper. Predict what you would see if you used blue paper. Try it! Did you predict correctly?

Compare your observations for the red paper and the blue paper. Draw a conclusion that explains why the observations were different. **5.d, 5.e**

163

VOCABULARY
absorb p. 166

SCIENCE CONCEPTS
▶ how light makes color
▶ how the color of light affects the color you see

Focus Skill CAUSE AND EFFECT
Look for ways different colors of light seem to change the color of an object.

cause ⟶ effect

Light and Color

In the Investigate, you saw sunlight go into the prism and colored light come out. The white light of sunlight is a mixture of all colors. Did you notice that the light bent as it went through the prism? It is this bending that causes white light to separate into its colors.

prism

white light

Light bends as it passes through a prism. Violet bends the most. Red bends the least. The bending is what causes the colors to separate.

For more links and animations, go to **www.hspscience.com**

How Rainbows Form

White light from the sun passes through drops of water in the air. The light bends as it enters and leaves each water drop. The light separates into many colors.

A drop of water is like a tiny prism.

The order of the colors in a rainbow is red, orange, yellow, green, blue, and violet.

Have you seen a rainbow? It takes sunlight and rain to make a rainbow. When the sun comes out after a rain, drops of water in the air act like tiny prisms. The sunlight enters them and bends. This separates the colors, causing a rainbow to form.

 **CAUSE AND EFFECT** What causes the colors that we see in a rainbow?

165

Objects in White Light

From the Investigate, you learned that white light is a mixture of all different colors of light. In white light, we see what we think of as the true colors of objects. We see yellow lemons. We see green limes.

When light hits an object, some of it is reflected. The color of the light that is reflected is the color we see. All the other colors are absorbed. To **absorb** something is to take it in. A lemon absorbs every color of light except yellow. A lime absorbs every color of light except green.

We see the colors that are reflected from the different kinds of fruit.

Which colors does each fruit absorb? Which color does each fruit reflect?

The colors that are absorbed and the colors that are reflected give objects their colors. Black objects absorb most of the light that hits them, so they reflect no colors. White objects absorb very little light. They reflect almost all of the white light. Dull objects absorb more light than shiny ones. Shiny things, such as mirrors, reflect most of the light that strikes them.

CAUSE AND EFFECT What causes objects to have color?

167

Objects in Colored Light

In white light, a lemon looks yellow. What color will it appear to be if the light that shines on it is not white? The color we see depends on the color of light that shines on an object. If you shine a blue light on a lemon, it will look dark. That's because the lemon absorbs all of the blue light. There is no yellow light for the lemon to reflect.

In red light, only the apple appears the way it would in white light.

In blue light, each kind of fruit looks dark.

168

In green light, the green grapes and the lime look green, as they would in white light.

Three things affect color. The first is the colors of light an object reflects or absorbs. The second is the color of light that hits an object. The third is how our eyes respond to light. If you change any one of these, an object's color will change.

Focus Skill **CAUSE AND EFFECT** If green light shines on a red apple, why does the apple look dark?

Insta-Lab

Color Switch

Tape blue cellophane over a flashlight. Shine the light on white paper. You see blue light. Now shine the blue light on objects. What colors do they appear to be? Try the same thing with red, green, and yellow cellophane. Why do the objects look different?

What causes color?

In this lesson, you learned that white light contains all the colors of the rainbow. An object has color because it absorbs some colors of light and reflects others. An object's color depends on the color of the light that shines on it.

Science Content Standards in This Lesson

2.c *Students know* the color of light striking an object affects the way the object is seen.

---

1. **(Focus Skill) CAUSE AND EFFECT** Draw and complete a graphic organizer to tell what causes a leaf to look green in sunshine. **2.c**

cause ⟶ effect

2. **SUMMARIZE** Identify the three things that affect color. **2.c**

3. **DRAW CONCLUSIONS** If you shine orange light on an orange, what color will the orange appear to be? Give a reason for your conclusion. **2.c**

4. **VOCABULARY** Explain why *absorb* and *reflect* are opposites. **2.c**

5. **Investigate and Experiment** Your teacher tells you that you can make white light by combining red, blue, and green light. Suppose you decided to shine red, blue, and green light together at the same spot on a sheet of black paper. Predict what would happen. **5.d**

6. A ball looks green under white light. Which is true?
   A The ball absorbs green light.
   B The ball reflects green light.
   C The ball bends green light.
   D The ball acts like a prism. **2.c**

The **Big** Idea

 Writing ELA–W 1.1

Write a Paragraph

Imagine that you are a beam of white light. Write a paragraph about what happens as you travel from a light source to an object. Tell how you make that object the color that people see. Write your paragraph so that someone younger can understand it.

 Math AF 1.1

Write a Number Sentence

Our eyes can see a range of colors, from violet to red. Violet light waves are 400 units long, and red light waves are 700 units long. Write and solve a number sentence to find the difference in the lengths of these two waves.

 Art VPA–VA 2.4

Categorize by Color

On poster board, draw the colors you see in a rainbow. You may use markers, crayons, colored pencils, or watercolors. Label each of the colors. For each color, draw a picture of one or more things that are this color.

 For more links and activities, go to **www.hspscience.com**

Science Content

2.d *Students know* an object is seen when light traveling from the object enters the eye.

Investigation and Experimentation

5.e Collect data in an investigation and analyze those data to develop a logical conclusion.

California Fast Fact

California Up Close

What's the best way to go sightseeing? Use binoculars! This family is using special binoculars to get a close-up view of San Francisco. Perhaps they are looking for the city's famous cable cars!

LESSON 3

Essential Question

How Do You See Objects?

San Francisco, California

172

opaque [oh•PAYK] Not able to let light pass through (p. 178)

How Light Travels

Start with Questions

It's not hard to tell where light comes from. It may be coming from the sun, a lamp, a candle, or a flashlight.

- How can you tell where light is traveling?

- How can you tell the direction in which it is traveling?

Investigate to find out. Then read to find out more.

Prepare to Investigate

Investigation Skill Tip

The information you collect during an investigation is called data. You might use a table, a chart, or a computer to record your data. You **communicate** data when you share it with others.

Materials
- ruler
- pencil
- 3 index cards
- clay
- small lamp without a shade

Make an Observation Chart

Diagrams of Card Positions	
Setup 1	Setup 2

Follow This Procedure

1. Using the ruler, draw lines on each card from corner to corner to make a large X.

2. Stack the cards, and use the pencil to make a hole in the center of each X.

3. Make a clay stand for each card. Stand the cards a few centimeters apart on a desk or table.

4. Place the lamp on the desk, and turn it on. Move the cards until you can see the light through all three holes at once.

5. Draw a diagram to record your setup.

6. Change the positions of the cards. Repeat Steps 4 and 5.

Step 1

Step 4

Draw Conclusions

1. In what position were the cards when you could see the light?

2. **Standards Link** Why couldn't you see the light when the cards were in different positions? **2.d**

3. **Investigation Skill** Scientists communicate their results in many ways. How did your drawings help you communicate your results?

Independent Inquiry

Analyze Data to Develop a Conclusion

In the Investigate, the cards were on a flat surface. Would the outcome be different if the surface were uneven?

Plan and conduct a simple investigation to find out. Collect and record data. From the results of both investigations, what can you conclude about the way light travels? **5.e**

VOCABULARY
opaque p. 178

SCIENCE CONCEPTS
▶ how light travels to the eye
▶ how you see things

SEQUENCE
Track the order of events needed for people to see things.

▢ → ▢ → ▢

Seeing Light

Light is all around you. The sun gives off light. So do streetlights and desk lamps. Light bounces off objects. When the light that bounces off an object reaches your eyes, you see the object.

How do you see light? First, it enters the front of the eye by passing through an opening called the *pupil*. The pupil is the black spot in the center of the eye. Around it is the *iris*, which is the colored part. The iris controls how much light comes into the eye.

Identify as many sources of light as you can in this photograph.

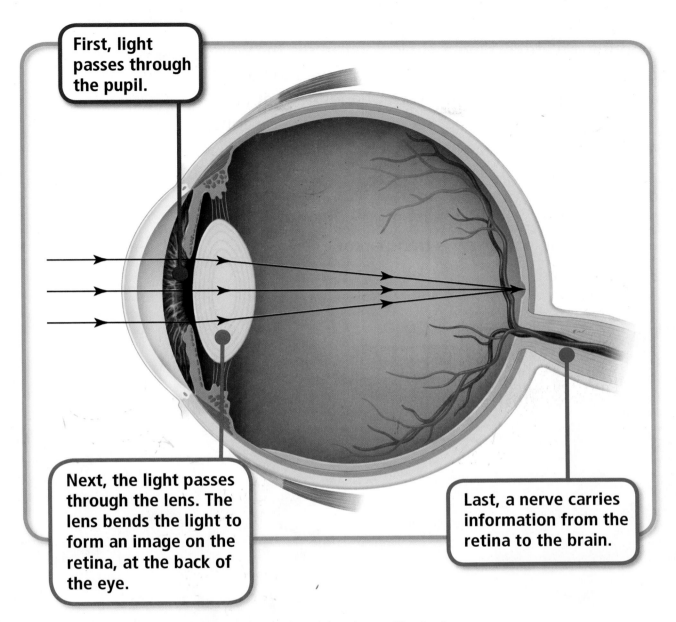

First, light passes through the pupil.

Next, the light passes through the lens. The lens bends the light to form an image on the retina, at the back of the eye.

Last, a nerve carries information from the retina to the brain.

In bright light, the iris makes the pupil small. Only a little light can get through. In dim light, the iris makes the pupil large so that more light can get through.

The light next passes through the clear *lens*. The lens bends the light so that it shines on a certain part of the *retina* (REHT•uh•nuh). The retina curves around the back of the eye. A nerve carries information about the light from the retina to the brain. Your brain tells you what you are seeing.

Focus Skill **SEQUENCE** List, in order, the things that must happen for people to see objects.

Stopping Light

Suppose you are reading a book. You can see the words because light bounces off the page and travels to your eyes. What happens if you hold your hands in front of your face? You can no longer see the book because light cannot pass through your hands. Objects that don't let any light pass through are **opaque**. Rocks, wooden desks, and people are opaque.

Transparent objects let most light pass through them. The clear glass in a window is transparent.

The stones are opaque.

The frosted marbles are translucent.

Translucent objects let some light pass through them. A "frosted" light bulb is translucent. Light passes through the glass of the bulb, but you can't clearly see what's inside it.

Focus Skill SEQUENCE What happens when light hits an opaque object?

The clear marbles and the vase are transparent.

The table shows an amount of light leaving a source. It also shows the amount that gets through three different materials—A, B, and C. Which material is translucent? Which is transparent? Which is opaque?

Material	Light from Source	Light Through Material
A	100	55
B	100	0
C	100	95

Insta-Lab

Look At and Through
Hold sheets of plastic wrap, aluminum foil, and wax paper up to the light. Try to see through each. Which is opaque? Which is translucent? Which is transparent?

Essential Question

How do you see objects?

In this lesson, you learned that we see objects because light that reflects off the objects enters the eyes. The eyes send information to the brain, which tells us what we are seeing. We can't see through an opaque object because no light passes through it.

Science Content Standards in This Lesson

2.d *Students know* an object is seen when light traveling from the object enters the eye.

1. **(Focus Skill) SEQUENCE** Draw and complete a graphic organizer to tell how light passes through the parts of the eye. **2.d**

2. **SUMMARIZE** Fill in the blanks. Light first passes through the _____. Light then passes through the _____, which bends it to focus on the retina. A _____ carries information to the brain. **2.d**

3. **DRAW CONCLUSIONS** A material lets through half of the light that hits it. Is the material transparent? Explain. **2.d**

4. **VOCABULARY** Draw a diagram that shows what happens when light hits an *opaque* object. **2.d**

5. **Investigate and Experiment** Light is shining through a window. The light outside the window is twice as bright as the light inside the window. What conclusion can you draw about the window? **5.e**

6. Light hits an object, and you see the object. In which direction is the light traveling?

   The Big Idea

   A into the eye
   B into the brain
   C into the object
   D into the ground   **2.d**

 Writing ELA–W 1.1

Write a Paragraph

Suppose your friends don't know that light travels in straight lines. Write a paragraph to help them understand this idea.

 Math NS 3.1

Draw Fractions

Material A blocks half of the light that hits it. Material B blocks one-fourth of the light. Draw pictures to show the fraction of the light that is blocked by each material.

 Health

Protect Your Vision

Find out how sunglasses protect the eyes. Make a poster to teach others what you learn.

 For more links and activities, go to **www.hspscience.com**

Using Lasers

What lights up the night sky but isn't the moon? What paints the sky with colors but isn't a rainbow? It's a beautiful show of laser light!

Laser light is different from ordinary light. It is light of a single pure color. Also, the light beam made by a laser does not spread out as it leaves its source. A laser is a tube with mirrors in it. Laser light gets more concentrated as it bounces back and forth between the mirrors before leaving the tube.

A laser light show

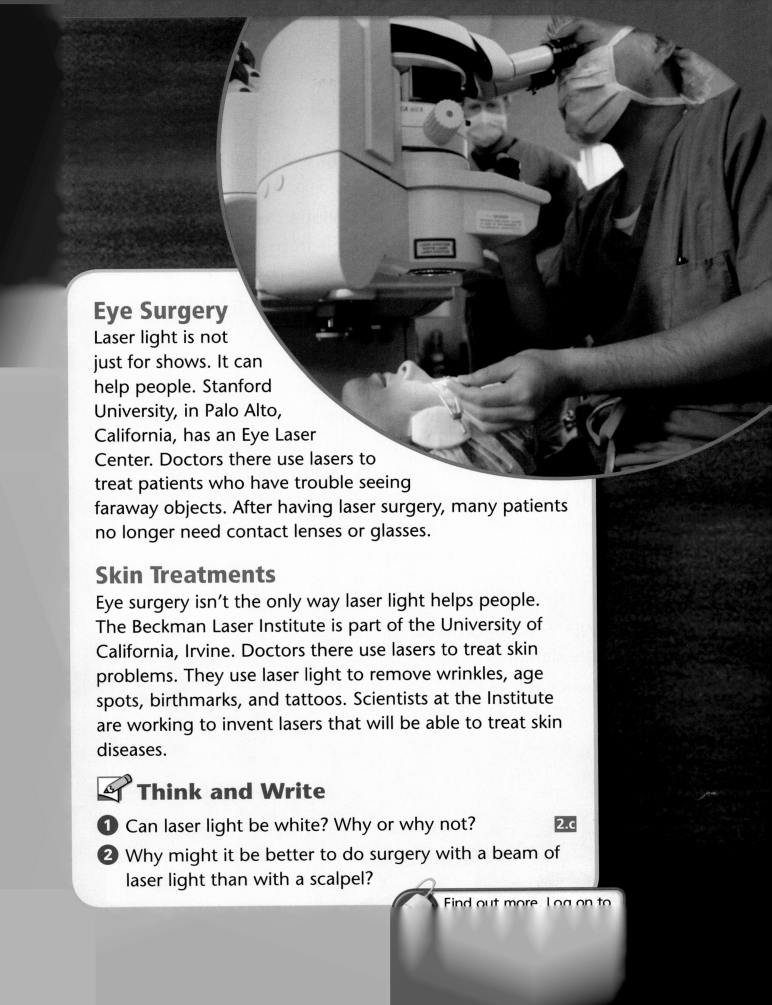

Eye Surgery

Laser light is not just for shows. It can help people. Stanford University, in Palo Alto, California, has an Eye Laser Center. Doctors there use lasers to treat patients who have trouble seeing faraway objects. After having laser surgery, many patients no longer need contact lenses or glasses.

Skin Treatments

Eye surgery isn't the only way laser light helps people. The Beckman Laser Institute is part of the University of California, Irvine. Doctors there use lasers to treat skin problems. They use laser light to remove wrinkles, age spots, birthmarks, and tattoos. Scientists at the Institute are working to invent lasers that will be able to treat skin diseases.

Think and Write

❶ Can laser light be white? Why or why not? **2.c**

❷ Why might it be better to do surgery with a beam of laser light than with a scalpel?

Find out more. Log on to

▶ **CHAD MOORE**

▶ **Physical Scientist**

▶ Studies light pollution

Chad Moore

You've heard of water pollution and air pollution. Have you ever heard of light pollution? It's the reason that people in big cities can't see the stars at night. There's too much human-made light on Earth's surface.

Chad Moore is a physical scientist. He's a member of the National Park Service's Night Sky Team. The team works in California and other western states. They have studied light pollution at Joshua Tree and Death Valley National Parks in California. With the information they gather, they can tell people if light pollution starts to get worse in the parks.

Think and Write

❶ Why is it important to protect the darkness of the night sky?

❷ Name a tool that Chad Moore might use in his work. **5.c**

Light pollution in Los Angeles

Lewis Latimer

Lewis Latimer was an inventor. He invented one of the first air conditioners. He also helped Alexander Graham Bell invent the telephone.

Latimer is best known for his work with Thomas Edison. Edison invented the electric light. Latimer was the only African American on Edison's team.

Latimer made a better carbon filament for the light bulb that burned much longer than Edison's paper filament. He patented his carbon filament. He developed a way to manufacture it and wrote a book on electric lighting. He supervised putting public electric lights in New York and other cities.

▶ **LEWIS LATIMER**

▶ **Engineer**

▶ Developed the carbon filament for the electric light bulb

Think and Write

1 Why do we need light to see? **2.d**
2 How did Latimer's work change how people live?

Today, the filaments in light bulbs are usually made of tungsten.

Visual Summary

Tell how each picture helps explain the **Big Idea**.

The Big Idea Light has a source and travels in straight lines.

2.a

Shadows
When light is blocked, you see a shadow.

2.b

Reflections
Light is reflected from mirrors and other surfaces.

2.c

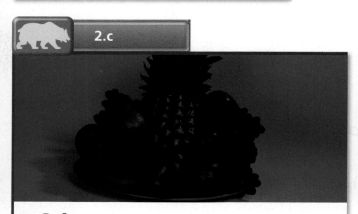

Color
The color of light striking an object affects the color you see.

2.d

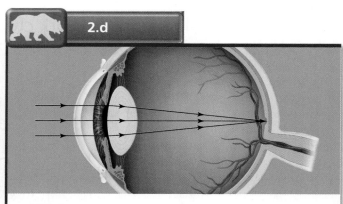

Vision
You see an object when the light traveling from the object enters your eyes.

Show What You Know

Unit Writing Activity

Write a Description

Draw a diagram that shows what light does when it strikes an opaque object. Write a sentence that describes the diagram. Write another sentence to describe what you see when you look at an opaque object. Then draw diagrams and write about what light does when it strikes translucent and transparent objects.

Unit Project

Build a Shadow Clock

On a sunny day, push a meterstick into the ground. Use string and craft sticks to mark the direction and length of its shadow. Add a label to record the time. Repeat the process four times during the day. Draw a picture of your results. Write a report telling how and why the shadows changed. Explain how shadows can be used to tell time.

Vocabulary Review

Use the terms below to complete the sentences. The page numbers tell you where to look in the unit.

shadow p. 152   absorb p. 166

reflect p. 154   opaque p. 178

1. Light _____ off smooth, shiny surfaces.   **2.b**

2. An object that does not let light pass through it is _____.   **2.d**

3. A dark area that forms when an object blocks light is a _____.   **2.a**

4. Dull objects _____ more light than shiny objects do.   **2.b**

Check Understanding

Choose the best answer.

5. **CAUSE AND EFFECT** Which of these bends light to form rainbows?   **2.c**
   A shadows   C sunshine
   B raindrops   D air particles

6. Which of these controls how much light enters the eye?   **2.d**
   A iris   C lens
   B pupil   D retina

7. **MAIN IDEA AND DETAILS** Which form of energy lets us see?   **2.d**
   A heat   C sound
   B light   D electricity

8. What happens to light when it strikes a mirror?   **2.b**
   A It bends.
   B It is absorbed.
   C It bounces off.
   D It makes a shadow.

Use the picture of the rose to answer questions 9 and 10.

9. Which color or colors are absorbed by the petals?   **2.c**
   A red   C all but red
   B black   D all but green

10. Under blue light, what color would the leaves seem to be?   **2.c**
    A red   C green
    B black   D white

11. Which of these bends light so that it falls on the retina?   **2.d**
    A iris   C lens
    B pupil   D nerve

12. Which kind of object blocks all the light that strikes it? `2.d`

A clear   **C** translucent

B opaque   **D** transparent

13. Which statement about light is **not** true? `2.b`

A Light has color.

B Light can be seen.

C Light has different sources.

D Light travels in curved lines.

14. Which of these is transparent? `2.d`

A    **C**

B    **D**

15. As white light passes through a prism, which color of light bends the **least**? `2.c`

A red   **C** green

B black   **D** violet

16. Erica was standing on a bridge over a pond. She could see herself. Which word names what she could see? `2.b`

A prism   **C** shadow

B source   **D** reflection

Investigation Skills

17. You stand in front of a mirror and wave your right hand. Predict what you will see in the mirror. `5.d`

18. Tomás opens the door from his bedroom to the hallway, and his pupils get smaller. What can you conclude about the light in Tomás's bedroom compared with the light in the hallway? Explain. `5.e`

Critical Thinking

19. Rory is choosing a T-shirt to wear on a hot day. What color shirt should he wear to keep him coolest when he is in the sun? Explain your answer. `2.c`

20. The picture shows a boy and his shadow. At what time of day was the picture drawn? Tell how you know. If the boy's shadow had been very long, what time of day would it have been?

The **Big** Idea

UNIT 3 LIFE SCIENCE

Adaptations

California Standards in This Unit

3 Adaptations in physical structure or behavior may improve an organism's chance for survival.

3.a *Students know* plants and animals have structures that serve different functions in growth, survival, and reproduction.

3.b *Students know* examples of diverse life forms in different environments, such as oceans, deserts, tundra, forests, grasslands, and wetlands.

3.c *Students know* living things cause changes in the environment in which they live: some of these changes are detrimental to the organism or other organisms, and some are beneficial.

3.d *Students know* when the environment changes, some plants and animals survive and reproduce; others die or move to new locations.

3.e *Students know* that some kinds of organisms that once lived on Earth have completely disappeared and that some of those resembled others that are alive today.

This unit also includes these Investigation and Experimentation Standards: **5.a 5.b 5.c 5.d 5.e**

What's the Big Idea?

Certain body parts and behaviors can help living things survive, grow, and reproduce.

Essential Questions

Salton Sea

Dear Jeff,

We just got back from camping at the Salton Sea! You really should go there! We caught lots of fish and saw thousands of birds. I learned that nearly all of the American white pelicans in this country live at the Salton Sea. I loved watching them scoop up fish in their big beaks.

Your friend,
Manuel

USA

Why don't all birds have beaks like the pelican's? How does this relate to the **Big Idea?**

Unit Inquiry

Choosing a Place to Live

If you could choose to live anywhere in the world, where would it be? Do other animals prefer to live in one place over another? For example, do mealworms like to live where it is wet or where it is dry? Plan and conduct an experiment to find out.

Science Content

3.a *Students know* plants and animals have structures that serve different functions in growth, survival, and reproduction.

3.b *Students know* examples of diverse life forms in different environments, such as oceans, deserts, tundra, forests, grasslands, and wetlands.

Investigation and Experimentation

5.a Repeat observations to improve accuracy and know that the results of similar scientific investigations seldom turn out exactly the same because of differences in the things being investigated, methods being used, or uncertainty in the observations.

5.d Predict the outcome of a simple investigation and compare the result with the prediction.

California Fast Fact

Life in the Desert

The beavertail cactus is found in the hot, dry Mojave Desert. Most of the part above the ground is the stem. The thick stem stores water to help the cactus survive in the desert.

LESSON 1

Essential Question

How Do Plant Parts Help Plants?

The Mojave Desert, California

trait [TRAYT]
A characteristic, or feature, of a plant or animal (p. 196)

survive [ser•VYV]
To stay alive (p. 196)

adaptation
[ad•uhp•TAY•shuhn] A trait that helps a living thing survive (p. 197)

reproduce
[ree•pruh•DOOS] To produce new living things (p. 200)

Desert Plants

Start with Questions

Living in the desert is not easy. Desert plants have parts and features that help them grow where there is not much water.

- What leaf shape is best for desert plants?

- In what ways do desert plants save water?

Investigate to find out. Then read to find out more.

Prepare to Investigate

Investigation Skill Tip

It's a good idea to do an investigation more than once. Then you can compare the results you got every time you did the investigation. If you get different results, you must find out why.

Materials
- water
- 3 paper towels
- large, flat baking pan
- wax paper
- paper clips

Make an Observation Chart

Desert Leaf Models	
Type of Leaf	My Observations
Flat	
Rolled	
Rolled, with waxy coating	

Follow This Procedure

1. Wet each paper towel. The paper towels will be models of leaves.

2. Place one towel flat on the pan. Roll up the second towel. Place it next to the flat towel.

3. Roll up the third towel. Fasten wax paper around it with paper clips. Place it on the pan.

4. Put the pan in a sunny place.

5. Wait two hours. Feel the towels and record your observations.

Draw Conclusions

1. Which towel felt the dampest? Which one was the driest?

2. **Standards Link** Why do you think desert plants have a waxy coating on their stems? **3.a**

3. **Investigation Skill** Compare your observations with the observations from other groups in the class. Did all groups have the same results? What could have caused any differences in the results between groups? **5.a**

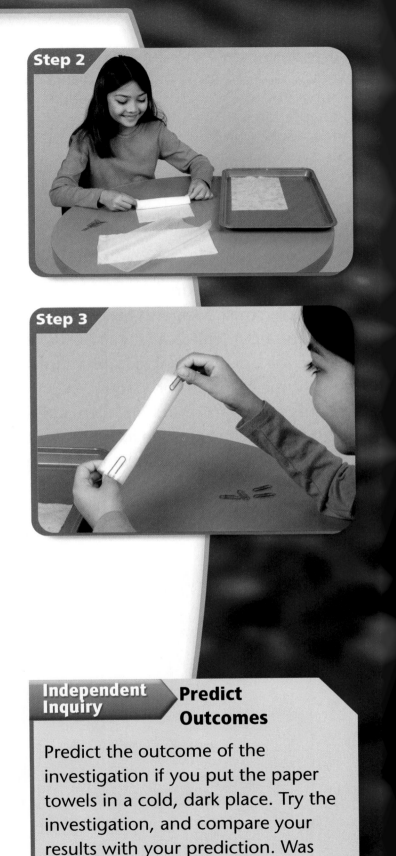

Step 2

Step 3

Independent Inquiry **Predict Outcomes**

Predict the outcome of the investigation if you put the paper towels in a cold, dark place. Try the investigation, and compare your results with your prediction. Was your prediction correct? **5.d**

VOCABULARY
trait p. 196
survive p. 196
adaptation p. 197
reproduce p. 200

SCIENCE CONCEPTS
▶ why plants have adaptations
▶ how adaptations help plants survive, grow, and reproduce

Focus Skill **MAIN IDEA AND DETAILS**
Look for examples of different kinds of adaptations.

Main Idea

detail   detail   detail

Plant Parts

It's easy to tell an apple and a carrot apart. They look, smell, feel, and taste different from one another. A **trait** is a characteristic, or feature, of a plant or animal. What are some traits of the plant on this page?

Plants have parts that help them **survive**, or stay alive. Their roots take in the water they need from the soil. Some plants also have thorns that keep animals from eating them.

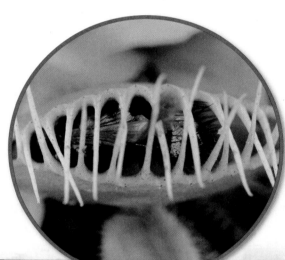

The Venus' flytrap has leaves that close when insects land on them. The plant gets nutrients from the insects.

▲ This corn plant has roots called prop roots. They are adaptations that help some plants stand up.

The thorns on this rosebush are an adaptation. They protect it from some animals that would eat it.

A trait that helps a living thing survive is called an **adaptation**. Sharp spines are one kind of adaptation. They protect plants such as cacti from being eaten by animals. Not many animals try to eat plants that have spines!

Some adaptations are not parts. They are ways plants or animals act that help them survive. Sunflowers turn slowly during the day to keep facing the sun. This helps them get as much sunlight as they can.

(Focus Skill) **MAIN IDEA AND DETAILS** What is an example of an adaptation that helps a plant survive?

197

Adaptations Help Plants Grow

Plants need nutrients, water, sunlight, and air. Many plants have adaptations that help them get these things so that they can grow.

Wood is an adaptation that helps trees grow tall. In a forest, the tallest plants get the most sunlight. Tree trunks are made of wood, which is very strong. It can support the tree as it grows upward. Without wood, a tree would bend or fall over.

Vines have an adaptation for growth, too. Their stems can wrap around other plants. This helps them grow toward the sunlight.

The stem of this vine has parts that hold on to other plants. This adaptation helps the vine climb upward.

The roots of beets, radishes, and carrots store food. The plants use this food to grow.

Roots are adaptations for getting water and nutrients. Some plants have fat roots, in which they store food. They use this food for growth.

Without water, a plant can't grow. Some desert plants have roots that grow deep into the soil. They reach water that is far under the ground. Other desert plants have roots that spread out just under the surface. This lets them take in water quickly when it rains.

Focus Skill **MAIN IDEA AND DETAILS** What is an example of an adaptation that helps a plant grow?

The leaves of this plant form a cup that collects rainwater. This adaptation helps the plant get the water it needs to grow. ▼

Adaptations That Help Plants Reproduce

Have you ever planted a seed and watched a new plant grow? Some plants use seeds to **reproduce**, or produce new living things. All living things reproduce.

The flowers of plants need pollen from other flowers to make seeds. They have adaptations that help them get that pollen. Their smell, color, and shape may attract insects and other animals. The animals get pollen on them and carry it from flower to flower.

Smell can be an adaptation. This carrion flower smells like rotten meat. The smell attracts flies, which carry the pollen to other carrion flowers.

Flowers make a sweet liquid called nectar. This adaptation attracts bees, which carry pollen from one flower to another.

A coconut is a giant seed. It travels from one island to another by floating on the water.

When seeds fall from a maple tree, they spin like helicopter blades. This adaptation helps the seeds "fly" to new places.

Soft fluff covers thistle seeds. These seeds can be blown by the wind to new places.

Sometimes seeds need to spread to new places to grow. Some plants have seeds that stick to animals. The animals spread the seeds as they move about. Other plants have tiny seeds that the wind can carry. Some seeds can float on water. They may be carried far from the parent plant.

Focus Skill **MAIN IDEA AND DETAILS** What is one adaptation that helps plants reproduce?

Insta-Lab

Hide and Seek
Put 10 peas and 10 kernels of corn on yellow paper. Close your eyes for a minute. Then open them and pick up the first 5 seeds you see. Which ones did you pick up? How can the color of a seed protect it?

Standards Wrap-Up and Lesson Review

How do plant parts help plants?

In this lesson, you read about many examples of plant adaptations. Plants have adaptations that help them survive, grow, and reproduce.

 Science Content Standards in This Lesson

3.a *Students know* plants and animals have structures that serve different functions in growth, survival, and reproduction.

3.b *Students know* examples of diverse life forms in different environments, such as oceans, deserts, tundra, forests, grasslands, and wetlands.

1. **MAIN IDEA AND DETAILS** Draw and complete a graphic organizer. Show the supporting details of the main idea *Plants have adaptations.* **3.a**

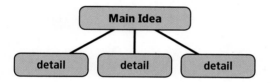

2. **SUMMARIZE** Write three sentences that tell what this lesson is mainly about. **3.a**

3. **DRAW CONCLUSIONS** What might happen to a cactus if it did not have spines? **3.a**

4. **VOCABULARY** Write a sentence for each vocabulary word. Show that you know what the word means. **3.a**

5. **Critical Thinking** Explain why a plant that lives under water can't survive in a desert. **3.b**

6. **Investigate and Experiment** You are working on a science fair project. You do an investigation, and you get interesting results. Why would you want to repeat the investigation? **5.a**

 Writing ELA–W 2.2

Write a Description

Make up an adaptation for a plant. Describe what the adaptation looks like. Tell how it helps the plant survive, grow, or reproduce.

 Math NS 3.1

Use Fraction Models

The mesquite tree grows long roots that reach water in the desert. In one area, water is 4 meters underground. One mesquite tree's roots are now 3 meters long. Make a drawing of the tree, its roots, and the water. Have the roots grown more or less than half the distance to the water?

 Social Studies HSS 3.5.1

California Plants

Find out more about giant sequoias. Make a poster showing where they grow. Tell what adaptations they have that help them survive, grow, and reproduce.

 For more links and activities, go to **www.hspscience.com**

Science Content

3.a *Students know* plants and animals have structures that serve different functions in growth, survival, and reproduction.

3.b *Students know* examples of diverse life forms in different environments, such as oceans, deserts, tundra, forests, grasslands, and wetlands.

Investigation and Experimentation

5.e Collect data in an investigation and analyze those data to develop a logical conclusion.

LESSON 2

Essential Question

How Do Animal Adaptations Help Animals?

California Fast Fact

All Ears

Black-tailed jackrabbits have ears that look too big for their bodies. Why are their ears so big? Do they help the rabbits hear better? No! The big ears help cool the animal's body on hot days.

Vocabulary Preview

hibernate [HY•ber•nayt]
To spend the winter in a
kind of deep sleep
(p. 210)

migrate [MY•grayt] To
travel from one place to
another and back again
(p. 211)

black-tailed
jackrabbit

Keeping Warm

Start with Questions

On a cold day, you might wear a jacket and a hat to keep warm.

- How do animals that live in cold places stay warm?

Investigate to find out. Then read to find out more.

Prepare to Investigate

Investigation Skill Tip

How do elephant seals stay warm in the cold ocean? To answer that question, scientists would plan an experiment. An experiment should test a possible answer to a question.

Materials
- large plastic bowl
- water
- ice
- spoon
- plastic bag
- solid vegetable shortening
- pair of plastic gloves

Make an Observation Chart

	Description of Hand
Hand with shortening	
Hand with no shortening	

Follow This Procedure

1 Fill the bowl with water and ice. Half-fill the bag with shortening.

2 Put on the gloves. Put one hand into the bag. Mold the shortening so that it evenly covers your hand.

3 Now put both gloved hands into the ice water. Compare the ways your hands feel. Record your observations.

Draw Conclusions

1. Which hand felt warmer in the ice water?

2. **Standards Link** How do you think the layer of blubber, or fat, under an elephant seal's skin is like the shortening? 3.a

3. **Investigation Skill** Scientists plan experiments to answer questions. What question did this experiment answer?

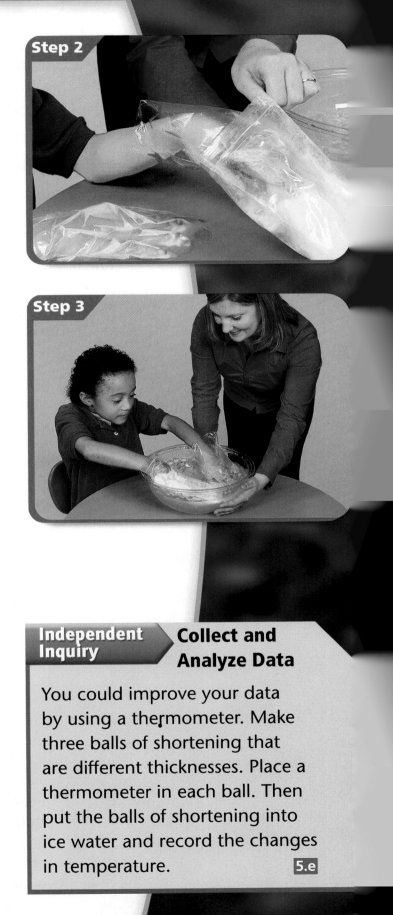

Step 2

Step 3

Independent Inquiry

Collect and Analyze Data

You could improve your data by using a thermometer. Make three balls of shortening that are different thicknesses. Place a thermometer in each ball. Then put the balls of shortening into ice water and record the changes in temperature. 5.e

VOCABULARY
hibernate p. 210
migrate p. 211

SCIENCE CONCEPTS
▶ some adaptations animals have
▶ how adaptations help animals survive, grow, and reproduce

Focus Skill CAUSE AND EFFECT
Look for ways that adaptations affect the lives of animals.

| cause | → | effect |

Adaptations for Survival

In Lesson 1, you read about some plant adaptations. Animals also have adaptations to help them survive.

For example, eagles have adaptations for flying and for catching food. An eagle's eyes can spot prey from a mile away! The birds' strong wings help them fly fast. Eagles have sharp claws they can use to grab and hold their prey. They also have sharp beaks for eating their food.

▲ Mother kangaroos have a pouch where their newborn babies live. The pouch protects the babies, giving them more time to grow.

Porcupines [PAWR•kyoo•pynz] have quills for protection. It hurts to get stuck by a quill, so other animals stay away from porcupines.

Some bears have short, curved claws for climbing. These claws help them reach fruit and leaves in trees.

◀ A crab's shell and claws protect it from other animals that would eat it. Their claws also help them catch food.

Male elephant seals live in the water most of the time. They hunt for food there. For three months of each year, however, they live on land. They can't hunt well there. Luckily, they are almost half blubber, and their blubber stores energy. This adaptation helps the seals live for three months without eating. Blubber also helps keep them warm in cold water.

Focus Skill CAUSE AND EFFECT What is one effect of an eagle's sharp eyes?

Insta-Lab

Thumbs Down

Tuck your thumb into the palm of your hand. Without moving your thumb, try to pick up an object. Now try to write your name. Share your observations with a classmate. How is the thumb a useful adaptation for humans?

Behaviors

Animals have behaviors, or ways of acting, that help them survive. You do, too. You eat when you are hungry. In winter, you wear a coat to stay warm.

Winter is hard for some animals. There is little food. In fall, some animals eat more and build up fat. Then they **hibernate**, or spend the winter in a kind of deep sleep. They do not use much energy. They live off their fat. Hibernating is an adaptation.

▲ A hibernating animal's body gets cold. The lower body temperature helps it use less energy.

This chipmunk spends the winter months hibernating. It curls into a ball and moves very little.

Math in Science
Interpret Data

When an animal hibernates, its heart beats more slowly. Use this graph to find each animal's active heart rate and hibernating heart rate. Find the differences between them.

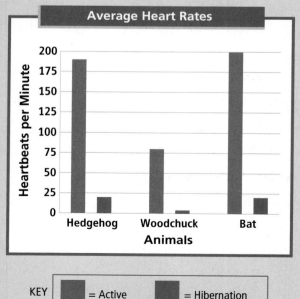

Average Heart Rates

KEY   = Active   = Hibernation

Migration Routes

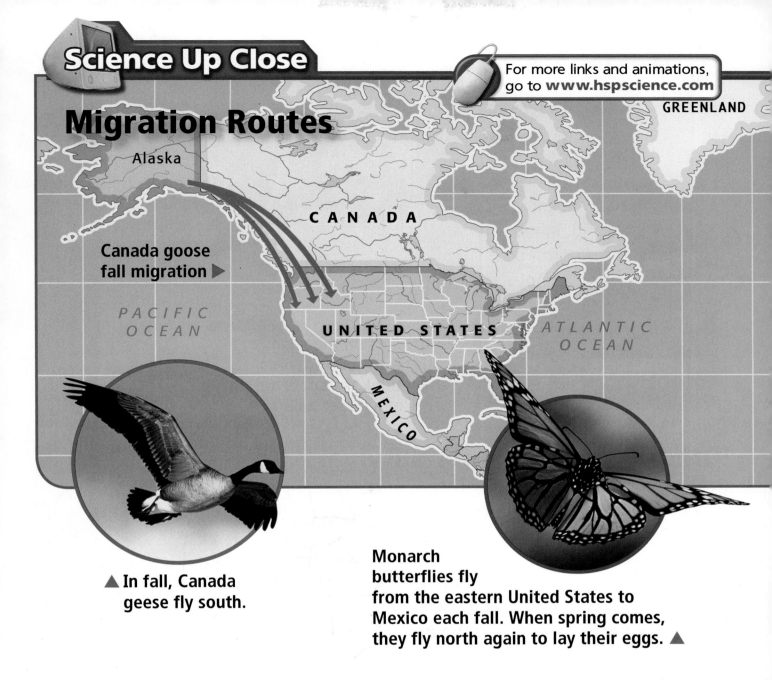

GREENLAND

Alaska

C A N A D A

Canada goose
fall migration ▶

PACIFIC
OCEAN

U N I T E D   S T A T E S

ATLANTIC
OCEAN

MEXICO

▲ In fall, Canada
geese fly south.

Monarch
butterflies fly
from the eastern United States to
Mexico each fall. When spring comes,
they fly north again to lay their eggs. ▲

Other animals **migrate** to survive. To migrate is to
travel from one place to another and back again. In
summer, gray whales live near Alaska. In fall, when the
ocean becomes colder, they swim south. They migrate to
warmer waters off the coast of California. In spring, they
swim north.

Animals do not need to learn how and when to
hibernate and migrate. They know these behaviors
without being taught. These behaviors are adaptations.

 CAUSE AND EFFECT   **What causes animals to hibernate?**

This insect is called a walking stick. It looks like a twig.

◀ The spots on the wings of this moth confuse birds. They think the spots are the eyes of a larger animal.

Other Adaptations for Survival

Some animals can hide well. Their shapes or colors match their environment. This adaptation helps them hide.

The Arctic hare has brown fur in the summer. The brown color matches the rocks and the ground. In winter, the Arctic hare's fur turns white. This makes the animal hard to see against the snow. Animals that eat hares may not see them.

▲ A chameleon [kuh•MEE•lee•uhn] can change colors to match its background so other animals do not see it.

◀ These stonefish look like rocks. Smaller fish swim close by and get eaten!

Some animals survive by looking like other animals. The milk snake is not deadly. The coral snake is. These snakes look very much alike. People can tell them apart. Animals that eat snakes cannot, so they leave both alone. Looking like the deadly coral snake keeps the milk snake safe.

Focus Skill **CAUSE AND EFFECT** **What is the effect of looking like a dangerous animal?**

Many animals do not take care of their eggs or young. Some frogs lay hundreds of eggs, as you see here. Laying large numbers of eggs is an adaptation that makes sure some eggs survive.

Some animals have only a few young, but they take care of them. Most of these young survive. ▼

Essential Question

How do animal adaptations help animals?

In this lesson, you learned that animals have adaptations. Adaptations help animals grow, survive, and reproduce. Adaptations help living things meet their needs in the environment in which they live.

 Science Content Standards in This Lesson

3.a *Students know* plants and animals have structures that serve different functions in growth, survival, and reproduction.

3.b *Students know* examples of diverse life forms in different environments, such as oceans, deserts, tundra, forests, grasslands, and wetlands.

1. (**Focus Skill**) **CAUSE AND EFFECT** Choose three animal adaptations. Complete a graphic organizer for each adaptation to show how the adaptation affects the animal's life. **3.a**

2. **SUMMARIZE** Write a summary of this lesson. Begin with the sentence *Animals have adaptations that help them survive.* **3.a**

3. **DRAW CONCLUSIONS** How can looking like another animal help a living thing survive? **3.a**

4. **VOCABULARY** Write a paragraph that explains how the terms *adaptation, hibernate,* and *migrate* are related. **3.a**

5. **Critical Thinking** Some small animals in the ocean migrate to the surface at night and back to deep water during the day. Why might they do this? **3.b**

6. **Investigate and Experiment** Which conclusion will be strongest?
   A one based on an idea
   B one based on a prediction
   C one based on an experiment
   D one based on an opinion **5.e**

 Writing ELA–W 2.1

Write a Narrative

Choose an animal that hibernates, such as a bat, a chipmunk, a ground squirrel, a hedgehog, or a woodchuck. Write a story about how that animal gets ready for hibernation.

 Math NS 2.5

Use Division

A gray whale comes to the surface every three minutes to take a breath. How many times will a gray whale come to the surface in 15 minutes?

 Art VPA–VA 2.5

Make-Believe Adaptations

Make up an animal with an adaptation that helps it survive. Then make a model of that animal out of clay, or draw it on a sheet of paper. Explain its adaptation to a small group or to the class.

 For more links and activities, go to **www.hspscience.com**

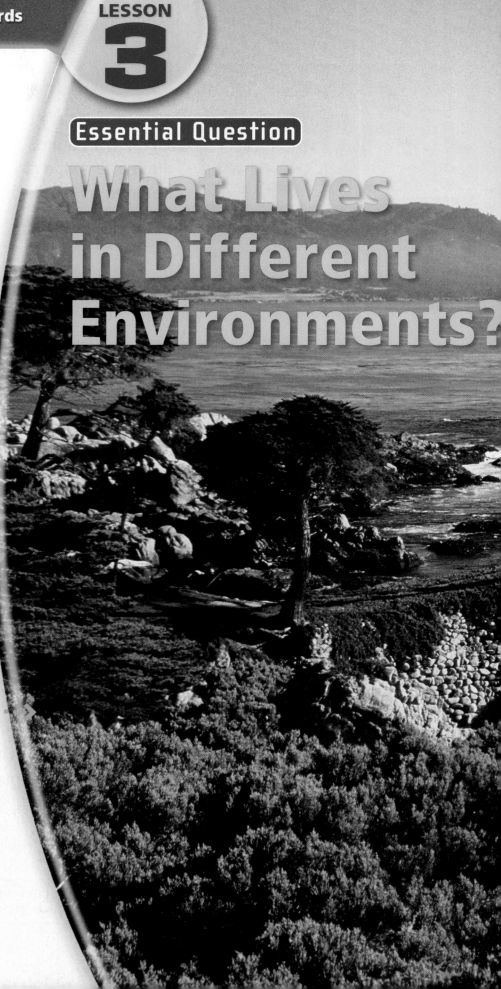

Science Content

3.a *Students know* plants and animals have structures that serve different functions in growth, survival, and reproduction.

3.b *Students know* examples of diverse life forms in different environments, such as oceans, deserts, tundra, forests, grasslands, and wetlands.

Investigation and Experimentation

5.e Collect data in an investigation and analyze those data to develop a logical conclusion.

LESSON

3

Essential Question

What Lives in Different Environments?

California Fast Fact

Having It All!

California has many environments. In different parts of the state, you can find forests, grasslands, wetlands, deserts, and ocean environments.

Monterey Peninsula
Carmel, California

environment
[en•vv•ruhn•muhnt]
Everything that is around
a living thing (p. 220)

habitat [HAB•ih•tat] The
place where something
lives in an environment
(p. 221)

climate [KLY•muht] The
weather a place has over
a long period of time
(p. 222)

Animal Homes

Start with Questions

You live in a home, and so do your friends.

- Do animals have homes?
- Are there different kinds of animal homes?

Investigate to find out. Then read to find out more.

Prepare to Investigate

Investigation Skill Tip

To draw a conclusion, use the data you have collected and what you already know. Then decide what makes sense.

Materials
- picture cards
- index cards
- markers
- reference books

Make an Observation Chart

Animal	Description of Home

Follow This Procedure

1 Observe each picture card that your teacher gives you. Notice each animal's home.

2 With your partner, write the name of each animal on an index card. Name or draw its home on another card. If you need help, look in reference books.

3 You have made a matching game. Play it with your partner. Then classify the animals by the kind of home they live in.

Draw Conclusions

1. Compare the homes of the foxes and the owl.

2. **Standards Link** Why do you think animals have different kinds of homes? `3.b`

3. **Investigation Skill** Analyze the data you have gathered and what you know about animals. What conclusions can you draw about animals' homes? `5.e`

Step 2

Step 3

Independent Inquiry **Collect and Analyze Data**

Use the index cards you made in the Investigate to compare kinds of homes. For animals that have the same kind of home, list ways that the animals are alike. Draw conclusions about the adaptations animals use to make the homes they live in. `5.e`

3.a, 3.b

SCIENCE CONCEPTS
▶ how environments are different
▶ how living things have adaptations for different environments

Focus Skill **COMPARE AND CONTRAST**
Compare and contrast different environments.

alike	different

Oceans

Have you ever seen a whale? Unless you live close to the ocean, you probably have not. An *ocean* is a large body of salty water.

An ocean is a whale's environment. An **environment** is everything that is around a living thing. Water, sunlight, seaweed, and fish are all part of a whale's environment.

The living things in the oceans have adaptations that help them live there. Fish have gills that take oxygen from the water, in the way that your lungs take oxygen from the air.

Focus Skill **COMPARE AND CONTRAST** How does your environment compare to an ocean environment?

▲ The sea otter's body is long and slim. This adaptation helps it swim quickly through the ocean.

Fish have gills that take oxygen out of the water. This adaptation allows fish to live in a water environment.

Deserts

A *desert* is a very dry environment. The plants and animals in a desert environment live in different habitats. A **habitat** is the place where something lives in an environment.

The desert lily usually lives in a flat, sandy area of the desert. This is one desert habitat. Ringtails and bighorn sheep live in the rocky hills of California deserts. Rocky hills are another desert habitat.

Many living things have adaptations for living in only one habitat. A cactus that lives in a flat, sandy habitat probably could not survive on a rocky hill.

Focus Skill **COMPARE AND CONTRAST** How are all the plants and animals in the desert alike?

▲ The ringtail lives in rocky parts of the desert. It can climb well, using its tail for balance.

The desert has little water. Many animals get water from the seeds and plants they eat.

Tundra

Different parts of the world have different weather. **Climate** is the weather a place has over a long period of time. The amount of sunlight and rain or snow a place gets is part of the climate. Seasons are also part of a place's climate.

The *tundra* is a place that has a very cold climate. Winters are long. Some of the soil stays frozen all the time.

The Arctic fox lives in the tundra. It has adaptations for surviving the cold weather. The fox has thick fur that helps it stay warm. Its fur is white in the winter, helping it hide in the snow.

Focus Skill **COMPARE AND CONTRAST** **Compare the tundra with the place where you live.**

Caribou spend part of the year in the tundra. When winter comes and food is hard to find, they migrate to a place with a warmer climate. ▼

Forests

There are many types of forests. A *forest* is an area that is covered with trees. Tropical rain forests have a hot and wet climate. Monkeys live there. They have fingers to grab branches and long tails for balance. These adaptations help monkeys move through the thick tangle of trees.

Some forests have warm summers and cold winters. In these forests, some trees stop growing in winter. They drop their leaves, helping them save energy in the cold weather. Then they grow new leaves in spring.

(Focus Skill) COMPARE AND CONTRAST How are tropical rain forests different from other kinds of forests?

▲ A long-eared owl uses its sharp eyes to search for food.

Squirrels eat nuts and fruits that grow in the forest. ▶

Forests have different habitats for many animals.

Grasslands

Grasslands are dry, flat places covered with grasses. They have hot summers and cold winters. Grasslands get more rain than deserts, but still not a lot of rain.

Grasslands have a dry climate with many fires. The grasses that grow there store food in their roots, where it will not burn in a fire. After a fire, the roots quickly grow again.

Bison and zebras are grassland animals. They eat grasses. Their flat teeth help them grind their food.

(Focus Skill) COMPARE AND CONTRAST How are a grassland and a desert alike? How are they different?

Little bluestem is one of many kinds of grasses. It can grow without much water.

During the 1800s, as many as 60 million bison lived on the grasslands of North America. ▼

Wetlands include bogs, marshes, and swamps.

leopard frog

Wetlands

Wetlands are areas that are wet all the time or most of the time. Many wetland plants have long stems that grow under water. If a wetland dries up or is drained, many of the plants do not survive.

Many wetland animals have adaptations for living in the wet environment. Some ducks dive under water to get food. Turtles have a hard shell for protection. Alligators can stay under water for a long time without breathing.

COMPARE AND CONTRAST How do plants in a wetland compare with plants in a grassland?

Insta-Lab

Getting to Know You
Choose an environment from this lesson. Use library resources to find at least two animals and two plants that live there. What adaptation does each have for surviving in that environment?

Essential Question

What lives in different environments?

In this lesson you learned about different environments. Each environment has a different climate. Plants and animals have adaptations that help them live in their environments.

Science Content Standards in This Lesson

3.a *Students know* plants and animals have structures that serve different functions in growth, survival, and reproduction.

3.b *Students know* examples of diverse life forms in different environments, such as oceans, deserts, tundra, forests, grasslands, and wetlands.

1. (Focus Skill) **COMPARE AND CONTRAST** Draw and complete a graphic organizer to compare and contrast the tundra and a tropical rain forest. **3.b**

2. **SUMMARIZE** Write a list of the main topics in this lesson. Include a little information about each main topic. **3.b**

3. **DRAW CONCLUSIONS** Why would plants from a forest not grow well in the tundra? **3.b**

4. **VOCABULARY** Write a sentence for each vocabulary word. Show that you understand what the word means. **3.b**

5. **Critical Thinking** Describe an adaptation a fish has for living in an ocean environment. **3.a**

6. A bird has a beak that helps it eat grass seeds. A fire burns the grasslands where it lives. Why will it probably not survive in another environment? **3.b**

The Big Idea

 Writing ELA–W 2.2

Write a Description

Write a travel brochure for an environment in this lesson. Describe things that visitors will enjoy about that environment.

 Math MR 2.3

Collect Data

Research an environment from this lesson. Find out its average monthly rainfall. Make a bar graph to show the information you collect.

 Social Studies HSS 3.2.2

Adapting to Nature

These Inuit know how to survive in a cold environment. Choose a California tribal nation. Find out how its early people adapted to their environment. How did their environment affect their food, clothing, and tools? Write a report to show what you learned.

 For more links and activities, go to **www.hspscience.com**

Joshua Tree

NATIONAL PARK

Joshua Tree National Park is in southeastern California, where two deserts meet. The Colorado Desert, to the east, has many cactus plants but no Joshua trees. The Mojave Desert, to the west, is cooler and has a little more moisture. The Joshua tree does grow here. Surviving in a desert is not easy, but the Joshua tree has adaptations that help it.

The Rain of Life

Many desert plants depend on spring rain. With the first rain, these plants sprout and bloom. They quickly produce seeds and then die. These new seeds might not sprout until the next spring's rain.

Plants like the Joshua tree grow only during longer wet periods. In between, they just survive. Like many other desert plants, the Joshua tree blooms after the spring rain.

Joshua trees can't reproduce without yucca moths. The moths spread pollen from one flower to another, so the trees can make seeds. Yucca moths also lay their eggs in the flowers.

The yucca seeds form soon. When the moth eggs hatch, the larvae eat some of the seeds. Still, without the yucca moth, there would be no seeds and no new Joshua trees.

The tallest Joshua trees are only 12 meters (39 ft) high. They grow only about $1\frac{1}{2}$ centimeters ($\frac{1}{2}$ in.) each year.

This yucca moth is gathering pollen from a Joshua tree flower.

✏️ Think and Write

❶ How do the Joshua tree and the yucca moth help each other survive? `3.a`

❷ Would the Joshua tree's adaptations help it survive in wetlands? Explain why or why not. `3.b`

Science Content

3.c *Students know* living things cause changes in the environment in which they live: some of these changes are detrimental to the organism or other organisms, and some are beneficial.

Investigation and Experimentation

5.d Predict the outcome of a simple investigation and compare the result with the prediction.

LESSON

4

Essential Question

How Do Living Things Change Environments?

California Fast Fact

Big Changes

Scientists estimate that 2 to 5 million acres of land will be developed in California in the next 20 years. Making changes to the land helps people but can harm other animals.

pollution
[puh•LOO•shuhn]
Harmful material
that is added to the
environment (p. 234)

**Orange County,
California**

Pollution and Plants

Start with Questions

All living things need water to survive. When pollution mixes with water, it can harm living things.

- What are some types of water pollution that harm plants?

- What happens to plants that take in polluted water from the soil?

Investigate to find out. Then read to find out more.

Prepare to Investigate

Investigation Skill Tip

When you compare, you notice how things are the same and how they are different.

Materials
- 3 clear plastic cups
- potting soil
- radish seeds
- marker
- clean water
- salty water
- oily water

Make a Data Table

Plant Growth							
Centimeters Grown Each Day							
Day	1	2	3	4	5	6	7
Clean							
Salty							
Oily							

Follow This Procedure

Step 1

1. Put soil in the cups. Plant a few seeds in each cup.

2. Label the cups *Clean, Salty,* and *Oily.* Water each cup with the kind of water on its label. Predict which seeds will grow best.

3. Place the cups near a sunny window. Each day for 10 days, water each cup with the kind of water on its label.

4. When the seeds sprout, measure the growth of the plants every day. Record your observations.

Step 3

Draw Conclusions

1. What did you observe? In which cup did the seeds grow best?

2. **Standards Link** Did it matter if the water you used was polluted? How can you tell? `3.c`

3. **Investigation Skill** Compare your results to your prediction. Which seeds did you predict would grow best? Were you correct? `5.d`

Independent Inquiry

Compare Results to Predictions

You can try this investigation using other kinds of water. Plan an investigation to test a prediction. Include your prediction, the materials you will need, and the steps you will follow. Compare your results to your prediction. `5.d`

VOCABULARY
pollution p. 234

SCIENCE CONCEPTS
▶ how living things can change the environment
▶ how the changes can be helpful or harmful

SEQUENCE
Watch for the order in which events happen.

☐ → ☐ → ☐

People Harm the Environment

People change the environment in many ways. Some ways are harmful to the environment. People cut down forests. This harms the living things that need trees.

Another way people harm the environment is by causing pollution. **Pollution** is harmful material that is added to the environment. Smoke from factories is one kind of air pollution. An oil spill is one kind of water pollution.

SEQUENCE What happens to forest animals when people cut down trees?

People cut down trees to make room for buildings and parking lots. The animals that lived in the forest must find new homes.

People build tunnels for animals so cars do not hit them.

◀ This sign asks people not to shine lights on the beach because lights confuse turtles when they hatch.

BEACHFRONT LIGHTS OUT
• MAY - OCTOBER •
Let's Save The Sea Turtles
Sponsored by
U.S. Fish and Wildlife Service

▲ A bird built its nest on this sign. Sometimes people help animals without meaning to.

People Help the Environment

People can make changes that help the environment. One way is to plant new trees after the trees in a forest are cut down. This helps the forest grow back faster.

Cars cause air pollution, but we need them for transportation. A special part on cars now reduces pollution. People can also clean up some kinds of pollution.

Focus Skill SEQUENCE What happens when people plant trees after a forest has been cut down?

Insta-Lab

Helping or Harming Write down one way people make changes to the environment. List living things that are harmed by the change. Then list living things that are helped by the change. Share your list with a partner.

Living Things Change Their Environments

Animals change their environments in many ways. Foxes dig holes and elephants knock over trees. Beavers build dams, which form ponds.

Plants also change their environments. Water hyacinths (HY•uh•sinths) grow in lakes and ponds. They grow fast and spread out to cover the water's surface. Sunlight can't reach other water plants below.

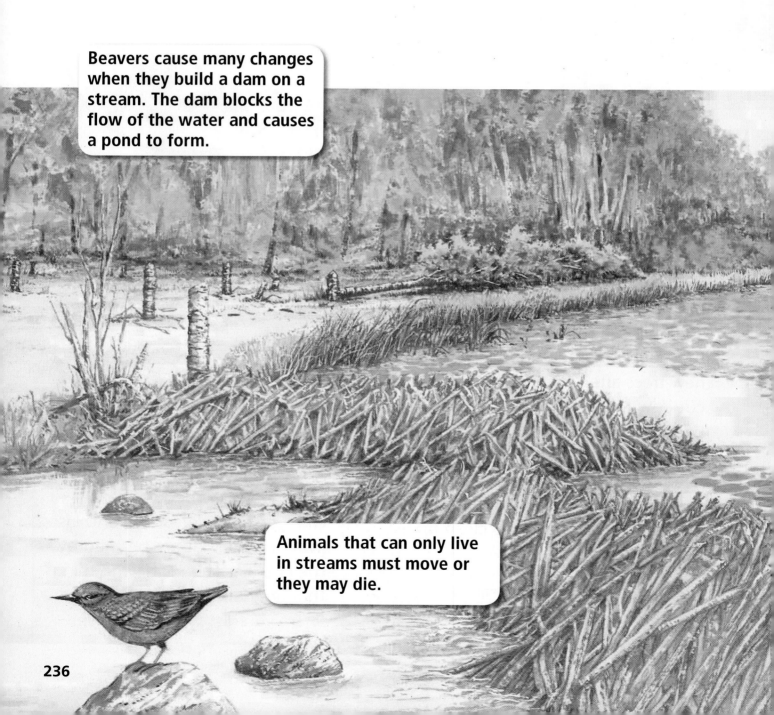

Beavers cause many changes when they build a dam on a stream. The dam blocks the flow of the water and causes a pond to form.

Animals that can only live in streams must move or they may die.

Suppose a tree falls in a forest. The area near it will get more sunlight. This will help plants that need a lot of sunlight to grow. However, the change will not be good for the birds and other animals that lived in the tree. They may need to find new homes.

How has the beaver dam in the picture changed the environment? Some changes in environments are helpful, and others are harmful. Many can be both.

 **Focus Skill** **SEQUENCE** What happens after a tree falls in a forest?

When beavers cut down trees, some birds and insects lose their homes.

The deeper water of the pond helps the beavers hide from animals that would eat them. The pond becomes a home for some kinds of plants and animals.

How do living things change environments?

In this lesson, you learned that people and other living things change their environments. Some changes are helpful, and others are harmful. Pollution is harmful to living things.

Science Content Standards in This Lesson

3.c *Students know* living things cause changes in the environment in which they live: some of these changes are detrimental to the organism or other organisms, and some are beneficial.

1. **Focus Skill** **SEQUENCE** Draw and complete a graphic organizer that shows what happens when a forest is cut down. **3.c**

2. SUMMARIZE Write a summary of the lesson. Include two helpful changes and two harmful changes. **3.c**

3. DRAW CONCLUSIONS Will living things ever stop changing the environment? Explain your answer. **3.c**

4. VOCABULARY Which choice about pollution is **not** correct?

  A Pollution harms the environment.

  B People cause pollution.

  C An oil spill is pollution.

  D A beaver dam is pollution. **3.c**

5. Critical Thinking Do you think more of the changes that people make to the environment are harmful or helpful? Explain your answer. **3.c**

6. Describe a change in an environment that helps some living things but harms others.

The Big Idea

3.c

 Writing ELA–W 2.3

Write a Letter

Write a letter to the editor of your community's newspaper. Ask people to protect the environment in some way. Explain why this action is important.

 Math NS 2.4

Solve Problems

Cutting down trees to make paper can harm the environment. We can recycle used paper by making it into new paper. Recycling 1 ton of paper saves 17 trees. How many trees would be saved if you recycled 4 tons of paper?

 Health

Breathe Deeply!

Find out how air pollution can affect your health. Then make a poster to share what you learned. Include tips on how to avoid polluted air to stay healthy.

 For more links and activities, go to **www.hspscience.com**

Science Content

3.d *Students know* when the environment changes, some plants and animals survive and reproduce; others die or move to new locations.

Investigation and Experimentation

5.b Differentiate evidence from opinion and know that scientists do not rely on claims or conclusions unless they are backed by observations that can be confirmed.

LESSON 5

Essential Question

How Do Changes to Environments Affect Living Things?

California Fast Fact

Growing Sideways!

Plants and animals are affected by their environments. This tree would normally grow upward. It has grown sideways because of a constant wind from the Pacific Ocean.

drought [DROWT] A long period of time with very little rain (p. 244)

balance [BAL•uhns] Not too many and not too few of a kind of living thing (p. 248)

Golden Gate National Recreation Area

Changing the Environment

Start with Questions

You have learned that plants have adaptations to help them survive in their environments. Some environments are very dry. Others are very wet.

- What happens if an environment changes and a plant doesn't get enough water?

- Can a plant get too much water?

Investigate to find out. Then read to find out more.

Prepare to Investigate

Investigation Skill Tip

There are many ways you can communicate the results of an investigation. When you have an idea you want to share, decide whether writing, speaking, or using pictures or diagrams will work best.

Materials
- 3 medium pots
- potting soil
- grass seeds
- watering can filled with water
- paper and pencil
- ruler

Make a Data Table

Plant Growth Data					
Day	1	2	3	4	5
No water					
Normal water					
Extra water					

Follow This Procedure

1 Half-fill the pots with potting soil.

2 Sprinkle grass seeds on top of the soil. Add a little soil to cover the seeds. Water each day to keep the soil moist.

3 When the seeds begin to grow, label the pots. One pot will continue to get the same amount of water. One pot will not get any water, and one pot will get twice as much water.

4 Each day, measure how tall the grass is in each pot. Record your observations.

Draw Conclusions

1. Compare the plants in the three pots. What differences did you notice in how the plants grew?

2. Standards Link How might a long period without rain affect a plant? How might a flood affect a plant? **3.d**

3. Investigation Skill Scientists can communicate their results by displaying their data. Use the data from your data table to make a graph. Display your data table and graph.

Step 2

Step 3

Independent Inquiry

Draw a Conclusion Based on Observations

Your partner concludes that all plants will die after a flood. What observations could you make that would prove your partner wrong? Design an investigation that could help you draw a different conclusion. Try it! **5.b**

3.d

SCIENCE CONCEPTS
▶ how climate and fire affect living things
▶ what living things do when their environment changes

CAUSE AND EFFECT
Look for changes to the environment caused by climate and fire.

| cause | → | effect |

Climate Affects Living Things

Environments have different climates. Plants and animals have adaptations that help them survive in their environments. What is the climate like where you live?

If the climate in a place changes, it affects all of the things that live there. A **drought** is a long period of time with very little rain. Plants that live in a place where it usually rains may not survive a drought.

▲ **Many plants die during a drought.**

These students are staying cool on a hot summer day.

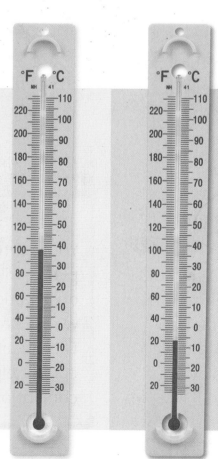

On cold days, people wear heavy clothing to stay warm.

During a flood, a river flows onto the land. Plants and animals may die. After the flood, the river goes back to its usual size. It leaves behind the soil it was carrying. Crops will grow well on this land.

The desert has a hot, dry climate. Few kinds of plants can grow in a desert because there is very little water. As a result, few animals live there. Those that do live there have adaptations that help them survive.

When it does rain in the desert, many plants begin to grow. After a rain, the desert may be covered with colorful wildflowers. These wildflowers grow quickly to make seeds before they die in the dry climate.

 **CAUSE AND EFFECT** What effect does a drought have on living things?

Fire Affects Living Things

A fire can cause a lot of changes to an environment. It can kill living things. Sometimes a fire can help an environment. If a tree burns, it is likely to fall. It leaves an open space in the forest. New plants can get more sunlight and have room to grow.

Fires can also be harmful. They can destroy animals' habitats. Those animals may not be able to survive in a new habitat.

Fire is helpful to some plants and animals. It is harmful to others.

This fire is causing many changes to the forest environment.

Firefighters set this small fire carefully to help plants and animals that need fires to survive.

◀ The cones of the lodgepole pine open and drop their seeds only when fire heats them. Without fire, the lodgepole can't reproduce.

Some plants have adaptations that help them live in places that have fires. There are many fires in grasslands environments. Grasses have many roots and can grow back quickly after a fire. Other plants cannot.

Ashes from burned plants add nutrients to the soil. The nutrients help new plants grow.

Focus Skill **CAUSE AND EFFECT** What is one helpful and one harmful effect of fire?

FIRE DANGER

HIGH

TODAY!

PREVENT FOREST FIRES

▲ This sign warns people that the forest is dry and a fire could spread easily.

Balance Between Living Things

An environment is in **balance** when there are not too many and not too few of any kind of living thing. An environment needs the right amount of the right plants. Without the plants, animals will have no food. The animals will have to find new places to live, or they will die.

This pond environment is in balance. More animals would upset this balance. More ducks would eat too many plants. Other animals would not have enough food. Some might leave the area. Others might die.

Science Up Close

Balance in a Pond

The living things here depend on one another. They also depend on this pond. If one kind of plant or animal was taken out of the pond, it could upset the balance of living things in the pond.

 For more links and animations, go to **www.hspscience.com**

Too many plants would also cause the pond environment to be out of balance. They might cover the surface of the pond and cause the fish to die. Then the birds that eat the fish would have to move or die.

Focus Skill CAUSE AND EFFECT

How does having too few plants affect an environment?

Insta-Lab

Upsetting the Balance

Make a pyramid of self-stick notes. In the bottom row of eight notes, draw grass. In the next row, draw four grasshoppers. In the next, draw two lizards. At the top, draw one owl. How would the owl be affected if you took away half of the grass?

If there were not as many plants, this bird would have nothing to eat. ▼

If there were more snails, they would eat all the plants.

249

Standards Wrap-Up and Lesson Review

Essential Question

How do changes to environments affect living things?

In this lesson you learned about changes to the environment, such as fires and changes in the climate. When these changes happen, living things may survive, may die, or may move to a new place.

Science Content Standards in This Lesson

3.d *Students know* when the environment changes, some plants and animals survive and reproduce; others die or move to new locations.

1. (Focus Skill) **CAUSE AND EFFECT** Draw and complete a graphic organizer to show the effects of a forest fire. **3.d**

2. **SUMMARIZE** Use the graphic organizer to summarize the important ideas in this lesson. **3.d**

3. **DRAW CONCLUSIONS** Do living things cause all the harmful changes in the environment? Explain your answer. **3.d**

4. **VOCABULARY** Explain how *climate* can affect the *balance* in an environment. Use both words in your answer. **3.d**

5. **Investigate and Experiment** Why should you use evidence to draw a conclusion instead of using your opinion? **5.b**

6. Which change will **most likely** have the greatest effect on an environment?

The Big Idea

   A A tree is cut down.

   B A piece of trash is thrown into a pond.

   C A fire burns down a forest.

   D There is no rain for a week in a desert. **3.d**

 Writing ELA–W 2.1

Write a Narrative

Choose an animal, and write a story about what happens to it when its environment changes. Explain the cause of the change, such as climate, fire, or an upset in the balance of living things.

 Math MR 2.3

Construct a Graph

Choose an animal that is disappearing from California, and find out why it is in trouble. Then make a bar graph. On it, show how many of these animals are alive now in California. Show how many were alive 10 years ago and 20 years ago.

 Drama VPA–T 2.1

Lights, Camera . . .

With a group, act out how living things change when their environment changes. One member can hold up a sign explaining the environmental change. The other members can wear labels telling which living things they are.

For more links and activities, go to **www.hspscience.com**

On the Prowl

Counting Jaguars

A sleek, spotted jaguar walks along the floor of the forest. As the jaguar passes a fig tree, there is a small whirring noise. A flashing light and a click follow. A camera has just snapped the jaguar's photograph.

No person was behind the camera's lens. The camera was triggered by motion and heat from the passing cat.

A Narrowing Range

Scientists from the Wildlife Conservation Society in New York have placed about 30 such cameras in trees throughout the tropical forest of Belize (beh•LEEZ). That is a country in Central America.

The cameras are helping researchers count the number of jaguars in some areas of Belize and other places where jaguars live.

This "camera trapping" will help scientists, because jaguars are hard to study. Despite the cats' large size, the thick jungle where they live make them difficult to spot. Also, the jaguars are very private.

"The cameras help researchers determine how many cats are out there and where they make their homes," said jaguar expert Kathleen Conforti to Weekly Reader.

A camera snaps a photograph of a passing jaguar.

The map shows how the range of jaguars has changed. ▶

KEY

■ Where jaguars live now

□ Where jaguars used to live

The researchers will use that information to help protect the endangered animals. They want to conserve, or save, the jaguars' habitat.

The actions of people have caused a decline in the jaguars' range. Cutting down trees has destroyed some of the animals' habitat. Hopefully, cameras will help researchers understand how to help protect jaguars.

Think and Write

1 How do you think the loss of trees might affect how jaguars live?

`3.d`

2 What adaptations of jaguars make them hard to study?

`3.a`

What a Roar

- Jaguars, which are carnivorous, can be as long as 1.8 meters (6 ft) and can weigh up to 136 kilograms (300 pounds).
- Jaguars are the third-largest cats, after tigers and lions.
- Most jaguars live alone and are very territorial. That means they protect their habitat from other jaguars.

Find out more. Log on to
www.hspscience.com

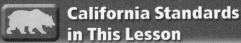
Science Content

3.e *Students know* that some kinds of organisms that once lived on Earth have completely disappeared and that some of those resembled others that are alive today.

Investigation and Experimentation

5.c Use numerical data in describing and comparing objects, events, and measurements.

5.e Collect data in an investigation and analyze those data to develop a logical conclusion.

California Fast Fact

Looking into the Past

Scientists have found the remains of many living things at the La Brea (BRAY•uh) Tar Pits near Los Angeles. Their findings include horses with three toes, cats with huge teeth, and elephant-like mammoths. These remains tell about California's past.

LESSON

6

Essential Question

How Have Living Things Changed over Time?

The Page Museum at the La Brea Tar Pits

fossil [FAHS•uhl] The hardened remains of a plant or an animal that lived long ago (p. 258)

extinct [ek•STINGT] Describes a kind of living thing that is no longer found on Earth (p. 262)

Animals from Long Ago

Directed Inquiry

Start with Questions

Scientists want to learn about animals that lived long ago. They can do this by looking at fossils. These are the remains of animals that lived long ago.

- Did the animals of long ago look like animals we see today?

- Were there animals long ago that did not look like any animals living today?

Investigate to find out. Then read to find out more.

Prepare to Investigate

Investigation Skill Tip

There are many ways to make observations. One way to improve your observation skills is by using numbers. Analyzing the data you collect can help you draw conclusions.

Materials

- shell fossil
- modern-day shell
- ruler
- elephant picture card
- woolly mammoth picture card

Make an Observation Chart

My Animal Observations		
	Alike	Different
Shell fossil and modern-day shell		
Woolly mammoth and elephant		

Follow This Procedure

❶ Observe the shell fossil and the modern-day shell. Record your observations.

❷ Use the ruler to measure the width and length of each shell. Record your measurements.

❸ Now observe the picture cards for the elephant and the woolly mammoth. Compare the two animals, and record your observations.

Draw Conclusions

1. How are the elephant and the woolly mammoth alike? How are they different?

2. **Standards Link** Do some shells from long ago look like ones we see today? If so, in what ways are they alike? `3.e`

3. **Investigation Skill** Use numbers to compare the shell fossil and the modern-day shell. Do you think the kinds of animals that lived in the shells have changed much over time? Explain. `5.e`

Step 1

Step 3

Independent Inquiry	**Use Numbers to Compare Things**

Research the size of the imperial mammoth. Then use a meterstick to mark its length and height on a flat surface outdoors. Draw its outline in chalk. Do the same for the elephant. How do the sizes of these two animals compare? `5.c`

SCIENCE CONCEPTS
▶ how some things that lived long ago have disappeared
▶ how some things living today look like some that lived long ago

COMPARE AND CONTRAST
Look for ways living things of long ago are like those of today.

alike ── different

Animals Then and Now

A **fossil** is the hardened remains of a plant or an animal that lived long ago. Some fossils, such as bones and teeth, look like the actual parts of the animals they came from. Other fossils, such as footprints, are only marks that the animals left behind.

▲ **Trilobites** [TRY•luh•byts] **lived in the sea millions of years ago, but there are none left on Earth now.**

Tyrannosaurus rex **was about 4.5 meters (15 ft) tall and had teeth as big as bananas.**

Modern-day camel

Small camel fossil

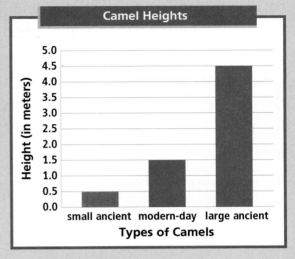

How much taller were large camels of long ago than camels are today?

Camel Heights

Height (in meters) / Types of Camels

small ancient   modern-day   large ancient

▲ Camels lived in North America many years ago. Fossils tell us that some of these camels were about the size of a rabbit. Others were about 4.5 meters (15 ft) tall.

Fossils show how animals have changed. There are no animals alive today that look like *Tyrannosaurus rex.* On the other hand, camels have not changed much. Camels of long ago were different in size, but they looked like the camels of today.

Focus Skill **COMPARE AND CONTRAST** How are footprint fossils different from bone fossils?

Scientists thought the kind of fish shown in this fossil no longer lived on Earth, until a live one was caught by a fisherman.

259

Plants Then and Now

Plant fossils are not as common as animal fossils. That's because the soft parts of plants are easily destroyed.

Some plant fossils are leaf prints in mud. Others are *petrified wood*, a type of fossil in which wood has turned to stone.

Scientists learn from fossils. From them, they know that some plants no longer grow on Earth. Other plants look like those we see today.

Focus Skill **COMPARE AND CONTRAST** How are fossil plants like fossil animals?

Making Fossils

Gather leaves and other plant parts. Press them into a flat piece of modeling clay. Look at the prints you made. What would they tell future scientists about the plants in your area?

Scientists can see how ferns have changed by comparing fossil ferns with modern-day ferns. ▼

Fern fossil

Modern-day fern

Modern-day ginkgo tree

The ginkgo tree is often called a living fossil because it has not changed much in 100 million years.

Ginkgo leaf fossil

Ginkgo leaves

Like ginkgo trees, there were bristlecone pine trees 100 million years ago. Fossils show that these trees have changed little over time. ▶

Bristlecone pinecones

Fossil pinecones

Bristlecone pine tree

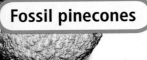

Extinct Plants and Animals

Many kinds of plants and animals are extinct. **Extinct** means a kind of plant or animal is no longer living. When the last *Tyrannosaurus rex* died, that animal became extinct.

Living things become extinct for many reasons. When an environment changes, some living things change, or adapt, to survive. Others find new habitats in which to live. Some cannot change, and they die.

The last great auk died in 1844. These birds are now extinct. ▼

◄ The saber-toothed cat is California's state fossil.

Saber-toothed cats were about 30 centimeters (12 in) shorter than today's lions. However, they were twice as heavy.

North America has had many Ice Ages. During these times, huge sheets of ice covered much of the land. Many plants and animals became extinct because they could not adapt to survive in the colder climate.

People can cause living things to become extinct. They cut down forests and drain wetlands. Plants and animals may lose their homes and become extinct.

▲ Woolly mammoths lived during the last Ice Age. However, they could not adapt as the climate became warmer after the Ice Age.

 **COMPARE AND CONTRAST** How was the climate during an Ice Age different from the climate today?

An Ice Age lasts for millions of years. This map shows areas that were covered by ice in the last Ice Age.

PACIFIC OCEAN

ATLANTIC OCEAN

Standards Wrap-Up and Lesson Review

How have living things changed over time?

In this lesson, you learned that living things have changed over time. Some living things today look like things that lived long ago. Some things that lived long ago have died out.

Science Content Standards in This Lesson

3.e *Students know* that some kinds of organisms that once lived on Earth have completely disappeared and that some of those resembled others that are alive today.

1. **(Focus Skill) COMPARE AND CONTRAST** Draw and complete a graphic organizer to compare and contrast a saber-toothed cat and a lion living today. **3.e**

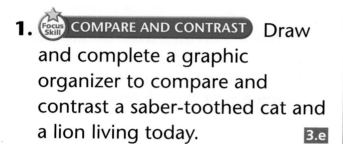

2. **SUMMARIZE** Write two sentences that tell the most important information in this lesson. **3.e**

3. **DRAW CONCLUSIONS** Suppose you found a fossil. Why should you be careful with it? **3.e**

4. **VOCABULARY** Explain how the words *fossil* and *extinct* are related to each other. Use both words in your answer. **3.e**

5. **Critical Thinking** Some animals of long ago are extinct. Why do you think other animals that look like ancient ones are still on Earth? **3.e**

6. **Investigate and Experiment** You read a report that says "Woolly mammoths were larger than elephants." Explain how you could use numbers to make the statement more exact. **5.c**

Writing

 ELA–W 2.2

Write a Description

Find a picture of a fish that lives today and looks somewhat like this one. Describe ways the two fish are the same and ways they are different. Explain whether you think the fish in this picture is a fossil of the living fish.

Math

 MR 1.1

Write a Word Problem

Write a word problem using information from this table. Ask a classmate to solve your problem.

Lengths of Dinosaurs	
Dinosaur	**Length (in meters)**
Stegosaurus	12
Tyrannosaurus	14
Brachiosaurus	25

Social Studies

 HSS 3.4.1

Endangered Species

Human activities can cause plants and animals to become extinct. Living things that may become extinct are said to be endangered species. Research the Endangered Species Act. Write a report about how the law helps protect a California plant or animal.

 For more links and activities, go to **www.hspscience.com**

Akira Okubo

▶ **AKIRA OKUBO**

▶ **Oceanographer**

▶ Learned why fish swim in large groups

When he was a boy, Akira Okubo watched schools of fish, or large groups of fish swimming together. He learned that fish form schools for protection. A school of tiny fish can look like one large fish, too big for other hungry fish to eat.

Okubo became an oceanographer, a scientist who studies oceans. He learned that a school of fish can have several million fish. All of the fish in a school are about the same size. Adult fish and young fish swim in different schools.

Tiny fish can't fight bigger fish, but they can fool them! Schooling is an adaptation that helps fish survive in their ocean environment.

✎ Think and Write

❶ How is schooling an adaptation? **3.a**

❷ Give two examples of animals that live together to survive in other environments.

> Some fish swim together their whole lives!

Lisa D. White

You would probably be excited to find a fossil of a dinosaur. Would you be as excited to find a fossil that is so small that you can barely see it?

Lisa D. White studies fossils of tiny living things in the oceans, such as diatoms. After ancient diatoms died, they sank to the ocean floor and became fossils. Even though the fossils are small, White can find out a lot about diatoms that lived long ago.

Millions of diatoms still live in the oceans. They are an important source of food for fish. Lisa D. White can compare diatoms living today with the fossils of diatoms she studies.

▶ **LISA D. WHITE**

▶ **Associate Professor of Geology, San Francisco State University**

▶ Studies tiny fossils

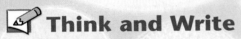

Think and Write

1. How can Lisa D. White learn about diatoms that lived long ago? `3.e`

2. What tools might Dr. White use to study diatom fossils?

Diatoms have many different shapes. Some are quite beautiful.

▶ Visual Summary

Tell how each picture helps explain the **Big Idea**.

The Big Idea Certain body parts and behaviors can help living things survive, grow, and reproduce.

3.a

Adaptations
A trait that helps a living thing survive, grow, and reproduce is an adaptation. A porcupine's quills are an adaptation.

3.a, 3.b

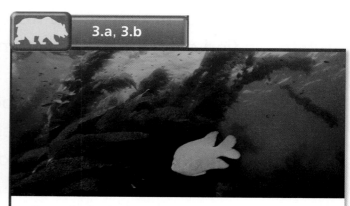

Surviving in Different Environments
Living things have adaptations to survive in certain environments. In the ocean, fish have gills.

3.c, 3.d

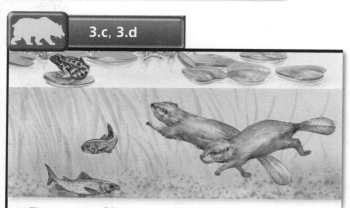

Responding to Change
Beavers change their environment to help themselves. The changes can affect other living things.

3.e

Change or Become Extinct
Some ancient living things changed with the environment. Others, like mammoths, became extinct.

Show What You Know

Unit Writing Activity

Write a Letter

Think of ways that your community could protect its plants and animals. One example might be using less weedkiller on lawns. Then write a letter to your city council. Tell your ideas for changes so that living things in your community will not have to adapt, move, or die.

Unit Project

Adaptations and Environments

Choose an environment, such as the desert or the tundra. Make an exhibit that shows how certain plants and animals are adapted to that environment. Use labels and pictures to explain their adaptations.

Vocabulary Review

Use the terms below to complete the sentences. The page numbers tell you where to look in the unit if you need help.

trait p. 196	pollution p. 234
adaptation p. 197	balance p. 248
hibernate p. 210	fossil p. 258
environment p. 220	extinct p. 262

1. Everything that is around a living thing is its _____. `3.b`

2. When there are not too many or too few of any living thing, there is _____. `3.d`

3. When a certain kind of living thing no longer exists, it is _____. `3.e`

4. The hardened remains of a plant or an animal that lived long ago are a _____. `3.e`

5. A feature of a plant or animal that makes it different from other plants or animals is a _____. `3.a`

6. Any harmful material in the environment is _____. `3.c`

7. To spend the winter in a deep sleep is to _____. `3.a`

8. A trait that helps a living thing survive is an _____. `3.a`

Check Understanding

Choose the best answer.

9. **CAUSE AND EFFECT** Which is caused by human actions? `3.c`
   A hibernation   C migration
   B instinct   D pollution

10. What have we **not** learned from fossils? `3.e`
    A how animals have changed
    B how animals will look someday
    C how climates have changed
    D how animals used to look

11. In which environment could the living thing shown below survive? `3.b`
    A desert
    B forest
    C tundra
    D wetlands

12. COMPARE AND CONTRAST How are a flood and a fire similar? `3.d`

A Both help all living things in an environment.

B Both harm all living things in an environment.

C Both can help some living things and harm others.

D Neither changes the balance of living things.

13. Which kind of adaptation does the animal in the picture have? `3.a`

A It migrates.

B It hibernates.

C It eats brown leaves.

D It blends in with its environment.

14. What happens to an animal when it hibernates? `3.a`

A Its heart beats faster.

B Its heart beats slower.

C Is breathing speeds up.

D It moves from one habitat to another.

15. Which of these is **not** a fossil? `3.e`

A a dinosaur footprint

B the shell of a snail that died last week

C petrified wood

D the outline of a bone in a rock

16. What can scientists learn from fossils? `3.e`

A how Earth formed

B what color an animal was

C what kinds of animals once lived on Earth

D which animals will become extinct

Investigation Skills

17. A scientist is studying how elk migrate. What conclusion can you draw using the scientist's data? `5.c`

Year	Kilometers Migrated
1999	122
2000	126
2001	130
2002	130
2003	132
2004	133
2005	133
2006	136

18. What do you predict will happen to a rain-forest plant that is moved to a desert? Explain. `5.d`

Critical Thinking

19. Houses are built near an area where raccoons live. How might this change be helpful and harmful to the raccoons? `3.c`

20. Choose a living thing and describe an adaptation it has. How does the adaptation help the living thing survive?

The **Big** Idea

UNIT 4
EARTH SCIENCE

Patterns in the Sky

What's the Big Idea?

We can predict where the sun, the moon, the stars, and the planets will be in the sky.

Sierra
Nevada

Dear Kenny,

I'm on a camping trip in the Sierra Nevada with my outdoors club. Last night, we stayed up to watch the stars and moon move across the sky. It was really neat. There were no city lights, so the stars looked brighter, and we could see more of them. I can't wait to tell you all about it!

Your friend,
Lisa

USA

What changes in the sky have you noticed? How do they relate to the **Big Idea?**

Unit Inquiry

Build a Model Solar System

Our solar system is made up of nine planets. Earth takes just over 365 days to travel around the sun. Do the other planets take the same amount of time to orbit the sun? To find out, build a model of the solar system and test your hypothesis.

Science Content

4.c *Students know* telescopes magnify the appearance of some distant objects in the sky, including the Moon and the planets. The number of stars that can be seen through telescopes is dramatically greater than the number that can be seen with the unaided eye.

4.d *Students know* that Earth is one of several planets that orbit the Sun and that the Moon orbits Earth.

Investigation and Experimentation

5.c Use numerical data in describing and comparing objects, events, and measurements.

Essential Question

What Planets Orbit the Sun?

VENUS • THE HOTTES

EARTH • OUR HOME PL

MARS • THE RED PLANET

ASTEROID BELT • SPACE R

JUPITER • THE GIANT

...E RINGED PLANET

...NUS ...EWAYS PLANET

...PTUNE ...HE LAST BIG ...

California Fast Fact

Earth's Neighbors

At the Chabot Space and Science Center in Oakland, you can see models of planets. Some planets are so far away that it would take years to travel to them.

Chabot Space and Science Center

planet [PLAN•it] A large body of rock or gas that orbits a star in space (p. 278)

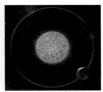

orbit [AWR•bit] To travel around an object (p. 278)

telescope [TEL•uh•skohp] A tool that makes faraway objects seem closer and larger (p. 279)

moon [MOON] A large body that orbits a planet (p. 279)

solar system [SOH•ler SIS•tuhm] The sun and the objects that orbit it, including the planets and their moons (p. 279)

275

The Planets

Start with Questions

Not all the points of light that fill the night sky are stars. Some of them are planets. Like Earth, they travel around the sun.

- How many planets are there?

- How far from the sun are the other planets?

Investigate to find out. Then read to find out more.

Prepare to Investigate

Investigation Skill Tip

There are many ways you can use numbers in science. You can use numbers to estimate and compare data. In this Investigate, you will use numbers to put things in order.

Materials
- pencil
- paper

Make an Observation Chart

Planet Data in Order		
Order from Sun	Name of Planet	Distance from Sun
1		
2		
3		
4		
5		
6		
7		
8		
9		

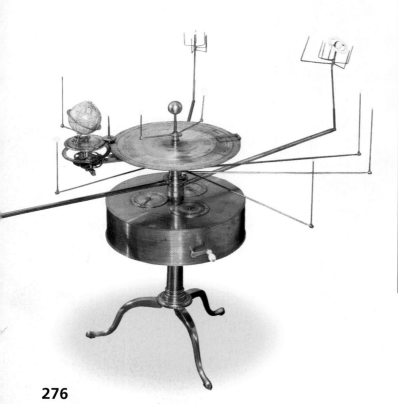

Follow This Procedure

1 Use numbers from the Planet Data Table to order the planets based on their distances from the sun, from closest to farthest.

2 Next to each planet's name, record its distance from the sun.

Draw Conclusions

1. How are the planets arranged? Start with the planet closest to the sun.

2. **Standards Link** How many planets are between Earth and the sun? `4.d`

3. **Investigation Skill** Scientists use numbers to describe and compare data. How did you use numbers in this investigation? `5.c`

In 2006, a group of scientists classified Pluto as a "dwarf planet."

Planet Data Table	
Planet	**Distance From Sun (in millions of kilometers)**
Earth	150
Jupiter	778
Mars	228
Mercury	58
Neptune	4,505
Pluto	5,890
Saturn	1,427
Uranus	2,869
Venus	108

Step 2

Independent Inquiry **Use Numbers**

Scientists sometimes use numbers to put things in order. Use pages 280–283 to list the planets in order by using different data. Then explain how you can use numbers to compare planets. `5.c`

VOCABULARY
planet p. 278
orbit p. 278
telescope p. 279
moon p. 279
solar system p. 279

SCIENCE CONCEPTS
▶ what the planets are like
▶ how planets move through the solar system

COMPARE AND CONTRAST
Look for ways to compare details about the planets.

alike ———— different

The Solar System

Do you wonder where we are in space? We live on the planet Earth. A **planet** is a large body of rock or gas in space.

Earth is always moving, but we can't feel this movement. Planets **orbit**, or travel around, stars. The sun is the star that Earth orbits. In all, nine planets orbit the sun.

In the night sky, you can see some of the planets with your eyes alone. Those planets look like stars, but they don't give off their own light. Planets reflect light from the sun. When you see a planet, you see that reflected light.

Nine planets orbit the sun. The largest one is Jupiter.

Mercury   Venus   Earth   Mars

Jupiter

To see some planets, you need a telescope. A **telescope** is a tool that makes faraway objects seem closer and larger.

Some planets have moons that orbit them. A **moon** is a large body that orbits a planet. Earth has only one moon, which we often see as a large object in the sky.

The word *solar* has to do with the sun. The **solar system** is the sun and the objects that orbit it. The solar system includes the planets and their moons. The sun is the center of the solar system. It is also the biggest object in the solar system.

Focus Skill **COMPARE AND CONTRAST** How is a moon's orbit different from a planet's orbit?

Modeling the Solar System

Work with a group. Use clay to make models of the planets. Use a basketball for the sun. Show how the planets orbit the sun. Where is Earth located in the solar system?

In 2006, a group of scientists classified Pluto as a "dwarf planet." Scientists are still discussing whether or not Pluto should be considered a planet.

Some of the brightest points of light you see in the night sky are planets, not stars.

Saturn

Uranus

Neptune

Pluto

The Inner Planets

The four planets closest to the sun are called the inner planets. The inner planets are Mercury, Venus, Earth, and Mars. You can sometimes see the three other inner planets at night. With a telescope, you may be able to see features such as the ice caps of Mars.

All the inner planets have rocky surfaces. The inner planets are small compared to some other planets. They are also warmer than some other planets, because they are closer to the sun.

Mercury

Fun Fact: In the daytime, much of Mercury's surface is hot enough to melt lead.
Length of Day: **about 59 Earth days**
Moons: **none**
Surface: **rocky, with many craters**
Distance Across: **4,900 kilometers (3,100 miles)**

Venus

Fun Fact: Venus may once have had oceans, but if so, they have dried up.
Length of Day: **about 243 Earth days**
Moons: **none**
Surface: **rocky, with thick clouds**
Distance Across: **12,000 kilometers (7,500 miles)**

Because Earth is moving, it is hard for scientists to study the movements of other planets. Scientists spent hundreds of years learning to understand the movement patterns of the other planets.

 COMPARE AND CONTRAST How are the inner planets different from the other planets?

Earth

Fun Fact: **Earth is the only planet that has liquid water on its surface.**
Length of Day: **24 hours (1 Earth day)**
Moons: **1**
Surface: $\frac{3}{4}$ water, $\frac{1}{4}$ land
Distance Across: **12,750 kilometers (7,900 miles)**

Mars

Fun Fact: **Mars has the largest volcano in the solar system.**
Length of Day: **about 25 Earth hours**
Moons: **2**
Surface: **rocky, with red dust and no water**
Distance Across: **6,800 kilometers (4,200 miles)**

The Outer Planets

The five planets farthest from the sun are called the outer planets. They are Jupiter, Saturn, Uranus, Neptune, and Pluto. Other than Pluto, the outer planets are made up mostly of gases. Most of them are very large and have moons. Only Jupiter and Saturn can be seen without a telescope.

 COMPARE AND CONTRAST How are most of the outer planets alike?

Jupiter

Fun Fact: Two planets the size of Earth could fit inside Jupiter's Great Red Spot. The Great Red Spot is a huge storm.
Length of Day: about 10 Earth hours
Moons: more than 60
Surface: no solid surface
Distance Across: 143,000 kilometers (88,900 miles)

Saturn

Fun Fact: Saturn has many rings, which reach out about 416,000 kilometers (260,000 mi) from its surface.
Length of Day: about 10 Earth hours
Moons: more than 55
Surface: no solid surface
Distance Across: 120,500 kilometers (74,900 miles)

Uranus

Fun Fact: Uranus spins on its side as it orbits the sun.
Length of Day: **about 18 Earth hours**
Moons: **more than 25**
Surface: **no solid surface**
Distance Across: **51,100 kilometers (31,800 miles)**

Neptune

Fun Fact: Neptune is the farthest planet from the sun for 20-year periods when Pluto crosses its orbit.
Length of Day: **about 19 Earth hours**
Moons: **more than 10**
Surface: **no solid surface**
Distance Across: **55,500 kilometers (34,500 miles)**

Pluto

Fun Fact: Pluto has a moon almost as large as itself.
Length of Day: **about 6 Earth days**
Moons: **at least 3**
Surface: **mostly ice and rock**
Distance Across: **2,400 kilometers (1,500 miles)**

Math in Science
Interpret Data

About how many Earth years does Saturn take to orbit the sun?

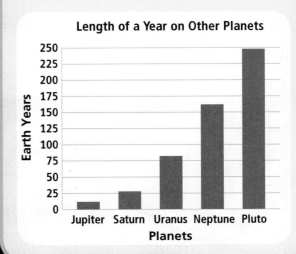

Length of a Year on Other Planets

Essential Question

What planets orbit the sun?

In this lesson, you learned that nine planets, including Earth, orbit the sun in our solar system. Each planet has different traits. Some planets have moons that orbit them. Earth has one moon.

Science Content Standards in This Lesson

4.c *Students know* telescopes magnify the appearance of some distant objects in the sky, including the Moon and the planets. The number of stars that can be seen through telescopes is dramatically greater than the number that can be seen with the unaided eye.

4.d *Students know* that Earth is one of several planets that orbit the Sun and that the Moon orbits Earth.

1. **(Focus Skill) COMPARE AND CONTRAST** Draw and complete a graphic organizer comparing and contrasting Earth and Saturn. **4.d**

   alike ——— different

2. **SUMMARIZE** Write a paragraph describing the solar system. **4.d**

3. **DRAW CONCLUSIONS** How do telescopes help scientists understand the solar system? **4.c**

4. **VOCABULARY** Write a sentence using the vocabulary terms *planet* and *solar system.* **4.d**

5. **Investigate and Experiment** How does using numbers in data help you compare and contrast the planets? **5.c**

6. Which statement is **not** true about Jupiter?

   A Jupiter is an outer planet.

   B Jupiter is part of the solar system.

   C Jupiter orbits the sun.

   D Jupiter is larger than the sun. **4.d**

The Big Idea

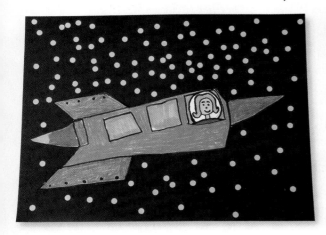

 Writing ELA–W 2.1

Write a Description

Choose one planet you read about in the lesson. Think about what a journey to that planet might be like. Describe what you would see along the way.

 Math MR 2.3

Construct Graphs

Make a bar graph showing about how many moons each planet has. Use the data on pages 280–283. Remember to label all parts of the graph.

 Art VPA–VA 2.2

Paint a Planet

Choose one planet. Make a painting that shows the colors and moons, if any, of that planet. Label the moons and special features of the planet.

 For more links and activities, go to **www.hspscience.com**

Ancient Planet Found

Can you guess what has been around for about 13 billion years? It's a planet that scientists recently discovered. If you think that 13 billion years sounds old, you're right. This planet is more than twice as old as Earth. In fact, the new discovery is the oldest planet known to exist.

However, don't rush out to try to look at the planet. It is too far away to be seen. Scientists found the planet only by using the Hubble Space Telescope.

A Faraway Planet

Scientists have found more than 100 planets outside of our solar system. This planet is different because it is so old. It is larger than Jupiter and is most likely made of gases.

A Special Telescope

The Hubble Space Telescope is a special kind of telescope. Rather than sitting in a dome on Earth, this telescope floats in space about 600 kilometers (375 mi) above Earth. Since this telescope is in space, it can take clearer pictures of stars and planets than telescopes on Earth can take.

Near the End?

Scientists say the Hubble's discovery is important. It means that planets probably began forming much earlier than scientists once thought. The Hubble's discoveries, however, may end soon. The telescope needs repairs and upgrades. Scientists now are working on a repair mission. The repairs would be done by robots. That could keep Hubble working longer.

The ancient planet is in this group of stars.

The arrow points to the ancient planet.

Large in Scope

Hubble is a lot bigger than many telescopes. It is 13.2 meters (43.5 ft) long and about 4.2 meters (14 ft) around the outside. This is about the size of a big tractor-trailer truck!

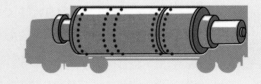

✏️ Think and Write

1 What can the Hubble Space Telescope teach scientists about the solar system?

4.c

2 Why do you think scientists want to discover new planets?

Find out more. Log on to
www.hspscience.com

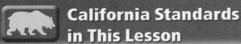

California Standards in This Lesson

Science Content

4.e *Students know* the position of the Sun in the sky changes during the course of the day and from season to season.

Investigation and Experimentation

5.b Differentiate evidence from opinion and know that scientists do not rely on claims or conclusions unless they are backed by observations that can be confirmed.

5.e Collect data in an investigation and analyze those data to develop a logical conclusion.

Essential Question

What Patterns Do Earth and the Sun Follow?

California Fast Fact

Sunrise and Sunset

In December, San Francisco gets only about $9\frac{1}{2}$ hours of daylight. In June, the city gets about $14\frac{1}{2}$ hours of daylight.

San Francisco, California

rotation [roh•TAY•shuhn] The spinning of Earth (p. 292)

axis [AK•sis] An imaginary line that runs through Earth from the North Pole to the South Pole (p. 296)

Northern Hemisphere [NAWR•thern HEM•ih•sfir] The northern half of Earth (p. 297)

Measuring Shadows

Start with Questions

On a sunny day, you can see your shadow. Shadows are sometimes long and sometimes short.

- What causes shadows?

- What causes the length of shadows to change?

Investigate to find out. Then read to find out more.

Prepare to Investigate

Investigation Skill Tip

At the end of an investigation, you draw conclusions from your observations and facts. You can make a list of things you know. Then use the list to draw a conclusion—a summary of what you learned in an investigation.

Materials
- scissors
- craft paper
- ruler
- marker
- tape measure

Make a Data Table

Shadow Data	
Time	Length of Shadow

Follow This Procedure

CAUTION: Be careful using scissors.

1. Cut a small hole in the center of the paper.

2. Find a location outdoors that will stay sunny all day. Lay the paper on the ground. Push the ruler through the hole in the paper and into the ground.

3. Trace the shadow of the ruler. Label the line with the time of day.

4. Repeat Step 3 every hour for several hours.

5. Measure the length of each shadow. Record the measurements.

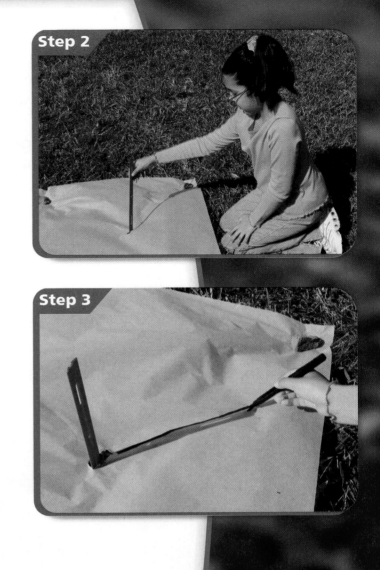

Step 2

Step 3

Draw Conclusions

1. Compare the lengths of your tracings. How did the ruler's shadow change?

2. **Standards Link** At what time was the ruler's shadow the longest? When was it the shortest? 4.e

3. **Investigation Skill** What conclusion can you draw about why the time of day affects the length of shadows? 5.e

Independent Inquiry

Support Conclusions with Observations

You think you could tell time by using the paper and ruler from the Investigation. You must be able to support your conclusion with observations. Set up the paper and ruler the same way. Tell what time it is without using a clock. How accurate were you? 5.b

VOCABULARY
rotation p. 292
axis p. 296
Northern Hemisphere
p. 297

SCIENCE CONCEPTS
▶ why the sun's position changes during the day
▶ why the sun's position changes from season to season

Focus Skill **CAUSE AND EFFECT**
Look for the effects of the movements of Earth.

cause → effect

Day and Night

You know that the sun rises and sets every day. To understand why this happens, you need to understand how Earth moves. Earth moves in two ways.

Rotation is the spinning of Earth. It takes Earth 24 hours—or one day—to make one rotation. Earth also orbits the sun, which takes about $365\frac{1}{4}$ days—or one year.

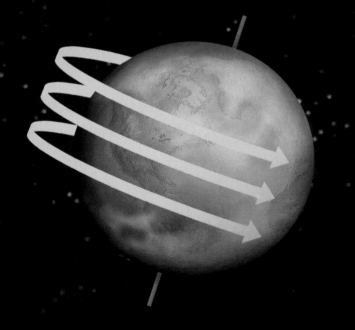

Rotation is the spinning of Earth as it travels through space.

It will take one year for Earth to orbit the sun.

Day and Night

The sun is always shining on one half of Earth while the other half is in darkness.

It is daytime in Sacramento.

At the same time, it is nighttime in Paris.

The sun always lights one half of Earth. It is daytime for the parts of Earth that face the sun. It is nighttime for the parts of Earth that face away from the sun. The part of Earth that is lit by the sun is always changing because of Earth's rotation.

Since some places have day while others have night, it isn't the same time everywhere. When it's 12 noon in Sacramento, California, it's 9 o'clock at night in Paris, France.

 **CAUSE AND EFFECT** What causes a part of Earth to have nighttime?

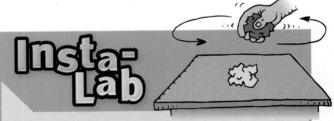

Modeling Motion
Crumple a sheet of yellow paper into a ball to model the sun. Then crumple a sheet of blue paper into a ball to model Earth. Use the models to show the two ways Earth moves. As Earth turns and travels, is the same part always facing the sun? Explain.

The Sun's Positions

Every day, the sun seems to rise in the east. At night, it seems to set in the west. Many years ago, people thought the sun traveled across the sky. Today, we know that it does not. Earth's rotation makes the sun seem to move across the sky.

As Earth spins, different parts of Earth face the sun. When a place on Earth faces the sun directly, the sun appears to be high overhead. As Earth rotates, that place moves away from the sun. This causes the position of the sun to seem to change.

In the morning, the sun is low in the sky, so shadows are long. At noon, the sun is directly overhead, so shadows are short. In the evening, the sun is low in the sky, and shadows are long again.

(Focus Skill) CAUSE AND EFFECT What causes the sun to appear to move across the sky?

This picture shows sunrise. How will the position of the sun change by noon?

Shadows Through the Day

The position of the sun in the sky changes during the day. This causes the length and direction of shadows to change.

Shadows are longer when the sun is low in the sky. In the morning, the shadows point in one direction. As the day goes on, the direction of the shadows changes.

The Seasons

Everyone has a favorite season. Perhaps you like warm summer days the best. Have you ever wondered why there are seasons?

Earth is shaped like a ball. Imagine a line through Earth from the North Pole to the South Pole. This line is called Earth's **axis**.

Earth's axis is not straight up and down. It is tilted. This causes the poles to tilt either toward or away from the sun as Earth orbits. The part of Earth tilted toward the sun has summer. The other part has winter.

In summer in California, the sun is higher in the sky, and the days are longer.

In winter in California, the sun is lower in the sky, and the days are shorter.

In July, the Northern Hemisphere is tilted toward the sun and has summer.

In January, Earth has traveled halfway around the sun. Now, the Northern Hemisphere is tilted away from the sun and has winter.

California is in the **Northern Hemisphere**, the half of Earth closer to the North Pole. In summer, the Northern Hemisphere is tilted toward the sun. The sun's rays are more direct, warming the Northern Hemisphere more. The days are longer. The sun appears higher in the sky.

Six months later, Earth has traveled halfway around the sun. The Northern Hemisphere is tilted away from the sun. The sun's rays are not as direct and do not warm the Northern Hemisphere as much. The days are shorter. The sun appears lower in the sky.

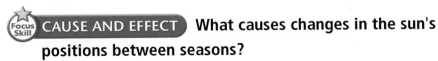 **CAUSE AND EFFECT** What causes changes in the sun's positions between seasons?

Standards Wrap-Up and Lesson Review

What patterns do Earth and the sun follow?

In this lesson, you learned that Earth moves in patterns. The movement of Earth causes the position of the sun in the sky to change during the day and from season to season.

 Science Content Standards in This Lesson

4.e *Students know* the position of the Sun in the sky changes during the course of the day and from season to season.

1. 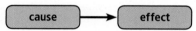 **CAUSE AND EFFECT** Draw and complete a graphic organizer to show the effect of the rotation of Earth.   4.e

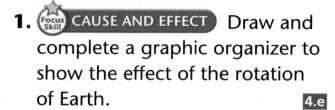

2. **SUMMARIZE** Write a summary of the lesson. Begin with the sentence *Earth moves in two ways.*   4.e

3. **DRAW CONCLUSIONS** Would Earth have seasons if its axis were not tilted? Explain.   4.e

4. **VOCABULARY** Draw and label a diagram that shows Earth's axis and the Northern Hemisphere. Show how the axis is tilted.   4.e

5. **Critical Thinking** It is spring in Australia, which is in the southern half of Earth. What season is it in California?

   A spring   **C** winter
   B summer   **D** fall   4.e

6. How does the position of the sun in the sky change from season to season?   4.e

 **The Big Idea**

 Writing ELA–W 2.3

Write a Letter

Think about which season is your favorite. What activities do you like to do? Write a letter to a friend telling why it is your favorite season. Be sure to describe what the weather is like during the season.

9÷3 **Math** NS 2.1

Add/Subtract Numbers

One fall morning, it was 57 degrees Fahrenheit in Los Angeles. In the afternoon, the sun warmed the air temperature to 91 degrees Fahrenheit. How much did the temperature change between the morning and the afternoon?

 Health

Sun Safety

Find out the hours of the day when the sun is the most harmful to your skin. List things you can do to protect yourself. Then make a poster of tips for staying safe in the sun.

 For more links and activities, go to **www.hspscience.com**

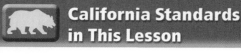

Science Content

4.a *Students know* the patterns of stars stay the same, although they appear to move across the sky nightly, and different stars can be seen in different seasons.

4.c *Students know* telescopes magnify the appearance of some distant objects in the sky, including the Moon and the planets. The number of stars that can be seen through telescopes is dramatically greater than the number that can be seen by the unaided eye.

Investigation and Experimentation

5.d Predict the outcome of a simple investigation and compare the result with the prediction.

LESSON 3

Essential Question

What Patterns Do *Stars* Follow?

California Fast Fact

Seeing Stars

This telescope is located at the Mount Wilson Observatory. It was the largest in the world from 1917 until 1948. Scientists still use the telescope today.

star [STAR] A huge, hot ball of glowing gases that gives off energy (p. 304)

constellation [kahn•stuh•LAY•shuhn] A group of stars that appears to form the shape of an animal, a person, or an object (p. 306)

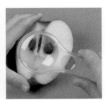

magnify [MAG•nuh•fy] To make an object appear larger (p. 308)

The Mount Wilson Observatory

Make a Telescope

Start with Questions

When you look through a telescope, you can see distant objects in detail. Telescopes help scientists see objects in space that are very far away.

- How does a telescope work?

- How do objects appear when you look through a telescope?

Investigate to find out. Then read to find out more.

Prepare to Investigate

Investigation Skill Tip

It is easier to compare two things when you make careful observations. Write or draw as many details as you can when you are making observations.

Materials
- modeling clay
- 1 thin (eyepiece) lens
- 1 thick lens
- 2 cardboard tubes

Make an Observation Chart

Telescope Observations	
Object 1: _____	
Drawing without Telescope	Drawing with Telescope
Object 2: _____	
Drawing without Telescope	Drawing with Telescope

Follow This Procedure

CAUTION: Never look directly at the sun.

1. With clay, fasten one lens in the end of each tube.

2. Slide the open end of one tube into the open end of the other tube.

3. Predict what will happen when you look through the telescope.

4. Choose a distant object to view. Draw the object without using the telescope. Then observe the object through the telescope. Make sure the thin lens is closer to your eye. Slide the small tube in and out until what you see becomes clear. Draw what you observe.

5. Repeat Step 4 with a different object.

Draw Conclusions

1. What did you predict would happen when you looked through the telescope?

2. **Standards Link** Compare your drawings with and without the telescope. `4.c`

3. **Investigation Skill** How did your observations compare with your prediction? `5.d`

Step 1

Step 2

Independent Inquiry

Predict the Outcome of an Investigation

What would happen if you looked through the other end of your telescope? Perform an investigation to find out. Compare the results of your investigation with your prediction. `5.d`

VOCABULARY
star p. 304
constellation p. 306
magnify p. 308

SCIENCE CONCEPTS
► why stars seem to move across the sky
► why many of the stars you can see in the sky change with each season

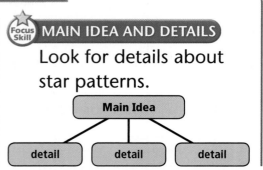

Focus Skill MAIN IDEA AND DETAILS

Look for details about star patterns.

Main Idea

detail detail detail

Stars Appear to Move

Have you ever gazed into the night sky and watched the stars? A **star** is a hot ball of glowing gases that gives off energy. On a clear night, you might see thousands of stars and other objects in the sky.

You know that the sun appears to move across the sky during the day. At night, the stars appear to move, just as the sun does during the day. The rotation of Earth causes stars to seem to move in the nighttime sky.

This student is observing how the stars appear to move across the sky.

7:00 P.M.

10:00 P.M.

5:00 A.M.

10:00 P.M.

The diagram on the left shows the stars that can be seen at 5:00 A.M. Can the same stars be seen at 10:00 P.M.?

Stars seem to rise in the east and set in the west. Stars in the sky near the poles seem to move in a circle.

The pattern of stars we see in the sky does not change. The Big Dipper is a pattern of stars you might know. It always looks like the Big Dipper, even though it isn't always in the same place in the sky.

 MAIN IDEA AND DETAILS What causes the stars to appear to move?

Star Patterns and the Seasons

You know that the stars seem to move across the night sky. The stars you can see also change from season to season. During spring and summer, you can see some star patterns that you cannot see in fall and winter. You can see other star patterns all year long.

People look for star patterns called constellations. A **constellation** is a group of stars that looks like the shape of an animal, a person, or an object. Long ago, people gave names to constellations they saw.

Some stars can be seen only at certain times of the year. Star patterns change with the seasons.

spring

summer

fall

winter

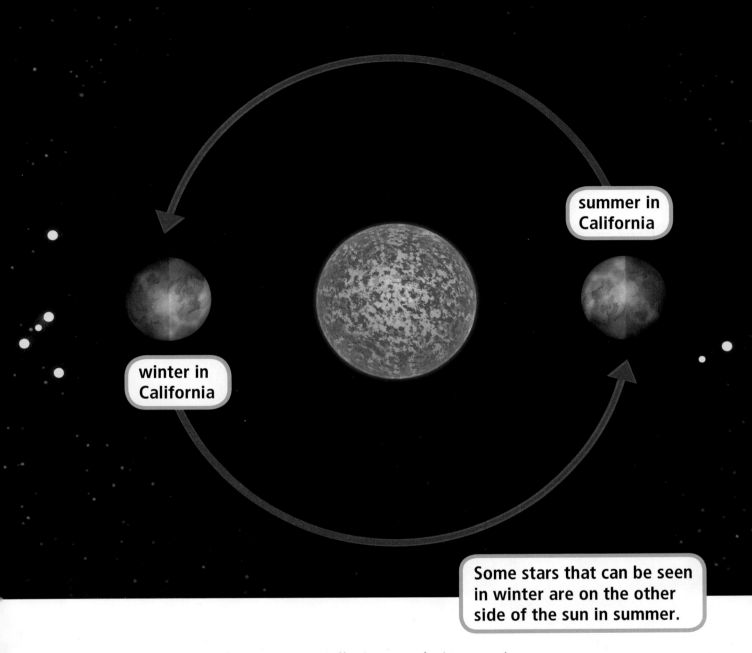

summer in California

winter in California

Some stars that can be seen in winter are on the other side of the sun in summer.

Why can you see some constellations only in certain seasons? The stars you can see depend on where Earth is in its journey around the sun.

On a cold winter night, people in California can see one set of stars. As Earth orbits the sun, the season changes. On a warm summer night, people in California can see a different set of stars. The stars you see in winter are on the other side of the sun in summer.

MAIN IDEA AND DETAILS **Why do stars change position with the seasons?**

Telescopes Help Us Observe Stars

When you look at stars, you may notice that some are very bright while others are hard to see. Stars give off light, which is why you can see them at night. On a clear night, you might see thousands of stars. A large group of stars is called a *galaxy*.

Scientists use telescopes to view stars. Through a telescope, you can see many more stars than you can see with just your eyes. A telescope will also **magnify** the stars, or make them appear larger.

A telescope lets you see small details of objects that are far away.

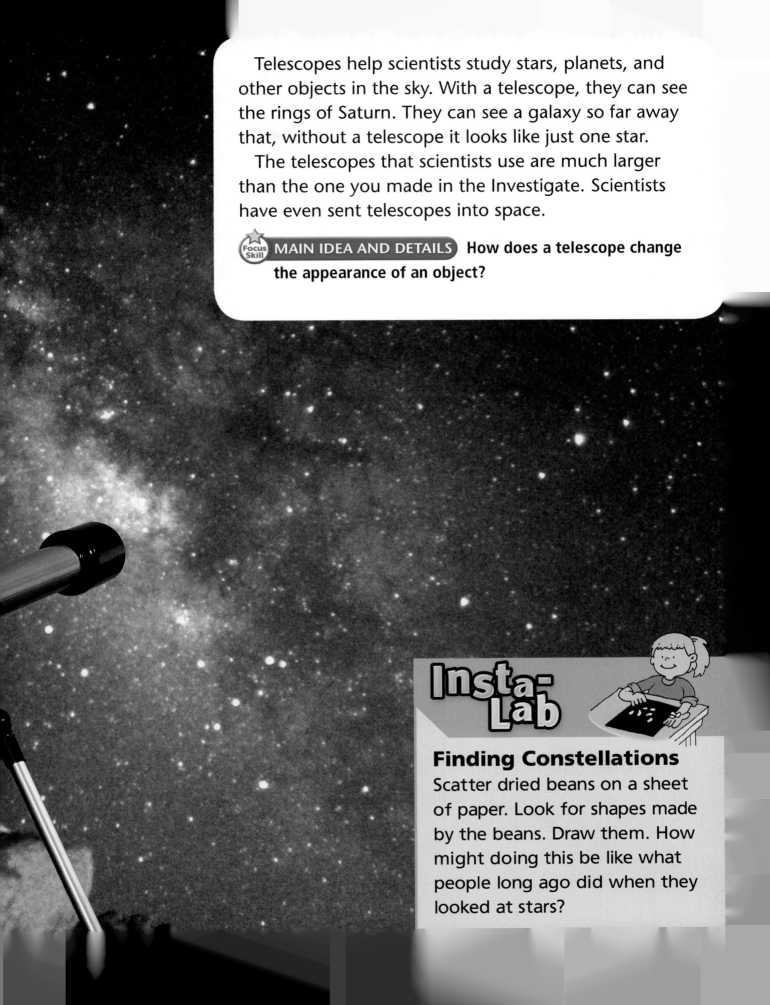

Telescopes help scientists study stars, planets, and other objects in the sky. With a telescope, they can see the rings of Saturn. They can see a galaxy so far away that, without a telescope it looks like just one star.

The telescopes that scientists use are much larger than the one you made in the Investigate. Scientists have even sent telescopes into space.

MAIN IDEA AND DETAILS How does a telescope change the appearance of an object?

Insta-Lab

Finding Constellations
Scatter dried beans on a sheet of paper. Look for shapes made by the beans. Draw them. How might doing this be like what people long ago did when they looked at stars?

Essential Question

What patterns do stars follow?

In this lesson, you learned that stars seem to move in the night sky. The stars that can be seen also change from season to season. You also learned that telescopes magnify the appearance of objects. Telescopes help us see objects and details we would not be able to see without a telescope.

Science Content Standards in This Lesson

4.a *Students know* the patterns of stars stay the same, although they appear to move across the sky nightly, and different stars can be seen in different seasons.

4.c *Students know* telescopes magnify the appearance of some distant objects in the sky, including the Moon and the planets. The number of stars that can be seen through telescopes is dramatically greater than the number that can be seen by the unaided eye.

1. **(Focus Skill) MAIN IDEA AND DETAILS** Draw and complete a graphic organizer. Show details that support the main idea *Stars seem to change position in the night sky.* **4.a**

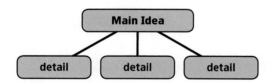

2. **SUMMARIZE** Use the information in the graphic organizer to write a summary of the lesson. **4.a**

3. **DRAW CONCLUSIONS** Your friend thinks that the stars really move across the sky at night. Why isn't this true? **4.a**

4. **VOCABULARY** Which word means "to make something appear larger"?
   A constellation
   B magnify
   C telescope
   D rotation **4.c**

5. **Critical Thinking** At 6:00 P.M., Marci saw a constellation in the eastern sky. At midnight, she saw the same constellation in the west. What happened? **4.a**

6. **Investigate and Experiment** How might you predict where you will see star patterns each night? **5.d**

 Writing ELA–W 2.2

Write a Description

Observe the movement of star patterns in the sky one night, or tell about a visit to a planetarium. Write a description of what you observe in the sky, or describe what you saw at the planetarium.

 Math MG 2.3

Complete a Shape

Look for constellations in the night sky, or find pictures of some in a book. Draw the constellations. Outline any geometric shapes, such as squares and triangles, in the star patterns.

 Social Studies HSS 3.2.1

Stories About the Stars

Many American Indian tribes have legends about the stars. Choose an American Indian tribe, and find a story its people tell about the stars. Draw pictures and write captions to go with the story.

 For more links and activities, go to **www.hspscience.com**

The Lick Observatory

Observatories are places where scientists use telescopes to study the stars and planets. The Lick Observatory, near San Jose, California, has several huge telescopes. They are kept in rooms with large domes. The domes open up to the sky.

This building houses one of the telescopes at the Lick Observatory.

Watching the Stars

One such telescope is the Lick Refractor. It has a lens that is 91 centimeters (36 in.) across. It was once the world's most powerful telescope. Now it is used to teach visitors about astronomy, the study of objects in space.

Operating the Telescopes

An operator uses a computer to point the telescopes at the part of the sky that scientists want to see. Scientists view the images in a control room next to the telescope. The images of planets and stars show details that scientists could not see with only their eyes. By using the powerful telescopes, scientists have learned much about objects in the sky.

✍ Think and Write

1 What is an observatory?

2 How do telescopes help scientists learn about stars and planets?

4.c

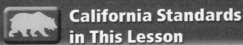

Science Content

4.b *Students know* the way in which the Moon's appearance changes during the four-week lunar cycle.

Investigation and Experimentation

5.c Use numerical data in describing and comparing objects, events, and measurements.

LESSON

4

Essential Question

Why Does the Shape of the Moon Seem to Change?

California Fast Fact

Earth's Satellite

The moon is about 384,500 kilometers (238,900 miles) from Earth. If you could drive a car to the moon without stopping, the trip would take about 180 days.

Joshua Tree, California

moon phases [MOON FAYZ•uhz] The different shapes the moon seems to have (p. 322)

full moon [FUHL MOON] The moon phase in which the moon looks like a circle (p. 322)

new moon [NOO MOON] The moon phase in which the lighted half of the moon cannot be seen from Earth (p. 322)

The Moon's Shapes

Start with Questions

One night, you look up at the moon and see a bright, shining ball. Two weeks later, you look up and see only half the moon.

- What happened?
- Why does the moon's shape seem to change?

Investigate to find out. Then read to find out more.

Prepare to Investigate

Investigation Skill Tip

When you infer, you draw a conclusion based on your observations. Check to see if your inferences agree with your observations and data.

Materials
- volleyball
- flashlight

Make an Observation Chart

Moon Phases Observations	
Position Number	Drawing of Volleyball
1	
2	
3	
4	

Follow This Procedure

1. Work in a group of three. One group member holds a volleyball at position 1. Another shines a flashlight on it. The third group member stands in the middle and observes the ball. Make a drawing of the ball that shows the ball's lighted side.

2. Make drawings of the ball at positions 2, 3, and 4. The person in the middle rotates to keep facing the volleyball. The person holding the flashlight should not move.

3. Switch roles so that everyone can observe the pattern.

Draw Conclusions

1. What does the ball represent? What does the flashlight represent? What does the person recording represent?

2. **Standards Link** How did the lighted part of the ball change at each position? **4.b**

3. **Investigation Skill** What can you infer causes the shape of the moon to seem to change?

Step 1

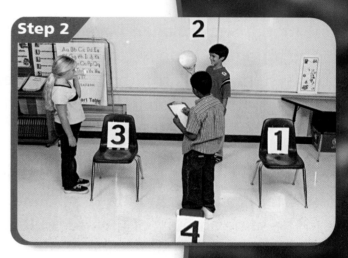

Step 2

Independent Inquiry **Collect Data**

The data you collected in the investigation helped you make inferences about the moon. To see if your inferences were correct, you need to collect more data. Predict how long it will take the moon to go through its pattern of changes. Then collect data to see if your prediction is correct. **5.c**

VOCABULARY
moon phases p. 322
full moon p. 322
new moon p. 322

SCIENCE CONCEPTS
▶ why the moon seems to shine
▶ what the moon's phases are

Focus Skill **SEQUENCE**

Look for sequences in the moon's pattern of changes.

The Moon and Earth

On some nights, you can see the moon shining brightly. Our planet, Earth, has only one moon. Some planets have many moons.

The moon is the body closest to Earth in the solar system. Like Earth, the moon moves in two ways. It rotates on its axis, and it orbits Earth.

Remember that Earth takes 24 hours to rotate once and one year to orbit the sun. The moon takes about one month to rotate once and the same amount of time to orbit Earth. This means that the same side of the moon always faces Earth.

The moon orbits Earth, just as Earth orbits the sun.

Focus Skill **SEQUENCE** How long does it take the moon to travel once around Earth?

This is what Earth looks like from the moon.

Modeling Earth and the Moon

Make a small ball, a medium ball, and a large ball out of clay. Use the balls as models to represent the moon, Earth, and the sun. Show the two ways the moon moves. How are the movements of the moon like the movements of Earth?

Why the Moon Seems to Shine

Like Earth and the other planets, the moon is shaped like a ball. Half the moon is always lit by the sun. The other half is dark.

The moon does not make light. The light you see shining from the moon comes from the sun. When sunlight strikes the surface of the moon, much of it is reflected. Some of the light reflects toward Earth. This reflected light is what you see when you look at the moon.

Light from the sun always lights one half of the moon.

When the moon is in the position below, this is how it appears from Earth. As the moon orbits Earth, its appearance changes.

The moon orbits Earth.

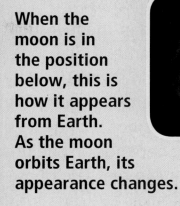

While one half of the moon is always lit, you can't always see that half from Earth. Sometimes, you can see only part of the lit half of the moon. Then the moon does not look like a full circle in the sky. The moon's shape seems to change as the moon orbits Earth.

Focus Skill SEQUENCE What happens to light that hits the moon's surface?

Phases of the Moon

As you modeled in the Investigate, the moon doesn't always look the same. It may look like a full circle, a half-circle, or just a thin sliver. The different shapes the moon seems to have are called **moon phases**.

The moon does not change its shape. From Earth, the shape you see depends on the phase, or how much of the lit half you can see. The phase changes as the moon orbits Earth. It takes $29\frac{1}{2}$ days for the moon to go through all of its phases.

When you can see all of the lit half, the moon looks like a circle. This is the **full moon**. Then the part you can see starts *waning* (WAYN•ing), or becoming smaller. In time, you cannot see the moon at all because the lit half is facing away from Earth. This is the **new moon**. Then the part you can see begins *waxing* (WAKS•ing), or getting bigger.

 **SEQUENCE** What happens after the new moon phase?

The moon goes through its phases every $29\frac{1}{2}$ days. ▼

Moon Phases

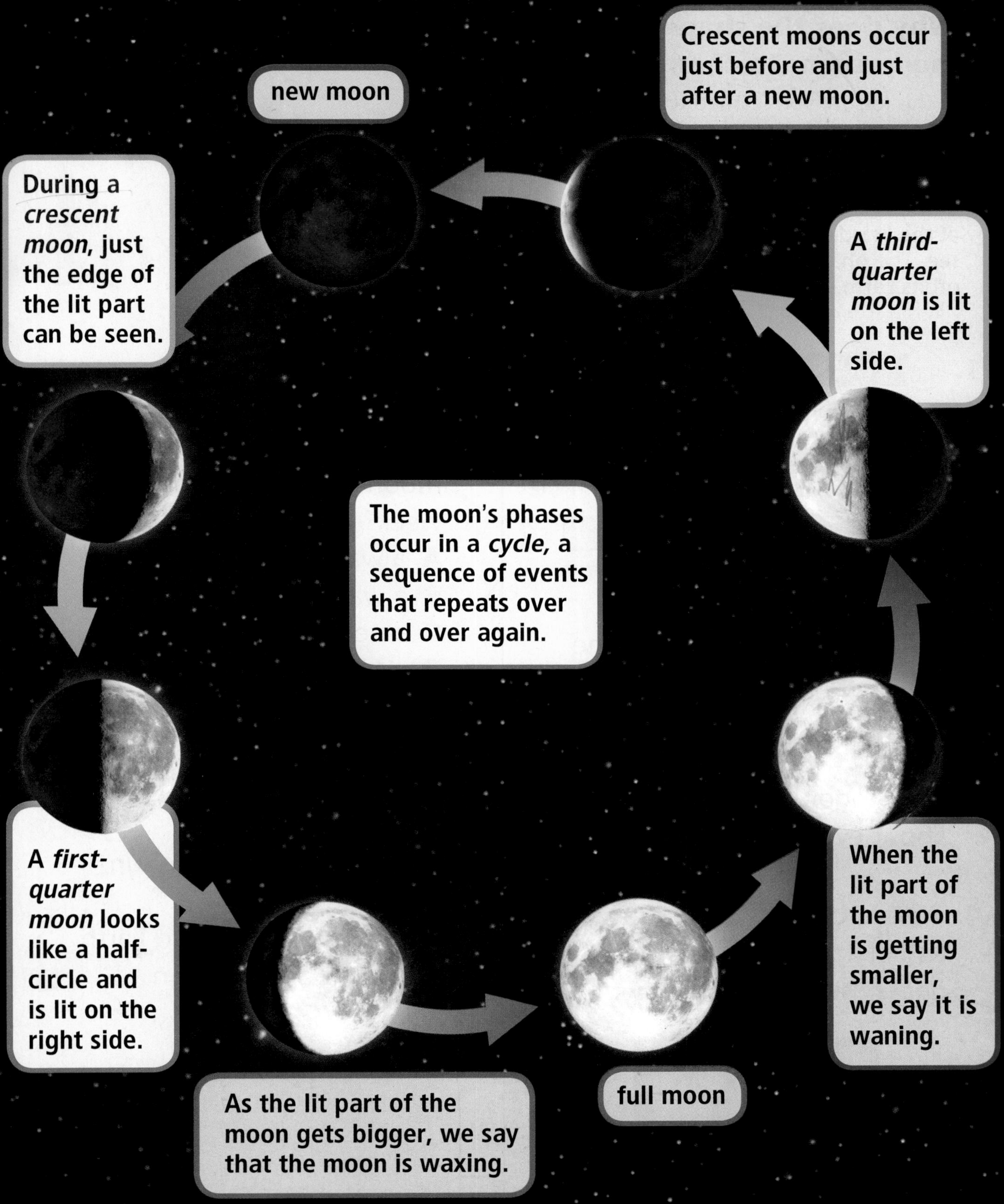

new moon

Crescent moons occur just before and just after a new moon.

During a *crescent moon*, just the edge of the lit part can be seen.

A *third-quarter moon* is lit on the left side.

The moon's phases occur in a *cycle*, a sequence of events that repeats over and over again.

A *first-quarter moon* looks like a half-circle and is lit on the right side.

When the lit part of the moon is getting smaller, we say it is waning.

As the lit part of the moon gets bigger, we say that the moon is waxing.

full moon

Essential Question

Why does the shape of the moon seem to change?

In this lesson, you learned that the moon has phases. It takes $29\frac{1}{2}$ days, or about 4 weeks, for the moon to go through all its phases. The phase of the moon depends on how much of the lit side of the moon we can see. The phase changes as the moon orbits Earth.

Science Content Standards in this Lesson

4.b *Students know* the way in which the Moon's appearance changes during the four-week lunar cycle.

1. **(Focus Skill) SEQUENCE** Draw and complete a graphic organizer showing the phases of the moon. **4.b**

2. **SUMMARIZE** Write a lesson summary explaining why the moon appears to shine. **4.b**

3. **DRAW CONCLUSIONS** Why does a full moon happen only once about every $29\frac{1}{2}$ days? **4.b**

4. **VOCABULARY** Make drawings to illustrate the terms *moon phase*, *waxing*, and *waning*. **4.b**

5. **Critical Thinking** Suppose you see a full moon on the first day of the month. What type of moon will you observe in one week?
   A a waxing moon
   B a waning moon
   C a new moon
   D a full moon **4.b**

6. What causes the moon's phases?
   A Earth's orbiting the sun
   B Earth's rotation
   C the moon's orbiting Earth
   D the moon's rotation **4.b**

The Big Idea

 Writing ELA–W 2.1

Write a Report

Find out about the first time humans landed on the moon. Write about the moon landing from the point of view of one of the astronauts.

 Math MR.1.1

Write Word Problems

Mark the phases of the moon on a calendar for this month. Write two word problems about the pattern of the moon's phases. Give them to a partner to solve.

 Art VPA–VA 2.3

The Night Sky

Draw or paint a landscape that shows the moon and other objects in the night sky. Label the phase of the moon and the other objects you can see in the sky.

 For more links and activities, go to **www.hspscience.com**

Galileo Galilei

▶ **GALILEO GALILEI**

▶ **Astronomer and mathematician**

▶ The first to view the moons of Jupiter

Galileo was an Italian scientist who died in 1642. He did not have the kinds of tools scientists use today. In fact, Galileo was one of the first astronomers to use a telescope!

Galileo spent many hours viewing bright points of light in the night sky with a telescope. Night after night, he recorded the positions of these points of light. Galileo analyzed his data and discovered many things. For example, he found that there are moons orbiting Jupiter.

Galileo also found that by using a telescope, he could see more stars in the sky than he could by using just his eyes. He could use it to learn more about space.

✎ Think and Write

1 What did Galileo discover about Jupiter's moons? `4.c`

2 Why was the discovery of the telescope `4.c` important to Galileo?

> Galileo used a telescope to study objects in the sky.

Adriana Ocampo

Have you ever wanted to know more about Earth's neighbors in space? Adriana Ocampo gets to research planets and their moons.

Ocampo works at the Jet Propulsion Laboratory in Pasadena, California. She used photos from the *Viking* mission to help make a map of Phobos, one of the moons that orbits Mars. Her work helped plan the routes for other space missions.

Ocampo is also studying pieces of an asteroid, a large rock from space, that struck Earth. The asteroid may have caused the dinosaurs to become extinct. She is researching how asteroids can affect Earth.

▶ **ADRIANA OCAMPO**

▶ **Research scientist for NASA**

▶ Worked on *Viking* and *Voyager* missions

✎ Think and Write

❶ How is Phobos like Earth's moon? 4.d

❷ Why is it important to study how Earth might be affected by an asteroid?

Phobos

Ocampo compares Earth's surface with other planets, such as Mars.

Visual Summary

Tell how each picture helps explain the **Big Idea**.

The Big Idea We can predict where the sun, the moon, the stars, and the planets will be in the sky.

4.d

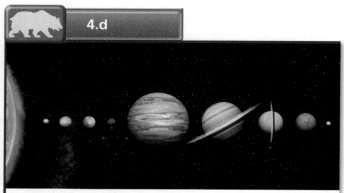

The Solar System
Earth is one of nine planets in the solar system. The planets orbit the sun. The moon orbits Earth.

4.c

A Closer Look
Telescopes make faraway objects seem closer. You can see more details by using a telescope.

4.a, 4.e

The Sun and the Stars
The patterns of the sun and the stars change because Earth rotates and orbits the sun.

4.b

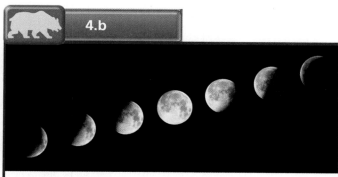

The Moon's Phases
The shapes the moon seems to be are called phases. It goes through its phases every $29\frac{1}{2}$ days.

Show What You Know

Unit Writing Activity

Write a Description

Imagine you and your classmates are on a journey through space. Write a story describing your trip. Include your observations of Earth, the sun, and the moon. Write about each planet you observe as you travel to the end of the solar system. You can include pictures with your story.

Unit Project

Make Science Center Displays

Work together as a class to set up a science center. Create and display a model of the solar system. Make posters or models for other topics covered in the unit. For example, you could use a flashlight to show how the sun appears to move across the sky in the summer and in the winter. You could also display some images that were made by using a telescope. Invite other classes to visit your science center. Explain the displays to the visitors.

UNIT 4 Review — EARTH SCIENCE

California Science Standards

Vocabulary Review

Use the terms below to complete the sentences. The page numbers tell you where to look in the unit if you need help.

planet p. 278

star p. 304

solar system p. 279

constellation p. 306

telescope p. 279

moon phases p. 322

rotation p. 292

full moon p. 322

1. The different shapes that the moon seems to have are the _____. **4.b**

2. A group of stars that looks like the shape of an animal, a person, or an object is a _____. **4.a**

3. A star and the planets that orbit it are called a _____. **4.d**

4. A _____ is a tool that magnifies objects that are far away. **4.c**

5. The _____ is a moon phase in which you see all the lighted half of the moon. **4.b**

6. A large body of rock or gas that orbits the sun is a _____. **4.d**

7. The turning of Earth on its axis is _____. **4.e**

8. A large ball of very hot gases in space is a _____. **4.a**

Check Understanding

Choose the best answer.

9. **COMPARE AND CONTRAST** How is Earth different from the other inner planets? **4.d**
   A Earth is made of rock.
   B Earth has liquid water.
   C Earth has no moons.
   D Earth rotates on its axis.

10. **CAUSE AND EFFECT** What causes day and night on Earth? **4.e**
    A Earth rotates on its axis.
    B Earth orbits the sun.
    C The sun moves around Earth.
    D Earth's axis is tilted.

11. Look at the diagram below. What season is it in the Northern Hemisphere? **4.e**
    A winter   C summer
    B spring   D fall

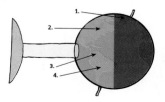

12. Which is **not** true about stars? `4.a`
 A They are balls of hot gases.
 B Stars orbit planets.
 C Stars appear to move in the sky.
 D The stars that can be seen in the sky change with the seasons.

13. Suppose there is a full moon tonight. How long will it be until the next full moon? `4.b`
 A about $8\frac{1}{2}$ days
 B about 15 days
 C about 22 days
 D about $29\frac{1}{2}$ days

14. Carlos wants to study details of the moon's surface. Which will help him do this **best**? `4.c`
 A He can wait for a full moon.
 B He can use a telescope.
 C He can wait for a new moon.
 D He can climb a mountain to be closer to the moon.

15. What does the red arrow in the diagram show **best**? `4.e`
 A how Earth rotates
 B how Earth orbits the sun
 C why the moon has phases
 D why Earth has seasons

16. In which season does the sun appear highest in the sky? `4.e`
 A fall   C spring
 B winter   D summer

Investigation Skills

17. Rosa reports that Jupiter has more moons than Saturn. How could she have used numbers in her report? Which is better? `5.c`

18. Shawn draws a picture of the moon each night for one week. How does collecting this data help him predict what the moon will look like two weeks from now? `5.e`

Critical Thinking

19. Janel looks out the window and sees the image below. What does she see? How can you explain why only a portion of what Janel sees is lighted? `4.b`

20. Many objects seem to move in the sky. What patterns could you observe by watching the sun's position in the sky for a year?

The **Big** Idea

References

Contents

Health Handbook

Reading in Science Handbook

Math in Science Handbook

Your Skin

Your skin is your body's largest organ. It provides your body with a tough protective covering. It protects you from disease. It provides your sense of touch, which allows you to feel pressure, textures, temperature, and pain. Your skin also produces sweat to help control your body temperature. When you play hard or exercise, your body produces sweat, which cools you as it evaporates. The sweat from your skin also helps your body get rid of extra salt and other wastes.

▼ The skin is the body's largest organ.

Epidermis
Many layers of dead skin cells form the top of the epidermis. Cells in the lower part of the epidermis are always making new cells.

Pore
These tiny holes on the surface of your skin lead to your dermis.

Oil Gland
Oil glands produce oil that keeps your skin soft and smooth.

Dermis
The dermis is much thicker than the epidermis. It is made up of tough, flexible fibers.

Hair Follicle
Each hair follicle has a muscle that can contract and make the hair "stand on end."

Fatty Tissue
This tissue layer beneath the dermis stores food, provides warmth, and attaches your skin to the bone and muscle below.

Caring for Your Skin

- To protect your skin and to keep it healthy, you should wash your body, including your hair and your nails, every day. This helps remove germs, excess oils and sweat, and dead cells from the epidermis, the outer layer of your skin. Because you touch many things during the day, you should wash your hands with soap and water frequently.

- If you get a cut or scratch, you should wash it right away and cover it with a sterile bandage to prevent infection.

- Protect your skin from cuts and scrapes by wearing proper safety equipment.

- Always protect your skin from sunburn by wearing protective clothing and sunscreen when you are outdoors.

Your Digestive System

Your digestive system is made up of connected organs. It breaks down the food you eat and disposes of the leftover wastes your body does not need.

Mouth to Stomach

Digestion begins when you chew your food. Chewing your food breaks it up and mixes it with saliva. When you swallow, the softened food travels down your esophagus to your stomach, where it is mixed with digestive juices. These are strong acids that continue the process of breaking your food down into the nutrients your body needs to stay healthy. Your stomach squeezes your food and turns it into a thick liquid.

Small Intestine and Liver

Your food leaves your stomach and goes into your small intestine. This organ is a long tube just below your stomach. Your liver is an organ that sends bile into your small intestine to continue the process of digesting fats in the food. The walls of the small intestine are lined with millions of small, finger-shaped bumps called villi. Tiny blood vessels in these bumps absorb nutrients from the food as it moves through the small intestine.

Large Intestine

When the food has traveled all the way through your small intestine, it passes into your large intestine. This last organ of your digestive system absorbs water from the food. The remaining wastes are held there until you go to the bathroom.

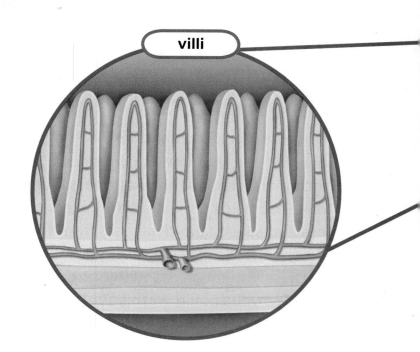

villi

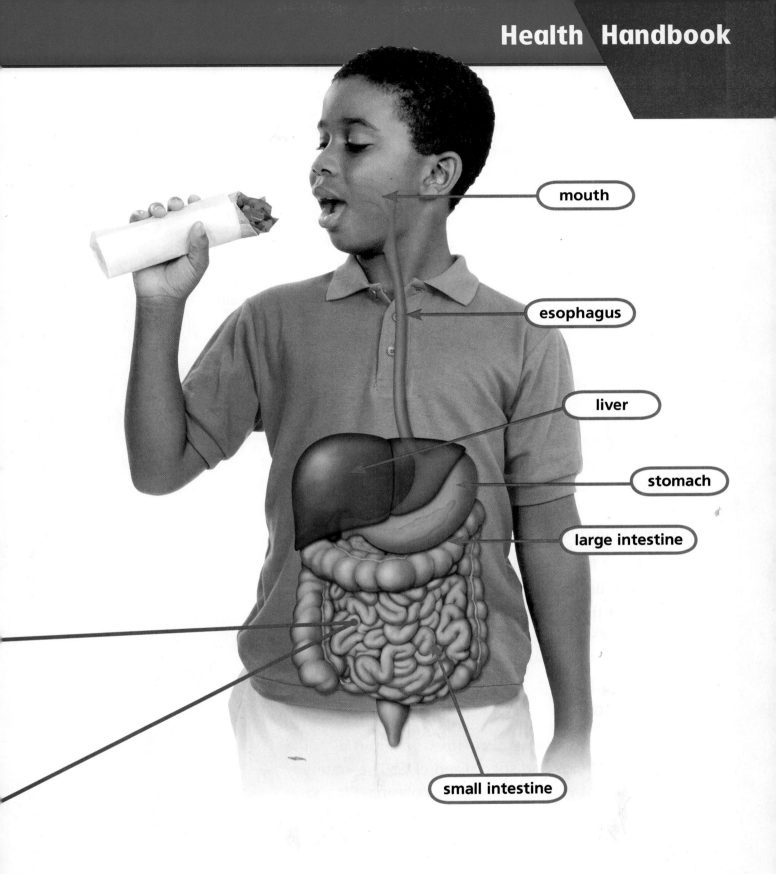

mouth

esophagus

liver

stomach

large intestine

small intestine

Your Circulatory System

Your circulatory system carries to every cell in your body the nutrients your digestive system takes from food and the oxygen your lungs take from the air you breathe. As your blood moves throughout your body, it also helps your body fight infections, control your temperature, and remove wastes from your cells.

vein

heart

Your Heart and Blood Vessels

Your heart is the organ that pumps your blood through your circulatory system. Your heart is a strong muscle that beats continuously. As you exercise, your heart adjusts itself to beat faster to deliver the energy and oxygen your muscles need to work harder.

artery

Blood from your heart is pumped through veins into your lungs, where it releases carbon dioxide and picks up oxygen. Your blood then travels back to your heart to be pumped through your arteries to every part of your body.

Your Blood

The blood in your circulatory system is a mixture of fluids and specialized cells. The watery liquid part of your blood is called plasma. Plasma allows the cells in your blood to move through your blood vessels to every part of your body. It also plays an important role in helping your body control your temperature.

Blood Cells

There are three main types of cells in your blood. Each type of cell in your circulatory system plays a special part in keeping your body healthy and fit.

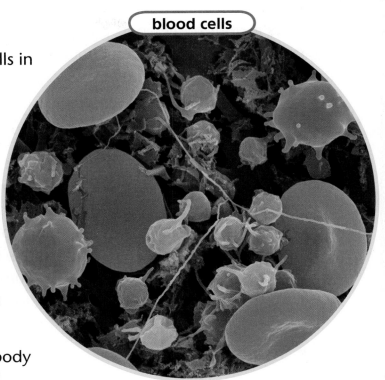

blood cells

Red Blood Cells are the most numerous cells in your blood. They carry oxygen from your lungs throughout your body. They also carry carbon dioxide back to your lungs from your cells, so you can breathe it out.

White Blood Cells help your body fight infections when you become ill.

Platelets help your body stop bleeding when you get a cut or other wound. Platelets clump together as soon as you start to bleed. The sticky clump of platelets traps red blood cells and forms a blood clot. The blood clot hardens to make a scab that seals the cut and lets your body begin healing the wound.

Caring for Your Circulatory System

- Eat foods that are low in fat and high in fiber. Fiber helps take away substances that can lead to fatty buildup in your blood vessels.

- Eat foods high in iron to help your red blood cells carry oxygen.

- Drink plenty of water to help your body replenish your blood.

- Avoid contact with another person's blood.

- Exercise regularly to keep your heart strong.

- Never smoke or use tobacco.

Your Skeletal System

Your skeletal system includes all of the bones in your body. These strong, hard parts of your body protect your internal organs, help you move, and allow you to sit and to stand up straight.

Your skeletal system works with your muscular system to hold your body up and to give it shape.

Your skeletal system includes more than 200 bones. These bones come in many different shapes and sizes.

Your Skull

The wide flat bones of your skull fit tightly together to protect your brain. The bones in the front of your skull give your face its shape and allow the muscles in your face to express your thoughts and feelings.

Your Spine

Your spine, or backbone, is made up of nearly two dozen small, round bones. These bones fit together and connect your head to your pelvis. Each of these bones, or vertebrae, is shaped like a doughnut, with a small round hole in the center. Your spinal cord is a bundle of nerves that carries information to and from your brain and the rest of your body. Your spinal cord runs from your brain down your back to your hips through the holes in your vertebrae. There are soft, flexible disks of cartilage between your vertebrae. This allows you to bend and twist your spine. Your spine, pelvis, and leg bones work together to allow you to stand, sit, or move.

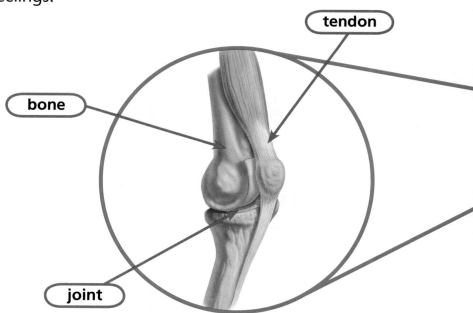

tendon

bone

joint

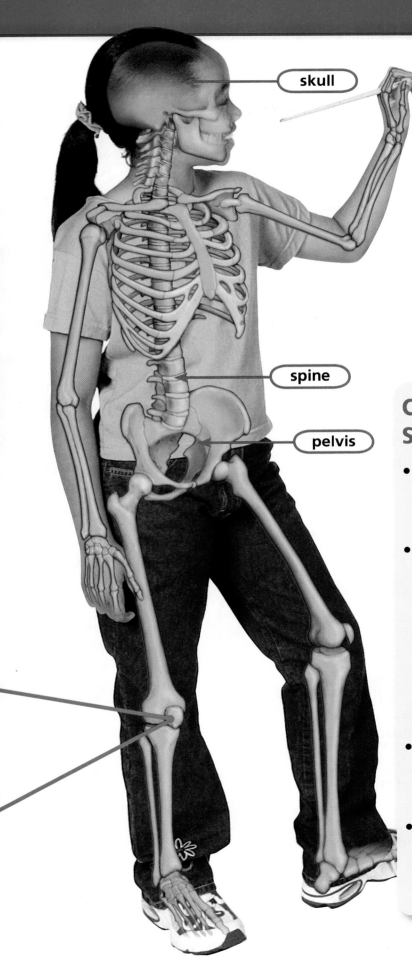

skull

spine

pelvis

Caring for Your Skeletal System

- Always wear a helmet and proper safety gear when you play sports, skate, or ride a bike or a scooter.

- Your bones are made mostly of calcium and other minerals. To keep your skeletal system strong and to help it grow, you should eat foods like milk, cheese, and yogurt that are high in calcium. Dark green, leafy vegetables like broccoli, spinach, and collard greens are also good sources of calcium.

- Exercise to help your bones stay strong and healthy. Get plenty of rest to help your bones grow.

- Stand and sit with good posture. Sitting slumped over puts strain on your muscles and on your bones.

Your Muscular System

A muscle is a body part that produces movement by contracting and relaxing. All of the muscles in your body make up the muscular system.

Voluntary and Involuntary Muscles

Voluntary Muscles are the muscles you use to move your arms and legs, your face, head, and fingers. You can make these muscles contract or relax to control the way your body moves.

Involuntary Muscles are responsible for movements you usually don't see or control. These muscles make up your heart, your stomach and digestive system, your diaphragm, and the muscles that control your eyelids. Your heart beats and your diaphragm powers your breathing without your thinking about them. You cannot stop the action of these muscles.

How Muscles Help You Move

All muscles pull when they contract. Moving your body in more than one direction takes more than one muscle. To reach out with your arm or to pull it back, you use a pair of muscles. As one muscle contracts to extend your arm, the other relaxes and stretches. As you pull your arm back, the muscles reverse their functions.

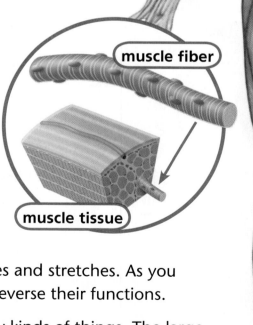

muscle fiber

muscle tissue

Your muscles let you do many kinds of things. The large muscles in your legs allow you to walk and run. Tiny muscles in your face allow you to smile.

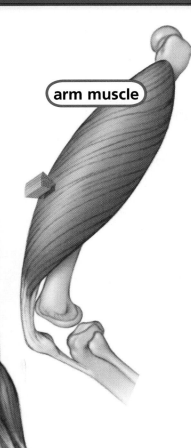

arm muscle

Your Muscles and Your Bones

The muscles that allow you to move your body work with your skeletal system. Muscles in your legs that allow you to kick a ball or ride a bicycle pull on the bones and joints of your legs and lower body. Your muscles are connected to your skeletal system by strong, cordlike tissues called tendons.

Your Achilles tendon, just above your heel, connects your calf muscles to your heel bone. When you contract those muscles, the tendon pulls on the heel bone and allows you to stand on your toes, jump, or push hard on your bicycle's pedals.

Caring for Your Muscular System

- Always stretch and warm up your muscles before exercising or playing sports. Do this by jogging or walking for at least ten minutes. This brings fresh blood and oxygen into your muscles and helps prevent injury or pain.

- Eat a balanced diet of foods to be sure your muscles have the nutrients they need to grow and remain strong.

- Stop exercising if you feel pain in your muscles.

- Drink plenty of water when you exercise or play sports. This helps your blood remove wastes from your muscles and helps you build endurance.

- Always cool down after you exercise. Walk or jog slowly for five or ten minutes to let your heartbeat slow and your breathing return to normal. This helps you avoid pain and stiffness after your muscles work hard.

- Get plenty of rest before and after you work your muscles hard. They need time to repair themselves and recover from working hard.

Your Eyes and Vision

Your eyes allow you to see light reflected by the things around you. This diagram shows how an eye works. Light enters through the clear outer surface called the cornea. It passes through the pupil. The lens bends the incoming light to focus it on the retina. The retina sends nerve signals along the optic nerve. Your brain uses the signals to form an image. This is what you "see."

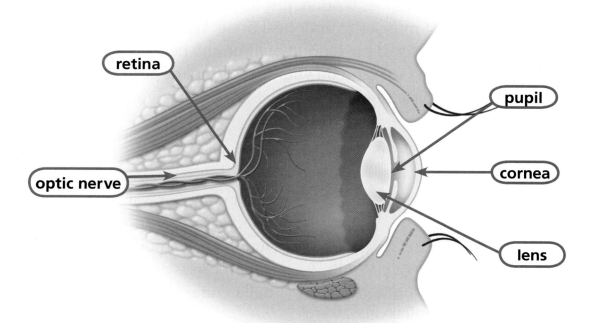

retina

optic nerve

pupil

cornea

lens

Caring for Your Eyes

- You should have a doctor check your eyesight every year. Tell your parents or your doctor if your vision becomes blurry or if you are having headaches or pain in your eyes.

- Never touch or rub your eyes.

- Protect your eyes by wearing safety goggles when you use tools or play sports.

- Wear swim goggles to protect your eyes from chlorine or other substances in the water.

- Wear sunglasses to protect your eyes from very bright light. Looking directly at bright light or at the sun can damage your eyes permanently.

Your Ears and Hearing

Sounds travel through the air in waves. When some of those waves enter your ear, you hear a sound. This diagram shows the inside of your ear.

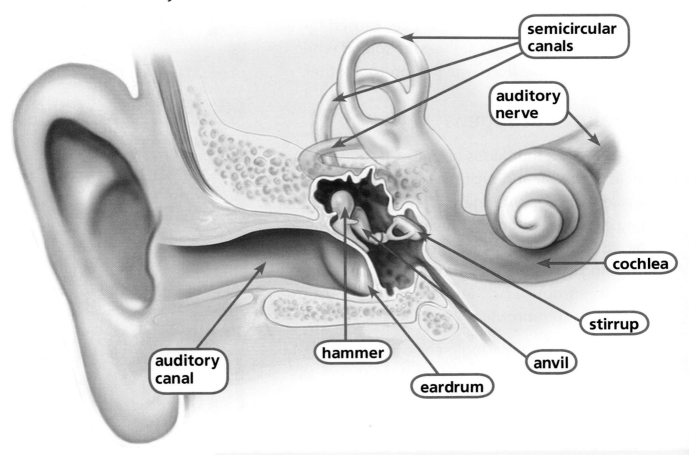

semicircular canals

auditory nerve

cochlea

stirrup

anvil

hammer

eardrum

auditory canal

Caring for Your Ears

- Never put anything in your ears.

- Wear a helmet that covers your ears when you play sports.

- Keep your ears warm in winter.

- Avoid loud sounds and listening to loud music.

- Have your ears checked by a doctor if they hurt or leak fluid or if you have any loss of hearing.

- Wear earplugs when you swim. Water in your ears can lead to infection.

Your Immune System

Pathogens and Illness

You may know someone who had a cold or the flu this year. These illnesses are caused by germs called pathogens. Illnesses spread when pathogens move from one person to another.

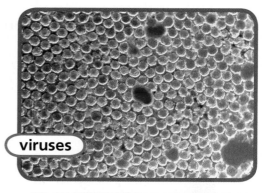
viruses

Types of Pathogens

There are four kinds of pathogens—viruses, bacteria, fungi, and protozoans. Viruses are the smallest kind of pathogen. They are so small that they can be seen only with very powerful electron microscopes. Viruses cause many types of illness, including colds, the flu, and chicken pox. Viruses cannot reproduce by themselves. They must use living cells to reproduce.

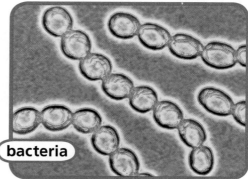
bacteria

Bacteria are tiny single-cell organisms that live in water, in the soil, and on almost all surfaces. Most bacteria can be seen only with a microscope. Not all bacteria cause illness. Your body needs some types of bacteria to work well.

The most common type of fungus infection is athlete's foot. This is a burning, itchy infection of the skin between your toes. Ringworm is another skin infection caused by a fungus. It causes itchy round patches to develop on the skin.

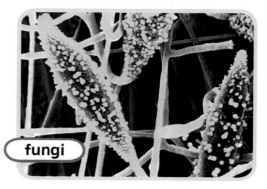
fungi

Protozoans are the fourth type of pathogen. They are single-cell organisms that are slightly larger than bacteria. They can cause disease when they grow in food or drinking water.

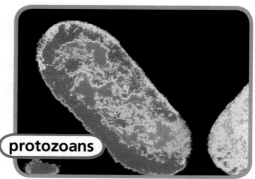
protozoans

Fighting Illness

Pathogens that can make you ill are everywhere. When you become ill, a doctor may be able to treat you. You also can practice healthful habits to protect yourself and others from the spread of pathogens and the illnesses they can cause.

The best way to avoid spreading pathogens is to wash your hands with warm water and soap. This floats germs off of your skin. You should wash your hands often. Always wash them before and after eating, after handling animals, and after using the bathroom. Avoid touching your mouth, eyes, and nose. Never share hats, combs, cups, or drinking straws. If you get a cut or scrape, pathogens can enter your body. It is important to wash cuts and scrapes carefully with soap and water. Then cover the injury with a sterile bandage.

When you are ill, you should avoid spreading pathogens to others. Cover your nose and mouth when you sneeze or cough.

Don't share anything that has touched your mouth or nose. Stay home from school until an adult or your doctor tells you that you are well enough to go back.

Even though pathogens are all around, most people become ill only once in a while because the body has systems that protect it from pathogens. These defenses keep pathogens from entering your body.

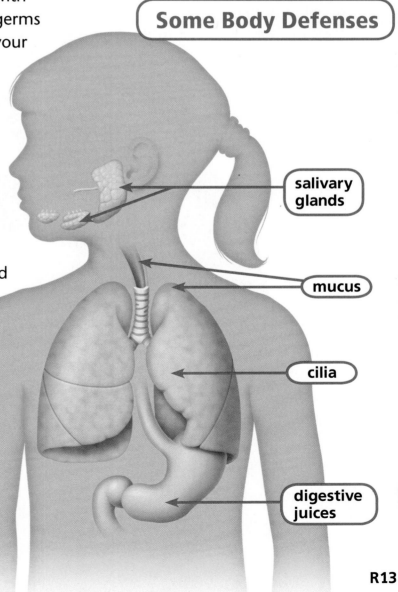

Some Body Defenses

salivary glands

mucus

cilia

digestive juices

Eat a Balanced Diet

Eating the foods that your body needs to grow and fight illness is the most important thing you can do to stay healthy. A balanced diet of healthful foods gives your body energy. Your body's systems need nutrients to function properly and work together.

Choosing unhealthful foods can cause you to gain excess weight and to lack energy. Inactivity and poor food choices can lead to you becoming ill more frequently. Unhealthful foods can also cause you to develop noncommunicable diseases. Unlike communicable diseases, which are caused by germs, these illnesses occur because your body systems are not working right.

Exercise Regularly

Exercise keeps your body healthy. Regular exercise helps your heart, lungs, and muscles stay strong. It helps your body digest food. It also helps your body fight disease. Exercising to keep your body strong also helps prevent injury when you play sports.

Exercise allows your body to rest more effectively. Getting enough sleep prepares your body for the next day. It allows your muscles and bones to grow and recover from exercise. Resting also helps keep your mind alert so you can learn and play well.

Identify the Main Idea and Details

This Reading in Science Handbook provides tips for using the 🔵 Reading Focus Skills you see throughout this book. Many of the lessons in this science book are written so you can understand main ideas and the details that support them. You can use a graphic organizer like this one to show a main idea and details.

Main Idea: The most important idea of a selection

| **Detail:** Information that tells more about the main idea | **Detail:** Information that tells more about the main idea | **Detail:** Information that tells more about the main idea |

Tips for Identifying the Main Idea and Details

- To find the main idea, ask *What is this mostly about?*

- Remember that the main idea is not always stated in the first sentence.

- Look for details that answer questions such as *Who, What, Where, When, Why* and *How*. Use pictures as clues to help you figure out the main idea.

Here is an example.

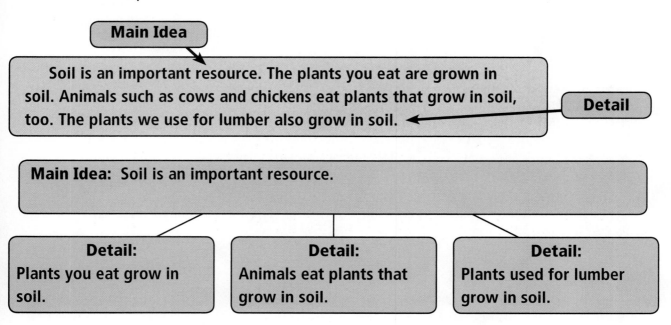

Main Idea

Soil is an important resource. The plants you eat are grown in soil. Animals such as cows and chickens eat plants that grow in soil, too. The plants we use for lumber also grow in soil.

Detail

Main Idea: Soil is an important resource.

| **Detail:** Plants you eat grow in soil. | **Detail:** Animals eat plants that grow in soil. | **Detail:** Plants used for lumber grow in soil. |

More About Main Idea and Details

Sometimes the main idea of a paragraph is at the end instead of the beginning. If the main idea is not given at all, look at the details to figure it out. Look at the graphic organizer. What do you think the main idea is?

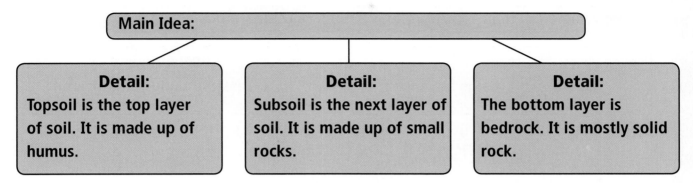

Main Idea:

Detail: Topsoil is the top layer of soil. It is made up of humus.

Detail: Subsoil is the next layer of soil. It is made up of small rocks.

Detail: The bottom layer is bedrock. It is mostly solid rock.

Sometimes a paragraph's main idea might contain details of different types. In this paragraph, identify whether the details give reasons, examples, facts, steps, or descriptions.

> Farmers and scientists have found a type of soil that is best for growing plants. It is soil that contains an equal mixture of sand, clay, and humus. Soil with this mixture can hold the right amount of water. It also has enough nutrients.

Skill Practice

Read the following paragraph. Use the Tips for Identifying the Main Idea and Details to answer the questions.

> Soil helps all living things meet their needs. It provides a home for some animals and plants. Soil is used to grow plants for food. It is also used to grow resources such as trees for lumber and paper.

1. What is the main idea of the paragraph?

2. What supporting details give more information?

3. What details answer any of the questions *Who, What, Where, When, Why* and *How?*

Compare and Contrast

Some lessons are written to help you see how things are alike or different. You can use a graphic organizer like this one to compare and contrast.

Topic: Name the topic—the two things you are comparing and contrasting.

Alike	**Different**
List ways the things are alike.	List ways the things are different.

Tips for Comparing and Contrasting

- To compare, ask *How are things alike?*
- To contrast, ask *How are things different?*
- When you compare, look for signal words and phrases such as *similar, alike, both, the same as, too,* and *also.*
- When you contrast, look for signal words and phrases such as *unlike, different, however, yet,* and *but.*

Here is an example.

Compare

Both dogs and cats have been kept by people for thousands of years. These four-legged companions have lived in our homes and shared our food. They are different in many ways. Cats help keep small animals like mice and rats out of the house. Dogs warn us of danger. Cats like to nap, but dogs like to play.

Contrast

Here is what you could record in the graphic organizer.

Topic: Dogs and Cats

Alike	**Different**
They live with humans, have four legs, and share our foods.	Cats chase mice, dogs bark at danger. Cats nap, dogs play.

More About Compare and Contrast

You can better understand new information about things when you know how they are alike and how they are different. Use the graphic organizer from page R18 to sort the following new information about cats and dogs.

Cats	Like fish	Afraid of dogs	Climb trees	Very independent

Dogs	Like meats	Bark at strange dogs	Run very fast	Will come when called

Sometimes a paragraph compares and contrasts more than one topic. In the following paragraph, the sentence that compares things is underlined. Find the sentences that contrast things.

> <u>The first boats and the first airplanes were both powered by using wooden parts.</u> People pulled wooden oars to move the first boats through water. Early airplanes were pulled through the air by wooden propellers. Wood is a strong, flexible material that is easy to shape into tools. A single oar can move a boat over water with each stroke, but a propeller must turn continuously to keep an airplane flying.

Skill Practice

Read the following paragraph. Use the Tips for Comparing and Contrasting to answer the questions.

> Both boats and airplanes seem to float easily. But water is much denser than air. Boats float on top of water because their weight is spread over the bottom of the boat. Airplanes are held up by the air under their wings. Boats can float when they are not moving. However, airplanes must move forward all the time. This creates the lifting force under their wings.

1. What is one likeness that boats and airplanes share?

2. What is one difference between boats and airplanes?

3. What are two signal words that helped you identify likenesses and differences?

Cause and Effect

Some of the lessons in this science book are written to help you understand why things happen. You can use a graphic organizer like this one to show cause and effect.

Cause	Effect
A cause is the reason, or why, something happens.	An effect is what happens.

Tips for Identifying Cause and Effect

- To find an effect, ask *What happened?*
- To find a cause, ask *Why did this happen?*
- Remember that events can have more than one cause or effect.
- Look for signal words such as *because, as a result, so,* and *therefore.*

Here is an example.

Effect

A gecko is a small lizard. It can climb up walls and walk upside down without falling. Scientists have found out how geckos stick on things so well. They have millions of tiny hairs on their feet. The hairs have flat ends that stick to almost anything. So, the gecko can walk on a ceiling without falling down.

Cause

Here is what you could record in the graphic organizer.

Cause:	Effect:
Geckos have tiny hairs on their feet with flat ends that stick to almost anything.	Geckos can climb walls and walk upside down.

More About Cause and Effect

Events can have more than one cause or effect. For example, suppose the paragraph on page R20 included a sentence that said *This helps the gecko escape from predators.* You could then identify two effects of geckos and their sticky feet.

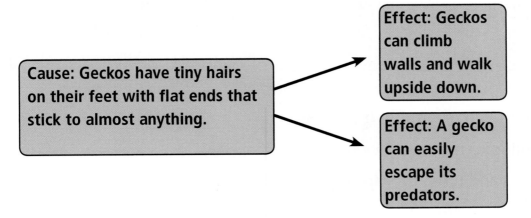

Cause: Geckos have tiny hairs on their feet with flat ends that stick to almost anything.

Effect: Geckos can climb walls and walk upside down.

Effect: A gecko can easily escape its predators.

Some paragraphs contain more than one cause and effect. In the following paragraph, one cause and its effect are underlined. Find the second cause and its effect.

> <u>**Birds have a body covering of feathers.**</u> <u>**The feathers keep birds warm and dry.**</u> **Feathers also give a bird's body a smooth surface over which air can easily flow. Another thing that helps birds fly is their bones. A bird's bones are filled with air pockets. As a result, the bird is very light, and this helps it fly.**

Skill Practice

Read the following paragraph. Use the Tips for Identifying Cause and Effect to help you answer the questions.

> **The viceroy butterfly would be a tasty meal for a bird. However, the viceroy looks a lot like the monarch butterfly. Birds often mistake the viceroy for a monarch, which tastes bad to birds. Therefore, birds usually leave the viceroy alone.**

1. What causes birds to not eat the viceroy butterfly?

2. What is the effect of the viceroy's looking like a monarch?

3. Name a signal word that helped you identify a cause or an effect.

Sequence

Some lessons in this science book are written to help you understand the order in which things happen. You can use a graphic organizer like this one to show sequence.

| 1. The first thing that happened | → | 2. The next thing that happened | → | 3. The last thing that happened |

Tips for Understanding Sequence

- Pay attention to the order in which events happen.
- Recall dates and times to help you understand the sequence.
- Look for time-order signal words such as *first, next, then, last,* and *finally.*
- Sometimes it is helpful to add time-order words yourself as you read.

Here is an example.

Suppose you have a mixture of rice, paper clips, and marbles. You need to separate the parts of the mixture. First, you separate the marbles with your hands. Then, you use a magnet to separate the paper clips. Finally, the rice is left.

Time-order words

Here is what you could record in the graphic organizer.

| 1. First, you separate the marbles by hand. | → | 2. Then, you use the magnet to separate the paper clips. | → | 3. Finally, the rice is left. |

More About Sequence

Sometimes information is sequenced by dates. Use a graphic organizer like the following to sequence the order in which water in a pond freezes and melts.

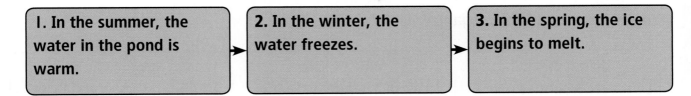

| 1. In the summer, the water in the pond is warm. | 2. In the winter, the water freezes. | 3. In the spring, the ice begins to melt. |

When time-order words are not given, add your own. Look at the underlined time-order word in the paragraph below. How many more time-order words can you add to help you understand the sequence?

When you cook food, you make new kinds of matter. <u>First,</u> flour, eggs, milk, and oil are mixed to make pancake batter. The batter is poured on a stove. The batter cooks and turns into pancakes. The pancakes will never be flour, eggs, milk, and oil again.

Skill Practice

Read the following paragraph. Use the Tips for Understanding Sequence to answer the questions.

A shiny iron bolt was left outdoors. It sat in the rain and moist air. After several days, the bolt began to turn dull. After a week, it turned an orange-brown color. When it was picked up a month later, the orange-brown iron bolt was flaky and soft. The orange-brown material was rust. When a metal turns to rust, it loses some of its strength.

1. What is the first thing that happens in this sequence?

2. About how long did the process take?

3. What three phrases helped you identify the sequence in this paragraph?

Draw Conclusions

At the end of each lesson in this science book, you will be asked to draw conclusions. To draw conclusions, use information from the text you are reading and what you already know. Drawing conclusions can help you understand what you read. You can use a graphic organizer like this one.

What I Read		What I Know		Conclusion:
List facts from the text.	+	List related ideas that you already know.	=	Combine what you just read in the text with what you already know.

Tips for Drawing Conclusions

- To draw conclusions, ask *What do I need to think about from the text?*

- To draw conclusions, ask *What do I really know that could help me draw a conclusion?*

- Be sure your conclusions make sense.

Here is an example.

When astronauts visited the moon, they left footprints. On the moon, there is no water. There is also very little air. Without air, there is no wind or weather. So the footprints that were left on the moon are still there.

Here is what you could record in the graphic organizer.

What I Read		What I Know		Conclusion:
The astronauts left footprints on the moon. The moon has no weather.	+	Footprints left on earth would be washed away by wind or rain.	=	The footprints on the moon will be there for a long time.

More About Drawing Conclusions

Text Information

| **What I Read**
The astronauts left footprints on the moon. The moon has no weather. | + | **What I Know**
Footprints left on earth would be washed away by wind or rain. | = | **Conclusion:**
The footprints on the moon will be there for a long time. |

Your Own Experience

Sometimes a paragraph might not contain enough information to draw a conclusion that makes sense. Read the paragraph below. Think of one right conclusion you could draw. Then think of a conclusion that would be wrong.

Venus is the second planet from the sun. It is about the same size as Earth. Venus is dry and covered with thick clouds. The thick clouds trap heat and make the planet's surface very hot.

Skill Practice

Read the following paragraph. Use the Tips for Drawing Conclusions to answer the questions.

The outer planets are Jupiter, Saturn, Uranus, Neptune, and Pluto. Four of these planets are large spheres made up mostly of gases. They are called the gas giants. Jupiter is the largest gas giant. Its atmosphere is very active.

1. What conclusion can you draw about the outer planets?

2. What information from your own experience helped you draw the conclusion?

3. What text information did you use to draw the conclusion?

Summarize

Retell what you have just read. Use the main idea and only the most important details.

Tips for Summarizing

- To write a summary, ask—What is the most important idea or the main thing that happened?

- Be sure the details you include are things the reader needs to know.

- Make your summary shorter than what you have read.

- Write a summary in your own words. Be sure to put the events in order.

Here is an example.

Main Idea

Fish are a type of animal group. They live their entire lives in water. Fish have gills that they use to take in oxygen from the water. Fish have a body covering of scales. The scales are small, thin, flat plates that help protect the fish. Fish also have fins they use to move in water.

Detail

Main Idea: Fish are a type of animal group.

Detail:
Fish have gills they use to take in oxygen.

Detail:
They are covered with scales.

Summary:
Fish are an animal group. They have gills, a body covering of scales, and fins.

> Here is what you could record in the graphic organizer.

Main Idea:		Detail:		Summary:
Fish are a type of animal group.	+	Fish have gills they use to take in oxygen. They are covered with scales	=	Fish are an animal group. They have gills, a body covering of scales, and fins.

More About Summarizing

Sometimes a paragraph has details that are not important enough to put in a summary. What if the paragraph on page R26 included a sentence about the color and size of a fish's scales? You would leave these details out of the summary. They would not be needed to understand the main idea.

Skill Practice

Read the following paragraph. Use the Tips for Summarizing to answer the questions.

> Amphibians are animals that begin life in the water and move onto land as adults. Amphibians lay eggs in the water. The eggs stay there until they hatch. Young amphibians, such as tadpoles, live in the water. They breathe with gills. As they grow, they develop lungs. Once they have lungs, their gills disappear. Tadpoles also develop other body parts, such as legs. These help them live on land. Most adult amphibians live on land.

1. If a friend asked you what this paragraph is about, what information would you include? What would you leave out?

2. What is the main idea of the paragraph?

3. What two details would you include in a summary of the paragraph?

Using Tables, Charts, and Graphs

As you do investigations in science, you collect, organize, display, and interpret data. Tables, charts, and graphs are good ways to organize and display data so that others can understand and interpret your data.

The tables, charts, and graphs in this Handbook will help you read and understand data. You can also use the information to choose the best ways to display data so that you can use it to draw conclusions and make predictions.

Reading a Table

A third-grade class is studying the lengths of different sea animals. They want to find out how the lengths vary. The table shows some of the data the students have collected.

LENGTHS OF SEA ANIMALS ← Title

Animal	Length (in feet)
Whale shark	60
White shark	40
Bottlenose dolphin	10
Giant squid	55
Gray whale	50

Header ←

Data ←

How to Read a Table

1. Read the title to find out what the table is about.

2. Read the headings to find out what information is given.

3. Study the data. Look for patterns.

4. Draw conclusions. If you display the data in a graph, you might be able to see patterns easily.

By studying the table, you can see the lengths of different sea animals. However, suppose the students want to look for patterns in the data. They might choose to display the data in a different way, such as in a bar graph.

Reading a Bar Graph

The data in this bar graph is the same as in the table. A bar graph can be used to compare the data about different events or groups.

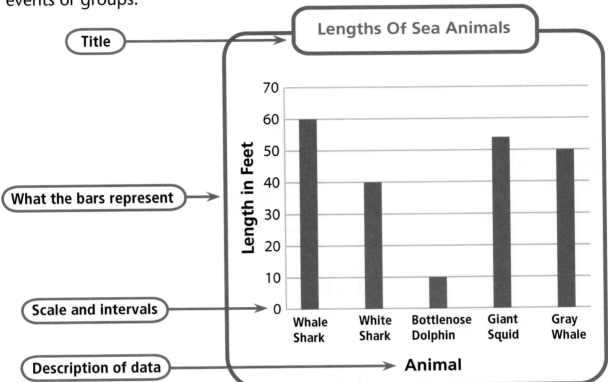

Title

What the bars represent

Scale and intervals

Description of data

Lengths Of Sea Animals

Length in Feet

Whale Shark | White Shark | Bottlenose Dolphin | Giant Squid | Gray Whale

Animal

How to Read a Bar Graph

1. Look at the graph to determine what kind of graph it is.

2. Read the graph. Use the labels to guide you.

3. Analyze the data. Study the bars to compare the measurements. Look for patterns.

4. **Draw conclusions.** Ask yourself questions like those on the right.

Skills Practice

1. How long is a gray whale?

2. How much longer is a whale shark than a white shark?

3. Which two sea animals vary in length by 40 feet?

4. **Predict** Which of these sea animals might you find in an aquarium at an animal park?

5. Was the bar graph a good choice for displaying this data? Explain your answer.

Reading a Line Graph

A scientist collected this data about temperatures in Anchorage, Alaska.

TEMPERATURES IN ANCHORAGE, ALASKA

Month	Normal Temperature in Degrees Fahrenheit
August	55
September	50
October	35
November	20
December	15

Here is the same data displayed in a line graph. A line graph is used to show changes over time.

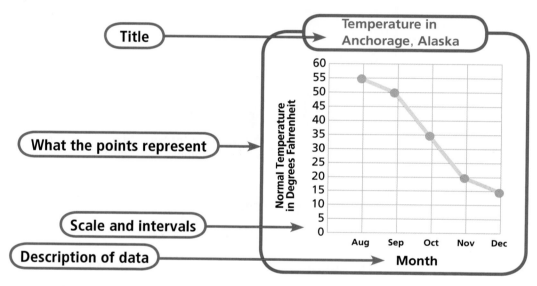

Title

What the points represent

Scale and intervals

Description of data

How to Read a Line Graph

1. Look at the graph to determine what kind of graph it is.

2. Read the graph. Use the labels to guide you.

3. Analyze the data. Study the points along the lines. Look for patterns.

4. **Draw conclusions.** Ask yourself questions like those on the right.

Skills Practice

1. In what month is the normal temperature 35 degrees?

2. **Predict** How will the temperature change from December to August?

3. Was the line graph a good choice for displaying this data? Explain why.

Reading a Circle Graph

A family went bird watching on an island. They counted 50 birds on the island. They wanted to know which birds they saw most often. They classified the birds by making a table. Here is the data they collected.

BIRD SIGHTINGS

Bird	Number Observed
Pelican	4
Bald Eagle	1
Osprey	10
Egret	15
Sandpiper	20

The circle graph shows the same data as the table. A circle graph can be used to show data as a whole made up of different parts.

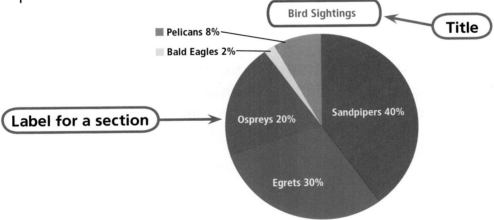

How to Read a Circle Graph

1. Look at the title of the graph to learn what kind of information is shown.

2. Read the graph. Look at the label of each section to find out what information is shown.

3. Analyze the data. Compare the sizes of the sections to determine how they are related.

4. **Draw conclusions.** Ask yourself questions like those on the right.

Skills Practice

1. Which type of bird did they see most often?

2. **Predict** If they return to the island in a month, should they expect to see a bald eagle?

3. Was the circle graph a good choice for displaying this data? Explain why.

Using Metric Measurements

A measurement is a number that represents a comparison of something being measured to a unit of measurement. Scientists use many different tools to measure objects and substances as they work. Scientists almost always use the metric system for their measurements.

Measuring Length in Metric Units

When you measure length, you find the distance between two points. The distance may be in a straight line, along a curved path, or around a circle. The table shows the metric units of length and how they are related.

Equivalent Measures
1 centimeter (cm) = 10 millimeters (mm)
1 decimeter (dm) = 10 centimeters (cm)
1 meter (m) = 1,000 millimeters
1 meter = 10 decimeters
1 kilometer (km) = 1,000 meters

You can use these comparisons to help you learn the size of each metric unit of length:

A **millimeter (mm)** is about the thickness of a dime.	A **centimeter (cm)** is about the width of your index finger.	A **decimeter (dm)** is about the width of an adult's hand.	A **meter (m)** is about the width of a door.

Sometimes you may need to change units of length. The following diagram shows how to multiply and divide to change to larger and smaller units.

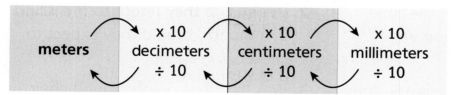

To change larger units to smaller units, you need more of the smaller units. So, multiply by 10, 100, or 1,000.

Example: 500 dm = ___ cm

Measuring Capacity in Metric Units

When you measure capacity, you find the amount a container can hold when it is filled. The table shows the metric units of capacity and how they are related.

A **milliliter (mL)** is the amount of liquid that can fill part of a dropper.

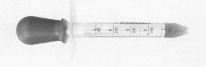

A **liter (L)** is the amount of liquid that can fill this plastic bottle.

You can use multiplication to change liters to milliliters.

You can use division to change milliliters to liters.

2 L = _____ mL

Think: There are 1,000 mL in 1 L.

2 L = 2 x 1,000 = 2,000 mL

So, 2 L = 2,000 mL.

4,000 mL = _____ L

Think: There are 1,000 mL in 1 L.

4,000 ÷ 1,000 = 4

So, 4,000 mL = 4 L.

Skills Practice

Complete. Tell whether you multiply or divide.

1. 4 L = _____ mL

2. 5,000 mL = _____ L

3. 3,000 mL = _____ L

4. 6 L = _____ mL

Measuring Mass

Matter is what all objects are made of. Mass is the amount of matter that is in an object. The metric units of mass are the gram (g) and the kilogram (kg).

You can use these comparisons to help you understand the masses of some everyday objects.

A paper clip is about 1 gram (g).	A slice of wheat bread is about 20 grams.	A box of 12 crayons is about 100 grams.	A large wedge of cheese is 1 kilogram (kg).

You can use multiplication to change kilograms to grams.

You can use division to change grams to kilograms.

2 kg = _____ g
Think: There are 1,000 g in 1 kg.
2 kg = 2 x 1,000 = 2,000 g
So, 2 kg = 2,000 g.

4,000 g = _____ kg
Think: There are 1,000 g in 1 kg.
4,000 ÷ 1,000 = 4
So, 4,000 g = 4 kg.

Skills Practice

Complete. Tell whether you multiply or divide by 1,000.

1. 2,000 g = ___ kg

2. 3,000 g = _____ kg

3. 4 kg = _____ g

4. 7 kg = _____ g

Measurement Systems

SI Measures (Metric)

Temperature
Ice melts at 0 degrees Celsius (°C).
Water freezes at 0°C.
Water boils at 100°C.

Length and Distance
1,000 meters (m) = 1 kilometer (km)
100 centimeters (cm) = 1 m
10 millimeters (mm) = 1 cm

Force
1 newton (N) = 1 kilogram x
  1 meter/second/second (kg-m/s²)

Volume
1 cubic meter (m³) = 1 m x 1 m x 1 m
1 cubic centimeter (cm³) =
    1 cm x 1 cm x 1 cm
1 liter (L) = 1,000 millimeters (mL)
1 cm³ = 1 mL

Area
1 square kilometer (km²) =
                    1 km x 1 km
1 hectare = 10,000 m²

Mass
1,000 grams (g) = 1 kilogram (kg)
1,000 milligrams (mg) = 1 g

Rates (Metric and Customary)
kmh = kilometers per hour
m/s = meters per second
mph = miles per hour
A liter (L) is the amount of liquid that
can fill a plastic bottle.

Customary Measures

Volume of Fluids
2 cups (c) = 1 pint (pt)
2 pt = 1 quart (qt)
4 qt = 1 gallon (gal)

Temperature
Ice melts at 32 degrees Fahrenheit (°F).
Water freezes at 32°F.
Water boils at 212°F.

Length and Distance
12 inches (in.) = 1 foot (ft)
3 ft = 1 yard (yd)
5,280 ft = 1 mile (mi)

Weight
16 ounces (oz) = 1 pound (lb)
2,000 pounds = 1 ton (T)

Safety in Science

Doing investigations in science can be fun, but you need to be sure you do them safely. Here are some rules to follow.

1. **Think ahead.** Study the steps of the investigation so you know what to expect. If you have any questions, ask your teacher. Be sure you understand any caution statements or safety reminders.

2. **Be neat.** Keep your work area clean. If you have long hair, pull it back so it doesn't get in the way. Roll or push up long sleeves to keep them away from your experiment.

3. **Oops!** If you spill or break something, or if you get cut, tell your teacher right away.

4. **Watch your eyes.** Wear safety goggles anytime you are directed to do so. If you get anything in your eyes, tell your teacher right away.

5. **Yuck!** Never eat or drink anything during a science activity.

6. **Don't get shocked.** Be especially careful if an electric appliance is used. Be sure that electrical cords are in a safe place where you can't trip over them. Never pull a plug out of an outlet by pulling on the cord.

7. **Keep it clean.** Always clean up when you have finished. Put everything away and wipe your work area. Wash your hands.

Visit the Multimedia Science Glossary to see illustrations of these words and to hear them pronounced. www.hspscience.com

Every entry in the glossary begins with a term and a *phonetic respelling*. A phonetic respelling writes the word the way it sounds, which can help you pronounce new or unfamiliar words.

The Pronunciation Key below will help you understand the respellings. Syllables are separated by a bullet (•). Small uppercase letters show stressed, or accented, syllables.

The definition of the term follows the respelling. An example of how to use the term in a sentence follows the definition.

If there is a page number in ( ) at the end of the entry, it tells you where to find the term in your textbook. Many of these terms are highlighted in yellow in the lessons. Most entries have an illustration to help you understand the term.

Pronunciation Key

Sound	As in	Phonetic Respelling	Sound	As in	Phonetic Respelling
a	bat	(BAT)	oh	over	(OH•ver)
ah	lock	(LAHK)	oo	pool	(POOL)
air	rare	(RAIR)	ow	out	(OWT)
ar	argue	(AR•gyoo)	oy	foil	(FOYL)
aw	law	(LAW)	s	cell	(SEL)
ay	face	(FAYS)		sit	(SIT)
ch	chapel	(CHAP•uhl)	sh	sheep	(SHEEP)
e	test	(TEST)	th	that	(THAT)
	metric	(MEH•trik)		thin	(THIN)
ee	eat	(EET)	u	pull	(PUL)
	feet	(FEET)	uh	medal	(MED•uhl)
	ski	(SKEE)		talent	(TAL•uhnt)
er	paper	(PAY•per)		pencil	(PEN•suhl)
	fern	(FERN)		onion	(UHN•yuhn)
eye	idea	(eye•DEE•uh)		playful	(PLAY•fuhl)
i	bit	(BIT)		dull	(DUHL)
ing	going	(GOH•ing)	y	yes	(YES)
k	card	(KARD)		ripe	(RYP)
	kite	(KYT)	z	bags	(BAGZ)
ngk	bank	(BANGK)	zh	treasure	(TREZH•er)

Multimedia Science Glossary: www.hspscience.com

A

absorb [ab•SAWRB] **To take in:** The color black *absorbs* all of the colors of light. (166)

accurate [AK•yuh•ruht] **Correct:** Mark measured the root twice to make sure his measurement was *accurate*. (8)

adaptation [ad•uhp•TAY•shuhn] **A trait that helps a living thing survive:** A giraffe's long neck is an *adaptation* for reaching leaves high on a tree. (197)

analyze [AN•uh•lyz] **To figure out what the data shows:** A model can help you *analyze* information. (19)

atom [AT•uhm] **The smallest particle of matter that has the properties of that matter:** Sugar is made of carbon, oxygen, and hydrogen *atoms*. (128)

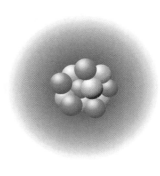

axis [AK•sis] **An imaginary line that runs through Earth from the North Pole to the South Pole:** Earth rotates around its *axis*. (296)

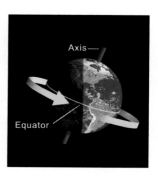

B

balance [BAL•uhns] **Not too many and not too few of a kind of living thing:** When people change the environment, they may change the *balance* among living things. (248)

bar graph [BAR GRAF] **A graph that uses bars to display data:** This *bar graph* can help you see differences in the lengths of animals that live in the sea. (32)

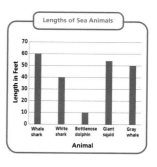

battery [BAT•er•ee]
An object that changes stored chemical energy into electrical energy: A *battery* contains stored energy. (73)

binoculars [bih•NAHK•yuh•lerz]
A tool you hold in your hands and look through with both eyes to make distant objects seem closer: *Binoculars* work the way a telescope does, but you use both eyes to look through them.

biome [BY•ohm] A part of the world with a certain climate and certain plants and animals that can survive there: This map shows the major *biomes* of the world.

boiling [BOYL•ing] A change from a liquid to a gas as a result of being heated quickly: After *boiling* for five minutes, the pot of water was almost empty. (108)

C

chemical change [KEM•ih•kuhl CHAYNJ] A change in which two or more substances combine to form a new substance: Rusting is one kind of *chemical change*. (118)

circuit [SER•kuht] A path that electricity follows: Electricity flows through this *circuit*, which connects a light bulb to a battery. (73)

climate [KLY•muht] The weather a place has over a long period of time: The *climate* in some parts of California is very cold in the winter. (222)

compare [kuhm•PAIR] To tell how two things are similar and different: You *compare* two animals by telling how they are the same and how they are different. (20)

conclusion
[kuhn•KLOO•zhuhn]
A statement based on data that summarizes what was learned in an inquiry: A *conclusion* should be written based on what you learn in an experiment. (23)

condense [kuhn•DENS]
To change from a gas to a liquid: Water in the air *condenses* when it loses heat and becomes cool. (109)

constellation
[kahn•stuh•LAY•shuhn] **A group of stars that appears to form the shape of an animal, a person, or an object:** Ursa Major is a *constellation* that many people think looks like a bear. (306)

crescent moon
[KRES•uhnt MOON]
The phase of the moon in which just the edge of the lit part can be seen: A *crescent moon* is seen just before and just after a new moon. (323)

cycle [SY•kuhl] **A sequence of events that happens over and over again:** The *cycle* of the moon's phases takes $29\frac{1}{2}$ days. (323)

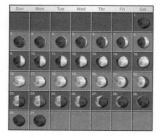

D

data [DAY•tuh]
Information: *Data* is collected by using measuring tools and recording the measurements. (19)

data table [DAY•tuh TAY•buhl] **A display that organizes data in rows and columns:** A *data table* helps you organize your data as you record it. (32)

desert [DEZ•ert]
**A very dry
environment:** A
desert gets very little
rain. (221)

Earth [ERTH] **The third
planet from the sun
in the solar system:**
We live on the planet
Earth. (280)

dissolve [dih•ZAHLV]
**To become
completely mixed
with a liquid:** Sugar
dissolves in water.
(117)

electricity
[ee•lek•TRIS•uh•tee] **A
kind of energy that
moves through a
wire:** *Electricity* runs
many of the things
we use at home and
at school. (73)

drought [DROWT] **A
long period of time
with very little rain:**
A *drought* can be bad
for farmers because
plants need water to
grow. (244)

element
[EL•uh•muhnt] **A pure
substance that has
only one kind of
atom:** Copper is an
element because it
is made of only one
kind of atom. (130)

E

eardrum [IR•druhm]
**A thin, skin-like
sheet inside your
ear; it vibrates when
sound energy strikes
it:** Sound waves
cause the *eardrum* to
vibrate, allowing us
to hear sounds. (85)

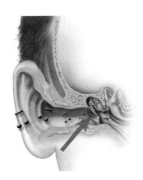

energy [EN•er•jee]
**The ability to cause
change:** *Energy* is
needed to push a
basket across the
floor. (56)

environment
[en•vy•ruhn•muhnt]
Everything that is around a living thing: Many kinds of living things can share the same *environment*. (220)

evaporation
[ee•vap•uh•RAY•shun] **The change of state from a liquid to a gas:** The footprints are drying up due to *evaporation* of the water by the sun. (107)

evidence
[EV•uh•duhns]
Information collected in a scientific inquiry: You must collect *evidence* to prove whether or not your prediction is correct. (23)

experiment
[ek•SPEHR•uh•muhnt]
A test done to find out if a hypothesis is correct: In this *experiment*, the only difference between the cups is the type of soil the plants are growing in. (41)

extinct [ek•STINGT]
Describes a kind of thing that is no longer found on Earth: Dinosaurs are *extinct*. (262)

F

first-quarter moon
[FERST KWAWRT•er MOON]
The moon phase in which the moon looks like a half-circle and is lighted on the right side: The *first-quarter moon* is one-quarter of the way through its phases. (323)

food [FOOD]
Substances from which plants and animals get energy and nutrients: *Food* gives you energy to run and play. (57)

forest [FAWR•uhst] **An area that is covered with trees:** Many kinds of animals live in a *forest*. (223)

fossil [FAHS•uhl] **The hardened remains of a plant or an animal that lived long ago:** We can learn about living things of long ago by studying *fossils*. (258)

freezing [FREEZ•ing]
The change from a liquid to a solid: *Freezing* turns liquid water into ice cubes. (108)

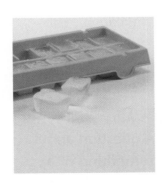

friction [FRIK•shuhn] **A force that slows the motion of objects that are touching:** Rubbing your hands together causes *friction*, which warms your hands. (87)

fuel [FYOOL] **A substance that is burned to release stored energy:** Some machines use gasoline as a *fuel*. (68)

full moon [FUHL MOON]
The moon phase in which the moon looks like a circle: A *full moon* is very bright in the night sky. (322)

G

galaxy [GAL•uhk•see]
A large group of stars: Earth is part of the Milky Way *Galaxy*. (308)

gas [GAS] **Matter that has no definite shape or volume:** As *gas* is pumped into the ball, the ball grows larger. (97)

grassland [GRAS•land] **A dry, flat area on which mostly grasses grow:** A *grassland* has many animals that eat grass. (224)

growth [GROHTH] **Getting larger in size:** You can use a ruler to measure the *growth* of a living thing. (198)

H

habitat [HAB•ih•tat] **The place where something lives in an environment:** In some grassland environments, prairie dogs live in an underground *habitat*. (221)

heat [HEET] **Energy that warms objects:** *Heat* from a stove cooks food. (60)

hibernate [HY•ber•nayt] **To spend the winter in a deep sleep:** When an animal *hibernates*, its breathing and heartbeat slow down and its body temperature drops. (210)

horizon [huh•RY•zuhn] **The line where the sky appears to meet the land:** Every evening, the sun sets on the *horizon*.

I

inquiry [IN•kwer•ee] **A question about something or a close study of it:** The students learned a lot from their *inquiry* about greenhouses. (6)

investigation
[in•ves•tuh•GAY•shuhn] **A scientific study:** The students performed an *investigation* to find out what substances dissolve in water. (40)

iris [EYE•ris] **The colored part of the eye that controls how much light enters the eye:** The *iris* of this eye is blue. (176)

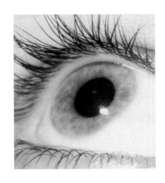

Jupiter [JOO•pit•er] **The fifth planet from the sun:** *Jupiter* is the largest planet in the solar system. (282)

L

lens [LENZ] **The part of the eye that bends light so that it shines on the retina:** The *lens* of your eye focuses light, the way the lens of a camera does. (177)

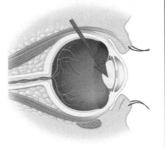

light [LYT] **A form of energy you can see:** Your eyes can sense *light* energy. (57)

line graph [LYN GRAF] **A graph that uses lines to display data:** You can see how temperature and time of year are related in this *line graph*. (33)

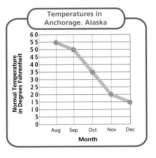

liquid [LIK•wid] **Matter that has a definite volume but no definite shape:** Water is a *liquid*; its shape can change but its volume does not. (96)

logical [LAHJ•ih•kuhl] **Based on facts; reasonable:** The conclusion was *logical* because it made sense. (20)

machine [muh•SHEEN]
An invention that uses energy to do work: Some *machines*, such as car engines, burn gasoline to get energy to do work. (72)

magnify [MAG•nuh•fy]
To make an object appear larger: Microscopes, hand lenses, telescopes, and binoculars all *magnify* objects. (308)

Mars [MARZ] **The fourth planet from the sun in the solar system:** The surface of *Mars* is covered with reddish dust. (280)

mass [MAS] **The amount of matter in an object:** A balance is used to measure how much *mass* an object has. (98)

matter [MAT•er]
Anything that takes up space: Everything that takes up space is *matter,* even if the matter is not visible to the eyes. (95)

melting [MELT•ing]
The change of state from a solid to a liquid: *Melting* causes water to drip from these icicles. (106)

Mercury [MER•kyoor•ee] **The planet closest to the sun in the solar system:** The surface of *Mercury* gets hotter than the surface of Earth. (280)

migrate [MY•grayt]
To travel from one place to another and back again: Some kinds of birds *migrate* south for the winter and return north for the summer. (211)

mirror [MIR•er] **A polished surface that reflects light:** You can see your reflection in a *mirror*. (154)

mix [MIKS] **To combine things:** You can *mix* colors of paint to make new colors. (116)

mixture [MIKS•cher] **A combination of two or more kinds of matter:** Lemonade is a *mixture* of water, sugar, and lemon juice. (116)

moon [MOON] **A large body that orbits a planet:** The *moon* orbits Earth about every 4 weeks. (279)

moon phases [MOON FAYZ•uhz] **The different shapes the moon seems to have:** The *moon phases* change as the moon orbits Earth. (322)

 N

Neptune [NEP•toon] **The eighth planet from the sun in the solar system:** Since *Neptune* is the next-to-last planet, it has very cold temperatures. (282)

new moon [NOO MOON] **The moon phase in which the lighted half of the moon cannot be seen from Earth:** It is easier to see stars at night when there is a *new moon*. (322)

Northern Hemisphere [NAWR•thern HEM•ih•sfir] **The northern half of Earth:** California is in the *Northern Hemisphere*. (297)

ocean [OH•shuhn] **A large body of salty water:** Whales live in the *ocean*. (220)

opaque [oh•PAYK] **Describes an object that does not let light pass through it:** You cannot see through *opaque* objects. (178)

opinion [uh•PIN•yuhn] **A personal belief that is not based on evidence:** Make sure you don't confuse your *opinions* with evidence that comes from an investigation. (23)

Cats are the best pets!

orbit [AWR•bit] **To travel around an object:** It takes about $365\frac{1}{4}$ days for Earth to *orbit* the sun. (278)

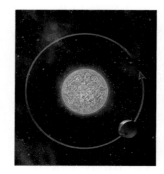

particle [PART•ih•kuhl] **A very small bit of something:** All matter is made of tiny *particles* called atoms. (128)

periodic table [pir•ee•AHD•ik TAY•buhl] **A chart that shows the elements:** Elements are arranged in order in the *periodic table*. (131)

planet [PLAN•it] **A large body of rock or gas that orbits a star in space:** Saturn is one of nine *planets* that orbit the sun. (278)

Pluto [PLOOT•oh] **The ninth planet from the sun in the solar system:** One year on *Pluto* is as long as 248 years on Earth. (282)

In 2006, a group of scientists classified Pluto as a "dwarf planet."

pollution
[puh•LOO•shuhn] **Harmful material that is added to the environment:** Oil spills are a kind of *pollution* that can kill many living things. (234)

predict [pree•DIKT]
To tell what you think will happen in the future: You *predict* the outcome of an experiment before you begin the experiment. (20)

property
[PRAHP•er•tee] **A characteristic of matter that you can observe or measure:** One *property* of lemons is their sour taste. (98)

pupil [PYOO•puhl]
The opening in the front of the eye, through which light passes: The *pupil* of your eye looks like a black dot. (176)

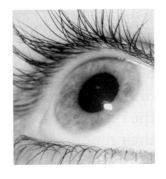

R

react [ree•AKT] **To combine and form a new substance:** When these clear and yellow liquids *react*, they form a new red substance. (118)

reflect [rih•FLEKT] **To bounce off a surface:** Light *reflects* off the shiny surface of a mirror. (154)

release [rih•LEES] **To give off:** Charcoal *releases* heat when it is burned. (68)

reproduce
[ree•pruh•DOOS] **To produce new living things:** Living things *reproduce* in many ways, such as by making seeds, laying eggs, or giving birth to live young. (200)

retina [RET•uh•nuh] **The back of the inside of the eye, where images are formed:** A nerve carries information from the *retina* to the brain. (177)

rotation [roh•TAY•shuhn] **The spinning of Earth:** One *rotation* of Earth takes 24 hours. (292)

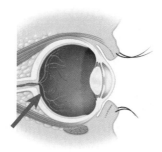

S

Saturn [SAT•ern] **The sixth planet from the sun in the solar system:** *Saturn* has a system of rings spinning around it. (282)

scientific method [sy•uhn•TIF•ik METH•uhd] **An organized plan that scientists use to conduct an investigation:** This student is using the *scientific method* to design an experiment. (40)

season [SEE•zuhn] **A time of year that has a certain kind of weather:** Spring, summer, fall, and winter are the four *seasons*. (296)

seismograph [SYZ•muh•graf] **A tool that records the strength of energy waves in an earthquake:** A *seismograph* can detect earthquakes that are not strong enough for us to feel. (83)

shadow [SHA•doh] **A dark area that forms where an object blocks the path of light:** When you move, so does your *shadow*. (152)

solar system [SOH•ler SIS•tuhm] **The sun and the objects that orbit it, including the planets and their moons:** Nine planets orbit the sun in the *solar system*. (279)

solid [SAHL•id] **Matter with a definite volume and shape:** Marbles, pasta, and grains of sand are *solids,* so their shapes and masses do not change. (96)

sound [SOWND] **Energy that can be heard:** The *sound* made by a drum is different from the sound made by a trumpet. (84)

Southern Hemisphere [SUHTH•ern HEM•ih•sfir] **The southern half of Earth:** When it is winter in the *Southern Hemisphere,* it is summer in the Northern Hemisphere.

species [SPEE•sheez] **One kind of living thing:** Wildebeests are one *species* living in Africa.

star [STAR] **A huge ball of hot, glowing gases that gives off energy:** There are many *stars* in the night sky. (304)

state [STAYT] **One form that matter can have:** Solid, liquid, and gas are three *states* of matter. (96)

stationary [STAY•shuh•nair•ee] **Not moving; fixed in one location:** Earth is not *stationary* but is constantly rotating on its axis as it orbits the sun.

summer [SUHM•er] **The season with warm weather and the longest days:** You can wear lighter clothing during the *summer* months. (296)

sun [SUHN] **The star at the center of the solar system:** The *sun* provides light and heat to Earth. (278)

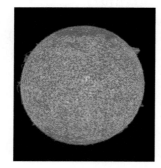

survive [ser•VYV] **To stay alive:** Plants and animals have adaptations that help them *survive.* (196)

symbol [SIM•buhl] **One or more letters that stand for an element:** *C* is the *symbol* for carbon on the periodic table of the elements. (131)

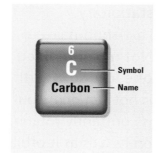

telescope [TEL•uh•skohp] **A tool that makes faraway objects seem closer and larger:** A *telescope* helps you see more clearly objects that are far away. (279)

third-quarter moon [THERD KWAWRT•er MOON] **The moon phase in which the moon looks like a half-circle and is lighted on the left side:** The *third-quarter moon* is three-fourths of the way through its phases. (323)

tilted [TILT•uhd] **Leaning in one direction; not straight up and down:** Earth's axis is slightly *tilted.* (296)

trait [TRAYT] **A characteristic, or feature, of a plant or animal:** The different *traits* of these flowers help you tell them apart. (196)

transfer [TRANZ•fer] **To carry energy or cause it to move from one thing to another:** The bowling ball *transfers* energy to the pins. (82)

translucent
[tranz•LOO•suhnt]
Describes an object that lets some light pass through it: You can see light through *translucent* objects, but you cannot see clearly through them. (179)

transparent
[tranz•PAIR•uhnt]
Describes an object that lets most light pass through it: You can see clearly through *transparent* objects. (178)

tundra [TUHN•druh] **A place that has a very cold climate:** Animals that live in the *tundra* all year have adaptations to survive in the cold. (222)

U

universe
[YOO•nuh•vers]
Everything that exists, including stars, planets, and energy: Many galaxies make up the *universe*.

Uranus
[YOOR•uh•nuhs] **The seventh planet from the sun in the solar system:** *Uranus* is the third-largest planet. (282)

V

Venus [VEE•nuhs] **The second planet from the sun in the solar system:** You do not need a telescope to see *Venus* in the night sky. (280)

vibrations
[vy•BRAY•shuhnz] **A series of back-and-forth movements:** The *vibrations* of a bell cause sound waves to move through the air. (84)

volume [VAHL•yoom] **The amount of space something takes up:** You can use a graduate to measure the *volume* of a liquid. (94)

waning [WAYN•ing]
Becoming smaller:
We say the moon is
waning during the
phases between a
full moon and a new
moon. (322)

wave [WAYV] **A**
disturbance that
moves energy to
other places: Light
travels in *waves* that
are similar to waves in
water. (82)

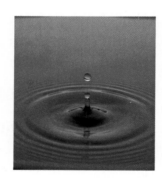

waxing [WAKS•ing]
Getting bigger:
We say the moon is
waxing during the
phases between a
new moon and a full
moon. (322)

wetland [WET•land]
An area that is
often flooded: Many
kinds of ducks live in
wetlands. (225)

winter [WIN•ter] **The**
season with cold
weather and the
shortest days: Many
trees lose their leaves
in *winter*. (296)

Index

CHARACTERISTICS The tufted puffin is named for the tufts of feathers that curl back on each side of its head.

CHARACTERISTICS Puffins are strong swimmers. They flap their wings to swim underwater.

MOVEMENT A puffin's webbed feet help it paddle through the water.

VOCALIZATION If puffins sense danger, they make warning sounds to alert the colony.

BEHAVIOR Puffins usually nest in large groups called colonies.